Volume 7
SAGE SERIES ON AFRICAN MODERNIZATION AND DEVELOPMENT

AFRICAN ISLANDS
and Enclaves

ROBIN COHEN
Editor

SAGE PUBLICATIONS
Beverly Hills / London / New Delhi

For information address:

SAGE Publications, Inc.
275 South Beverly Drive
Beverly Hills, California 90212

SAGE Publications India Pvt. Ltd.
C-236 Defence Colony
New Delhi 110 024, India

SAGE Publications Ltd
28 Banner Street
London EC1Y 8QE, England

Printed in the United States of America

Library of Congress Cataloging in Publication Data

Main entry under title:

African islands and enclaves.

(Sage series on African modernization and development ; v. 7)
    Bibliography: p.
    Contents: Introduction / Robin Cohen — Interpreting dependency in the Canary Islands / Miguel Sanchez-Padron — From colonialism to confederation / Arnold Hughes — [etc.]
    1. Islands—Africa—Addresses, essays, lectures.
2. Africa—Politics and government—1960- —Addresses, essays, lectures. 3. Africa—Economic conditions—1960- —Addresses, essays, lectures. 4. Africa—Dependency—Addresses, essays, lectures 5. Africa—Colonial influence—Addresses, essays, lectures.
6. States, Small—Addresses, essays, lectures.
I. Cohen, Robin. II. Series.
DT30.5.A364   1983   960'.32   83-2997
ISBN 0-8039-1966-2

FIRST PRINTING

CONTENTS

ACKNOWLEDGMENTS

The collection of material for this volume has been greatly aided by the support of a number of colleagues. Prior to the early months of 1982, when the Falklands/Malvinas crisis aroused a general interest in the study of small islands, the editorial board of the Sage Series on African Modernization and Development showed confidence in an enterprise that looked, at the time, to be a rather esoteric pursuit. In particular, the series editor, Peter Gutkind, provided encouragement to both the editor and the contributors. Ed Dommen of UNCTAD, whose knowledge of island societies is unrivaled, acted as a friendly adviser.

Three of the chapters were presented at a special conference in September 1981 on Small Island Economies, organized by one of the contributors, Miguel Sanchez-Padron, together with the Illustre Colegio de Economistas de Canaria and the Facultad de Ciencias Económicas y Empresariales of the University of La Laguna in the Canaries. The overseas guests were provided with a level of hospitality by the local government, the Chamber of Commerce, and our university colleagues for which it is difficult to express adequate thanks.

I would also like to record my gratitude to secretarial staff in the Department of Sociology at Warwick. Lesley Holmes initially kept the flow of correspondence going with contributors in seven countries. Later, Pam Smitham gave invaluable help on the manuscript itself and drew the location map. It was a great pleasure to work with her on this book.

—*Robin Cohen*
University of Warwick

LOCATION MAP
African Islands and Enclaves

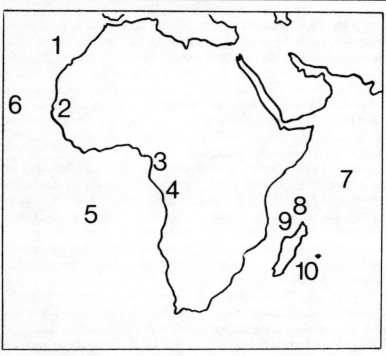

Key: 1. Canary Islands   6. Cape Verde Islands
      2. The Gambia   7. Diego Garcia
      3. Equatorial Guinea 8. Seychelles
      4. Cabinda   9. The Comoros
      5. St. Helena   10. Mauritius

INTRODUCTION

ROBIN COHEN
University of Warwick

Even President Reagan's staunchest political opponent must have felt some sympathy for his expression of bewilderment at Britain going to war for an "ice-cold bunch of land" in the South Atlantic during the early months of 1982. But however irrational this outburst of British militarism appeared, the dispute over the Falklands/Malvinas Islands simply drew to the public's attention what had been apparent to specialist scholars and strategists for a number of years: that small territories and islands are significant flashpoints in the contemporary world order. They are both exposed to the vissicitudes of international power rivalries and find it difficult to sustain a stable internal political and economic order. The contours of this dual exposure are derived in some respects from the very fact of their size, their characteristic economic weakness, and their historical dependence on larger countries for budgetary support and political protection.

It is true that size alone is not an absolute index of economic unviability. Witness the case of Hong Kong, which ranked fifteenth in the world in the value of manufactured exports in 1978 (World Bank, 1981: 156-157). The per capita incomes of the United Arab Emirates, Luxembourg, and Kuwait also show that small populations and territories can occasionally take advantage of a bonanza (like oil) or a special status in the financial markets. But the general association between smallness and weakness is clear. Of the 45 territories listed in United Nations statistics as having GDPs under U.S. $500 million (1977), no less than 26 are island countries. Even the smallest continental economy (the enclave of Djibouti, with a GDP of U.S. $90 million) has an economy larger than sixteen independent island economies. The smallest independent state in the world in terms of GDP is the Maldives, with no more than U.S. $11 million (Dommen, 1981: 1). An equally salient measurement is that of the 31 countries that are members of the United Nations and the World Bank with populations under 1 million, 24 have GNPs per capita of under U.S. $3,000, 19 of them being islands or small enclaves surrounded by other territories (World Bank, 1981: 185).

ECONOMIC AND POLITICAL REALITIES

The reasons for this demoralizing economic performance are not hard to find. Islands (and, to a lesser degree, enclaves) are rarely able to take advantage of economies of scale. They are frequently remote from major markets; they face adverse factor constraints (like limited fresh water supplies and inadequate personpower); their markets are wide open to market fluctuations; they often record high rates of emigration; the cost of their administrations is disproportionate to the populations they serve; and so on. Ed Dommen has also shown that hurricanes are more frequent on islands (affecting some two-thirds of island countries); fewer animal species are able to survive; and island countries are more densely populated than are their continental counterparts, while their populations are growing at a lower rate—the effect of lower crude birthrates and high emigration (Dommen, 1980: 931-943).

By the standards of the development agencies, then, small island countries and enclaves are being left behind in the race to "development." As the globalization of production and distribution reaches out toward the periphery, micro states remain in or are pushed further toward the margins of the world system. Paradoxically, however, smallness and weakness have not been important constraints on the attainment of self-determination and the international recognition of sovereignty. Many islands, of course, remain dependencies of larger political units—including, in this collection, the islands of St. Helena, the Canaries, and Diego Garcia. But many more have achieved formal independence—an extraordinary triumph considering the size of some of the territories concerned—of nineteenth-century notions of national self-determination. The proliferation of micro states has led to the anomalous situation in which the Maldives and Comoros islands have a combined voting strength in the UN General Assembly equivalent to that of China and the USSR. Naturally, this equality is merely a nicety of international law and in no way mirrors the strengths of the countries concerned. Nevertheless, the recognition of national status is not without significance. States, however small, have the right to levy tariffs, customs, and import duties; to print currency; to raise taxes; to be eligible for all kinds of international grants and assistance; to operate free ports; to be a home for international bankers and investors; down to the right to print postage stamps. It is a formidable set of advantages and (this is the point) a feature that permits small sovereign islands to evince a degree of power totally disproportionate to their size or their factor endowments. It is for access to the possibilities conferred by international recognition that so many nationalist and independence movements have been started in island countries, normally by the wealthy and dominant elements. The attainment of political independence has provided numerous opportunities for the more unscrupulous individuals in island societies to enrich themselves, an intriguing example being the case of James Mancham, formerly president of the Seychelles and the subject of a fawning biography (Lee, 1976).

But with these opportunities for some, come dangers for the islands' populations. Casinos, hotel chains, and hot money often held by criminal elements in metropolitan societies seize the advantages conferred by international law. The massive seesaws in the currency market experienced over the last few years owe not a little to the protective haven that small islands confer on currency speculators. Local governments are often hopelessly weak, ill-organized, or incapable of resisting the gifts and onslaughts of international finance. Where micro states are independent, the ruling parties tend to be precarious alliances of a local comprador bourgeoisie and its administrative supporters. The result tends to be a sharp polarization of wealth and opportunities within the island. Older notions of equality and harmony are rapidly transformed as the effects of the penetration of international capital are differentially spread among the populace. In some cases, the local leadership is able to maintain the sharp inequalities only by resort to terror. Ibrahim Sundiata's chapter on Equatorial Guinea provides a detailed account of one such regime, which has unfortunately escaped much public attention. Other independent island states discussed in the book (the Seychelles, the Comoros) have witnessed a successful revolt against the ruling groups and a precarious attempt to move to a more egalitarian path of development.

Dissent does not, however, always stem from internal forces. Island and micro states are also increasingly prone to secessionist tendencies characteristically resulting when a fraction of foreign capital can find a local leader—for them a pliant client—to use the rights conferred by independence in the interests of his paymasters. The tone of this new form of domination was perhaps best captured by an article in *Esquire* called "The Amazing New-Country Caper." This article describes how a group of businesspersons, including a firearms manufacturer, sought to subvert and ultimately seize by military force, the Abaco Islands in the Bahamas. The islanders, leading lives that were described as "ranging from quiet stagnation to mute poverty," were enjoined to fight for the status of a self-governing community in order better to further the conspirators' plans (St. George, 1975). Though the Abaco scheme soon floundered, in June 1980 the attempt to foment a rebellion in Espiritu Santo, part of the New Hebrides in the Pacific, very nearly succeeded. The rebel leader, Jimmy Stevens, was able to take advantage of the multiple confusions wrought by the joint British and French condominium of the islands with the help of his sponsors, the Phoenix Foundation of America, which, according to one source, has "right-wing views and a good deal of money" (Guardian Weekly, 1980). As far as newspaper reporters were able to discern, Mr. Stevens enjoyed a minimal level of popular support.

THE HISTORICAL LEGACY

The foregoing examples concern islands that were to be "decolonized" in the interests of private enterprise. In some cases, like those of the Canary Islands and St. Helena, decolonization is barely on the agenda. The Canaries are seen by official sources as an integral part of Spain, though the pressures for autonomy, as Sanchez Padron shows, have increased with the prospect of the islands losing their favored trading status when Spain joins the Common Market. Historically, the forms of dependence the island has on the mainland have conditioned the ways local powerful interests can dominate the island. In a sustained theoretical analysis, Sanchez Padron argues that "rent" and "profit" have intertwined to support the local oligarchy/bourgeoisie, but that this form of domination now depends on the continuing reconciliation of local and national interests. It is this protective relationship that is challenged by the autonomy movement.

Even though it is also under direct metropolitan control, the case of St. Helena offers a strong contrast to the Canaries, since there is no basis for local accumulation. The British rule of the island is hinged, rather, on that country's inability to escape an administrative burden acquired first during a period of relative prosperity and strategic significance of the island.

Many islands had their basic economies established during the mercantile period of capitalism's expansion. Some, like St. Helena, were settled and populated precisely to service the ships carrying the expanded trade of the European economy. Historically, the island was in effect a vegetable garden, a ship's chandlery, and a refreshment station for sailing ships going to the East via the Cape route. Once the steamship was invented and the Suez Canal opened, there was simply no reason to call there any more. The island drifted into a debilitating decay, that has not been arrested to this day.

Other islands, equally structured and conditioned by mercantile trade, have managed to achieve a precarious independence. Mauritius, the Cape Verdes, Equatorial Guinea, the Seychelles, and the Comoros (discussed in subsequent chapters) all have independent administrations, yet the burden of the past weighs heavily on them. Whatever level of internal reproduction existed, this was typically dependent on a monoculture, a plantation economy worked by imported slave labor. A number of the islands described in this book share with their Caribbean counterparts the heritage of a plantation-based economy. Of the islands surveyed, only in the Seychelles does there appear to be, as Kaplinsky argues, some basis for local accumulation.

The general pattern, however, seems to follow that proposed by Geoff Kay (1975), who argued in opposition to André Gunder Frank that dependence does not arise automatically from capitalist expansion; rather, the underdeveloping effects of capitalism are seen when *merchant* capital predominates and where therefore there is little basis for indigenous capital accumulation (the profits of trade being realized in the metropoles) and no growth of the local means of production beyond a small range of simple commodities or a single crop. Many island communities are still living with the underdeveloping effect of merchant capital. Fluctuation in the world demand for their products—normally sugar, coffee, bananas, and copra—leave them totally at risk. Even when prices are historically high, they are insufficient to wipe out previous troughs in world demand. Competitive advantage is difficult to exploit where the shipping lines are in control of their dominant trading partners, there are no regional markets, and the islands are located far from their principal markets.

While many islands have barely escaped and still show many signs of their mercantilist character, one recent development has been the attempt to start export-oriented manufacturing industries on a number of islands. The trend is not wholly new, though it has been rapidly accelerated in recent years. Such a strategy was pioneered by Hong Kong, Taiwan, and

Puerto Rico, but now there is scarcely an island in the world that does not have plans for at least a modest export manufacturing sector, often encouraged by agencies like the United Nations Industrial Development Organization (UNIDO) and the World Bank. What prospects of success do the attempts at peripheral industrialization have? The case of Puerto Rico (a state in "free association" with the United States) does not auger well for subsequent imitators of this development. Some 55 percent of the population take advantage of the food stamp scheme, costing the federal government $1 billion. Some 2 million islanders and their descendents live on the mainland, as opposed to 3.2 million on the island. Between 30 and 40 percent are unemployed or have given up seeking work, one-third of the work force works for the government or its agencies, the government of Puerto Rico owes $7 million to the mainland banks. This is on an island where the undoubted growth in GDP consequent on the U.S.-sponsored Operation Bootstrap has been deemed a great success, even an economic miracle, by its defenders.

THE COLLAPSE OF THE STATE OF NATURE

All this evidence of economic stagnation and political weakness—the implosion of the effects of world economic forces on remote islanders—is in marked contrast to a romantic view of island societies that is deeply embedded in Western cultures. David Pitt has pointed out that the interest in islands goes back at least to the Mediterranean odysseys. The European Age of Discovery (so-called, for of course the islanders themselves had already discovered their own islands) provided a good deal of new imagery for poetry and fiction and for scientific and social comment. As Pitt goes on to argue, the published work of explorers, missionaries, castaways, and traders had a great appeal to the Western consciousness and led to the publication of some of the most enduring works of fiction: *Robinson Crusoe, Treasure Island,* and a host of lesser imitations. The imagery of the South Sea islands, in particular, contrasted with the drab, back-to-back, urban landscapes of the industrial revolution. Islands also held out a prospect that was both exotic and erotic—Rousseau's State of Nature gained its artistic expression, for example, in the paintings of Gauguin. Again, the assumed permissiveness of many island cultures contrasted with the repressive social norms of the eighteenth- and nineteenty-century bourgeoisie and the asceticism that accompanied the growth of capitalism in Western Europe and North America. Even in the twentieth century, this imagery was hard to dispel, and the work of leading anthropologists like Bronislaw Malinowski (*Argonauts of the Western Pacific,* 1922) and Margaret Mead (*Coming of Age in Samoa,* 1928) undoubtedly gained more attention precisely because of their exotic settings (Pitt, 1980: 1051).

In many ways, then, islands represent to Western industrial culture an alternative vision—one that is marked by an exchange economy, a naturalness, a simple division of labor—an image often of the preindustrial age in the metropolitan culture. Seen more at the level of individual psychology rather than at the social level, to participate in island culture has become an expression of another side of the human personality—a form of escape into fantasy, warmth, and romance. It is this side of the appeal of islands that has now been transmuted through international travel and tourism into a consumer good, to be purchased through the local travel agent. Here escape is packaged into neat two-week periods, with any element of threat removed by the provision of the identikit hotels, similar cuisine (spiced occasionally by some local recipe), and guaranteed sea, sun, and sand. One of the dominant characteristics in the modern economies of small islands has thus become the fulfillment of an ersatz, temporary, plastic version of the adventures of the early explorers.

While the package tourist cannot easily reach St. Helena, would be excluded from the joys of observing the military maneuvers of the U.S. fleet on Diego Garcia, or would be terrified by the macabre and random violence Sundiata depicts in Equatorial Guinea, of the cases covered in this collection, the tourist impact in the Seychelles, The Gambia, Mauritius, and the Canary Islands is especially evident. While it is difficult to generalize across all islands in this respect, the growth of tourism presents an increasingly sharp choice between the economic benefits to islands in terms of the growth of the service industries and the acquisition of foreign exchange on the one hand, and, on the other hand, the damaging environmental and social costs incurred. Sometimes even the economic benefits of tourism have been challenged by some who show that the infrastructure of island economies can be easily distorted by a too-dominant tourist industry. The food-and-luxury-item import bill goes up to serve both the visitors and the locals who have acquired their consumer tastes, while foreign tour operators, hotel chains, and airline companies are able to extract a lion's share of the profits, to the detriment of the local economy. The environmental costs of tourism are increasingly evident in many places, as pollution, unsightly development, and overdevelopment impose strains on the local ecology—in particular, in the need to provide new sources of fresh water, sewage disposal systems, and agricultural land for airport and road development. The social costs of tourism can also be extremely heavy, and the gross disproportion of wealth between the islanders and the visitors then leads to a loss of confidence in the local culture, an imitative style of behavior and conduct, and, in some cases, the turning of the local population into waiters, pimps, and prostitutes. Only recently have we become aware of another possible cost of tourism: the political one. In The Gambia, the local population (some of them Muslim and fundamentalist, others simply trying to retain some of their own cultural norms) were long resentful of the tourist invasion of their country. School attendance rolls dropped as children left to beg money, while the tourists' standards of dress offended the locals. This feeling of resentment and dependence on foreign visitors undoubtedly triggered the recent violent attempted coup in that country—a country that, as Hughes shows, had hitherto been marked by an adherence to a parliamentary system of government, unusual in Africa.

STRATEGIC FACTORS

If tourism—an apparently innocent twentieth-century fulfillment of a nineteenth-century dream—has shown such a capacity for producing destructive social, political, and environmental effects, we are clearly dealing with societies that are highly brittle, highly exposed, and highly vulnerable to outside forces. But even if sophisticated tourist operators are able to insulate the romantic dreams of their clients from the harsher realities of island life, the final collapse of romanticism must follow the newly rediscovered strategic importance of islands. This importance derives from three principal factors. First, many islands sit astride important sea lanes. This mattered little to the imperialist powers when Britain, and later the United States, monopolized naval power on a worldwide scale. It matters a great deal more when Soviet naval power is expanding so dramatically and a host of medium-sized powers (including India, Argentina, and Brazil) have substantial merchant and naval fleets. The incoming conservative prime minister of Jamaica, for example, was not slow to point out to his potential U.S. backers that 61 percent of U.S. oil is routed through the Caribbean. Again, following the Suez crisis of 1956 and the oil cartel crisis of 1973, Western nations have become acutely conscious of their need to move strategic materials through waters not fully controlled by them. As Britain once used Gibraltar to police the sea lanes to the Mediterranean, so now the U.S. and a number of other countries have constructed military and naval facilities on islands.

This leads to the second factor enhancing the strategic attractiveness of islands. The stationing of dangerous warheads, missiles, and bomb stores, plus security-tight operations like space satellites and radio and other electronic transmission stations, can conveniently be sited on islands. The populations can be expelled (as in Diego Garcia), and many governments are easily coerced into compliance by the dominant power. Moreover, with the growth of antinuclear sentiment in Europe and the attempts by the peace movement to have Europe declared as a nuclear free zone, the temptation to take over an island solely for military purposes must be great. Although there is already a storm of protest building up in the Canary Islands over the proposed siting of NATO facilities there, perhaps the most brutal reminder of big-power realities is the case of Diego Garcia, now entirely given over to U.S. military use. Jooneed Khan has employed his skills in investigative journalism to expose the dubious moral standards of the departing colonial power, Britain, made all the more visible by its supposed principled stance in the analogous case of the Falklands. The election in Mauritius of a socialist government with historical claims on Diego Garcia and a program calling for the demilitarization of the Indian Ocean ushers in what could be a period of considerable instability. Both Kaplinsky's chapter on the Seychelles and Selwyn's analysis of the Mauritian economy and social structure provide information integral to an evaluation of the strategic significance of the Indian Ocean. The region as a whole is indeed fraught with uncertain geopolitical considerations. Are we to regard the U.S. facilities on Diego Garcia as a surrogate for its loss of influence in Iran? Will the South Africans intervene in Mauritius, bearing in mind that former members of the South African Military Reconnaissance Unit were responsible for the attempted invasion of the Seychelles late in 1981 (Financial Times, 1981)? Will the Soviet Union expand its naval presence in the area? Will the Indian or East African governments support the Mauritian call for the neutralization of the region?

The final factor influencing the strategic salience of islands and enclaves is that they happen sometimes to be located either where important mineral resources exist or where they can serve as gateways to hitherto unexploited resources. In the case of Cabinda, analyzed by dos Santos, the oil reserves operated by Gulf Oil in the enclave triggered a series of contradictory positions taken by the U.S. State Department. On the one hand, the intervention by Cuba and the accession to power in Angola by what was seen as a Marxist government impelled some sections of the State Department to lend covert support to South Africa's sustained attempts to destabilize the Angolan regime. On the other hand, Gulf's need to evolve a working relationship with the Angolan government eventually forced a *modus vivendi*. Nonetheless, as dos Santos shows, any attempts to develop Cabinda socially and economically are severely constrained by the security situation. Where strategic materials are not located *in* enclaves or islands, they nonetheless might provide bases for the expanded development of fishing resources, mining of the seabeds, and aquaculture, particularly since successive Law of the Sea conferences have expanded the territorial limits surrounding a coast line. While some of these developments are still somewhat speculative (U.S. Council on Environmental Quality, 1982: 105-116), at least some commentators on Britain's military expedition to the Falklands pointed to the possible exploitation of oil and mineral resources in the South Atlantic and Antarctica as an explanation for the action supplementary to that provided by the British prime minister.

SOME FINAL COMMENTS

Most of the chapters in this book speak for themselves. It would be misleading to try to impose an artificial unity of theme on all the contributors. But it may be helpful to readers if I make a few comments on the criteria I employed for selection. There are, by one estimate, some 77 micro states with populations of less than half a million people out of a total of 224 identifiable inhabited regions in the world (Caldwell et al., 1980: 953). In and around Africa alone, there are about two dozen islands and enclaves that could qualify for our attention. What I sought to achieve here was a reasonable balance between enclaves and islands, between Indian and Atlantic Ocean territories, and between territories that were self-governing and those that were still integrated into metropolitan political units.

What the authors share is a close familiarity with the territories they surveyed, one that goes beyond the tourist brochure or a traditional anthropological fiction into a direct and sometimes brutal appreciation of the difficulties and realities of constructing a modern life in such limiting contexts. The contributors, in short, transcend the view of islands as self-sustaining utopias fostered during the Age of Discovery. The possibilities of autarky, if they ever existed, passed with the underdevelopment occasioned by mercantile neglect and monoproduction in the eighteenth and nineteenth centuries. This heritage remains an indelible legacy of many islands and small territories today. The twentieth century has seen the emergence of new opportunities for islands—possibilities essentially of using their sovereignty to foster tourism, protect shady operators, and promote industrial development. These possibilities, as I have argued, have their own dangers and problems. But perhaps the real crisis, the crisis born of the increased recognition of the strategic significance of islands, is yet to come. Islanders have traditionally responded to such threats to their survival by migration, as Meintel shows in her contribution on the Cape Verdes. But with the avenues of international mobility increasingly closed off to them, islanders are going to have to evolve autonomous solutions to the challenges that confront them. I cannot but help express some pessimism as to their eventual capacity to resist the powerful extraneous forces I have described.

REFERENCES

CALDWELL, J. C. et al. (1980) "The demography of micro-states." World Development 8: 953-967.

DOMMEN, E. (1980) "Some distinguishing characteristics of island states." World Development 8: 931-943.

——— (1981) "Invisible exports from islands," presented at the Conference on Small Island Economies, Universidad de La Laguna, Canary Islands, September, 1981.

Financial Times (1981) November 27.

Guardian Weekly (1980) June 6.

KAY, G. (1975) Development and Underdevelopment: A Marxist Analysis. London: Macmillan.

LEE, C. (1976) Seychelles: Political Castaways. London: Hamish Hamilton.

MALINOWSKI, B. (1922) Argonauts of the Western Pacific. London: Routledge & Kegan Paul.

MEAD, M. (1928) Coming of Age in Samoa. New York: Morrow.

PITT, D. (1980) "Sociology, islands and boundaries." World Development 8: 1051-1059.

ST. GEORGE, A. (1975) "The amazing new-country caper." Esquire (February).

U.S. Council on Environmental Quality (1982) The Global 2000 Report to the President. Harmondsworth: Penguin.

World Bank (1981) World Development Report, 1981. Washington DC: International Bank for Reconstruction and Development.

1

INTERPRETING DEPENDENCY IN
THE CANARY ISLANDS

MIGUEL SANCHEZ-PADRON
Universidad de La Laguna, Canary Islands

This chapter starts by providing background information on the basic geographical, political, demographic, and historical features of the Canary Islands. Having set the scene, I begin with a critical assessment of the standard interpretation of the Canary Islands' economic evolution, seeking to show the conceptual and methodological weaknesses of such studies. The deficiencies and limitations of previous research are then examined. The lack of relevant statistical data limits the possibilities of these studies, studies that usually take the form of a sector-by-sector (agriculture, industry, and services) analysis. However, it is my contention that this type of analysis fails to provide a global perspective of the Canary Islands' socioeconomic system. To avoid these shortcomings, conceptual categories are proposed as guidelines for a new line of inquiry, with which empirical evidence can be easily interrelated, thus allowing a more comprehensive interpretation of the data. In order to illustrate the new perspectives and explanatory power of this proposal, the recent growth process of the Canaries' economy is then analyzed.

The last section is dedicated to a recapitulation of the main theoretical issues developed in the chapter: the *forms* taken by the reproduction of labor and the accumulation of capital. Finally, I emphasize the theoretical role that rent can play as an explanatory link between the economic and the sociopolitical levels of analysis.

BACKGROUND

Geography. The Canary Islands Archipelago lies a short distance from the Tropic of Cancer and 100 kilometers from the West coast of Africa. It is formed by a cluster of seven islands: Tenerife, Fuerteventura, Gran Canaria, Lanzarote, La Palma, La Gomera, and El Hierro. There are also six smaller islands; of these only La Graciosa is inhabited, by a very small community of fishing people. The archipelago has been an integral part of Spain since its conquest at the end of the fifteenth century.

The original inhabitants of the islands—the Guanches—and their culture have virtually disappeared.[1] The few that survived the conquest intermarried with the colonizers; thus the original language is unknown except in several towns and villages that still bear unaltered Guanche names. Some words have also survived.

The administrative organization of the islands is like that of any other part of Spain and is formed by two provinces, Santa Cruz de Tenerife (Tenerife, La Palma, Gomera and Hierro) and Las Palmas (Gran Canaria, Lanzarote, Fuerteventura and the other six very small islands). In 1852 the archipelago was granted, by royal decree, the status of duty free port.

Demography. Since 1920, the archipelago experienced continuous demographic growth: Between 1920 and 1975 (the date of the last local census), the population tripled, reaching a total of 1,394,276. This was the result of crude birthrates, which if not very high by Third World standards, have been much more pronounced than Spanish averages. Between 1936 and 1945, the crude birthrate was around 30 births per 1000 population, while the Spanish average was 21.6 births per thousand. The corresponding figures for the 1969-1975 period are approximately 25 births (Canary Islands) and 19 births (Spain) per thousand population.

Another demographic variable of great significance is emigration. Although there has been a more or less continuous flow of emigrants from the Canary Islands to Spanish America in general, three distinctive periods clearly stand out. During the first (1678-1778) there was forced emigration: For every 100 tons of goods exported from these islands to Spanish America, five local families were forced to leave in order to settle the new Spanish colonies. The second (1875-1925) and third (1940-1960) were directed mainly to Cuba and Venezuela, respectively.

As in most cases, emigration figures are not very reliable, but it has been estimated that between 250,000 and 300,000 people of Canary Islands origin live at present in Venezuela. There has also been a considerable amount of migration between the islands following a center (Gran Canaria and Tenerife) periphery (the rest of the islands) relationship.

Economy. An almost total lack of resources, as these are traditionally understood, is perhaps one of the most common topics in the descriptions of the archipelago—an assertion that is also generally supplemented with much-quoted references to the warm climate and strategic location of the islands as positive assets. At this point, however, it is necessary to stress that resources are a relative concept. This may be obvious, yet two observations need to be made. On the one hand, the beneficial aspects of most resources (but not all) are relative to and "can be assessed only in the context of particular social and economic structures and market situations" (Selwyn, 1978: 4). Indeed, it can be argued that the so-called advantage provided by certain resources may also have negative consequences.[2] On the other hand, who would have guessed that the Canary Islands' excellent location for astronomical observation would become a valuable natural resource (Sanchez, 1981)? More specifically, land and water are resources generally accepted to be scarce[3]—especially water; the water situation is considered to be critical, particularly in Gran Canaria (see Table 1.1). But here again, it must be asked to what extent the present situation is due to the institutional structure. Before developing this point, it will be necessary to describe briefly the main features of the archipelago's economic evolution. To this end it is useful to describe the model[4] that has been used in the past to summarize this evolution.

According to this model, the economic history of the region has been characterized by a succession of cycles, each of which is associated with a dominant export crop. Thus from the conquest of the islands by the Castilian crown the region has been integrated in the world economy by means of an international division of labor imposed from the outside that has oriented the economy to a number of productive activities that move chronologically from sugar cane (1500-1600), wine (1600-1800), cochinilla, an insect used in making dyes (1800-1850), bananas and tomatoes (from 1890), and tourism (from 1960). The change from one crop to another was caused by the loss of competitiveness as low-cost manufacturers or new synthetic products entered the world market. These shifts were also marked by crises in which emigration played the role of a safety valve, thus explaining the apparent contradiction between the changes just described and the fact that since the conquest "the structure of production and the appropriation of the social product has remained unchanged" (Bergasa and Gonzalez Vietez, 1969: 29). In the words of the authors who

TABLE 1.1   Basic Statistics of the Canary Islands

	Area (km²)	Water Extraction (Rm³/Year)	Water Consumption (M³/Person/Year)
Tenerife	2,057	225.65	382
La Palma	730	86.80	1.240
Gomera	378	12.58	620
Hierro	277	2.39	352
Total Province	3,442	327.42	477
Gran Canaria	1,532	147.54	233
Fuerteventura	1,731	5.21	208
Lanzarote	836	2.22	45
Total (Province E)	4,099	154.97	219
Total (Region)	7,541	482.39	346

SOURCE: Institute de Reforma y Desarrdlo agrario and Proyecto MAC-21.
Proyecto de Planificacion de la Explotacion y Uso racional de los recursos de Agua en las Iskey Canarias.

have expounded this latter thesis: "Emigration has constituted throughout Canary Islands' history, the conjunctural form of transcending structural conflicts, which reappear systematically as the causes which originated them remained unaltered" (Bergasa and Gonzalez Vietez, 1969: 32). Finally, tourism would constitute the last phase of change, a new cycle whose crisis is developing now that the emigration safety valve closed.[5] Herein lies the novelty of this crisis and its social importance. With this apparently structural crisis, the economy of these islands faces the exhaustion of its growth model.

But as in all summaries, the above gives an incomplete picture of the situation[6] and several qualifications are in order:

(1) The crises of the different crops have not been followed by their complete disappearance from cultivation, though they have certainly meant the loss of a significant contribution from each successive crop. Further, the beginning of tourism did not coincide with a crisis in the production of bananas and tomatoes;[7] its beginning was rather juxtaposed to previous economic activities—although with consequences for the rest of the system that will be analyzed later.

(2) The importance attributed to the different monocultures may give the wrong impression about their actual economic importance within the agricultural sector. In fact, as we shall see, domestic food production had performed a significant economic, albeit indirect, role.

(3) Further, the above description not only distorts the picture of the agricultural sector, but also, as Table 1.2 and 1.3 show, of the economy as a whole. Besides providing some background information, these tables show the basic statistics of the region insofar as they relate to our present concerns. It is sufficient to note at this point the importance of the service sector, the significance of which predates the upsurge of tourism. In fact, although this is not shown in the statistics cited, commerce even now claims a higher share of employment than tourism does.

A further elaboration on these points does not pertain to this brief introduction, which merely intends to provide some factual information. As I have already said, one of the main purposes of this chapter is precisely to show the shortcomings of the kind of approach partially summarized in the above exposition. To this I now turn.

CRITICAL EVALUATION OF PREVIOUS RESEARCH

Previous research[8] on the Canary Islands' economy is, generally speaking, empirical rather than theoretical. To a certain extent this type of approach was justified because the research was intended to obtain knowledge of a reality that had not been studied much; it was necessary, therefore, to delineate a "map" of the different economic sectors. This highly descriptive phase of research has had a clear impact on the "state of the matter" about Canary Islands' problem. Later, this description was completed with explanations and interpretations that, despite their brilliance, lacked a *theoretical* framework. Such a framework is needed both to unite those interpretations into a coherent whole and to show the interrelationships among the different economic sectors of the different islands that form the archipelago.

However, it is not accurate to say categorically that earlier research totally lacked a framework. Nor is it true that the approach used was simply a question of personal error. The framework was a natural division of the economy by sectors, main activities, and institutions (agriculture, industry, building, tourism, external trade, and so on). To a certain extent, this approach was the result of a combination of factors.

TABLE 1.2 Gross Domestic Product by Industrial Origin, 1955 and 1977 (current prices)

Year	Agriculture		Fishing		Manufacturing		Building and Construction		Services		Total
	a	b	a	b	a	b	a	b	a	b	
1955											
Las Palmas	1,286	26.0	105	2.1	589	11.6	378	7.7	2,583	52.3	4,941
Santa Cruz de Tenerife	1,190	25.2	55	1.2	852	18.0	279	5.9	2,345	49.7	4,721
Canarias	2,176	25.6	160	1.7	1,441	14.9	657	6.8	4,928	51.0	9,662
1977											
Las Palmas	7,830	6.0	3,434	2.6	15,227	11.6	11,568	8.8	93,249	71.0	131,308
Santa Cruz de Tenerife	9,435	7.5	671	0.5	14,798	11.8	12,729	10.1	88,033	70.1	125,666
Canarias	17,265	6.7	4,105	1.6	30,025	11.7	24,297	9.5	181,282	70.5	256,974

SOURCE: Renta Nacional de Espana y su distribucion provincial del Banco de Bilbao 1955 and 1977.
a. Millions of pesetas.
b. Percentage of GDP.

TABLE 1.3 Distribution of Employment by Sector, 1955 and 1977

Year	Agriculture Total	%	Fishing Total	%	Industry Total	%	Construction Total	%	Services Total	%	Total	Wage Employment Total	%
1955													
Las Palmas	85,111	51.4	5,322	3.2	23,764	14.4	9,372	5.7	41,933	25.3	165,502	91,971	55.6
Santa Cruz de Tenerife	103,935	62.2	1,890	1.1	16,753	10.0	8,133	4.9	36,427	21.8	167,138	84,397	50.5
Canarias	189,046	56.8	7,212	2.2	40,517	12.2	17,505	5.3	78,360	23.5	332,640	176,368	53.0
1977													
Las Palmas	32,176	15.8	5,964	2.9	25,425	12.5	21,662	10.6	118,505	58.2	203,732	154,624	75.9
Santa Cruz de Tenerife	46,531	22.3	2,073	1.0	23,858	11.4	24,108	11.6	112,187	53.7	208,754	145,068	69.5
Canarias	78,707	19.1	8,037	2.0	49,283	11.9	45,770	11.1	230,689	55.9	412,486	299,692	72.7

SOURCE: Renta Nacional de Espana y su distribucion provincial del Banco de Bilbao, 1955 and 1977.

The first factor was (and is) of a statistical nature, in the sense that the available data (basically figures about demography, production and transport, tourism, external trade, incomes of local government institutions, and some financial flows) made an approach based on more strictly economic concepts very difficult. For example, the typical short-term analysis based on income, employment, consumption and investment cannot be made because a continuous evaluation of most of these factors for Canary Islands has not been done.

To the inherent difficulties of the classic sectoral framework without any specific theoretical content must be added two other kinds of conceptual problems that face any type of global approach to economic systems like the one being considered here. First, a basic feature of many underdeveloped[9] economies in general, and of small economies in particular, is that

> they are made up of atoms which are relatively juxtaposed and not integrated, the density of the flow of external exchanges of these atoms being relatively greater and that of the flow of internal exchanges very much less. It is said that this economy is "disarticulated," "astructural" or else that the developed economy is "auto-centric" whereas that the underdeveloped countries is extraverted [Amin, 1974: 288].

Second, and much more important, is the question of whether the unit concerned can be treated as an "economy." As Selwyn (1978: 11) argues:

> Brewster in an empirical study of the relations between a number of key variables such as employment, wages, exports, the import coefficient, productivity, the G.D.P., capital formation and prices in Trinidad, found a notable absence of association between them: this economic incohesiveness, and the limits it imposes consequentially on the internal ability to manipulate the system give rise to some doubt about the extent to which such a country can be treated analytically as if it were an economy.

In this case, we find partial evidence of the above features when we consider the peculiar forms taken by the economic crisis in the Canaries: a paradoxical coexistence of "good" indices of agricultural production and increases in the number of visitors together with high (and growing) unemployment figures and a decrease in the activity of the building industry.

These conceptual problems explain why studies about the Canary Islands' economy based on a sectoral framework could not shed light on the functioning of the system as a whole. The reason is obvious; the sectors in which the system is "divided" for its analysis are parts so weakly integrated[10] that they provide too narrow a base on which to reconstruct a theoretical whole in its totality and thus facilitate a global interpretation. My own previous work about the Canary Islands' economy, to the extent that it was also guilty of using a sectoral framework, also suffered from the same shortcomings. Furthermore, any new, fundamental reevaluation—theoretical or empirical—about the functioning of the system that we tried to introduce would be finally diluted or "vanish" inside the Procrustean bed created by the sectoral analysis. Thus despite the positive advance provided by power approaches, "descriptive theory represents a phase in the constitution of the theory. The accumulation of facts," as Althusser notes, "although it furthers the illustration, does not advance the scientific theory of the object under study. Thus, every descriptive theory runs the risk of blocking the necessary development of the theory" (Althusser, 1974: 23). One of the first requisites to a more comprehensive understanding of the Canary Islands' economic reality is, therefore, a different framework of analysis that can overcome the difficulties so far mentioned.

But there is another aspect of this line of research with which we must deal. This is the model of the historical evolution of the Canary Islands previously summarized. (To be more precise, this model was the vision of the economic history into which the research was inserted, and which, to a large extent, conditioned this approach.) I am referring to the emphasis given by this model to the continuity of "extraversion" and external dependency throughout the different cycles—from my point of view one of its most positive and insightful aspects. The external side of the economy certainly is a good starting point to explain the dynamics of the region. This is so not only because that sector is the locus through which part of the economic surplus is obtained, but also because the infrastructure, as well as part of the economic and social structure of the region, is organized on the basis of the "external side" of the economy.

Indeed, one of the features of the economy of the Canary Islands shares with the other island economies, is the importance of the external sector. Table 1.4 shows the evolution of foreign and total (which include those from mainland Spain) imports and its relation to total regional income. But it is one thing to talk of the external trade sector in general and another thing to concentrate, as the model does, on the dominant export crops to explain the evolution of the region's economy. In fact, as Table

TABLE 1.4 Total Regional Income (RI) Imports (in millions of pesetas), 1962-1977

Year	RI	Imports				Imports as Proportion of RI			
		Foreign		Total					
	(1)	(2)	(3)	(4)	(5)	(2)/(1)	(3)/(1)	(4)/(1)	(5)/(1)
1962	15,660	10,713.3	5,817.1	12,449.1	7,552.9	68.41	37.14	79.49	48.22
1964	22,729	13,812.9	8,203.2	16,009.6	10,339.9	60.77	36.09	70.43	45.75
1967	34,625	20,200.8	13,465.0	24,724.4	17,978.3	58.34	38.88	71.40	51.92
1969	46,736	25,664.1	17,772.2	43,712.4	34,415.9	54.91	38.02	93.53	73.63
1971	66,336	32,878.7	22,181.6	58,089.5	47,174.5	49.56	33.43	87.56	71.11
1973	102,396	41,157.3	31,467.0	81,700.9	70,958.1	41.17	30.73	79.78	69.29
1975	147,746	60,526.4	33,838.7	111,764.1	84,511.5	40.9	22.90	75.64	57.20
1977	237,856	109,632.6	58,111.6	181,188.5	129,667.5	46.09	24.43	76.17	54.51

SOURCE: Renta Nacional y su distribucion provincial del Banco de Bilbao Direccion General de Aduanas. Anuarios de Comercio Exterior.

(1) Regional income.
(2) Foreign imports.
(3) Foreign imports (excluding oil).
(4) Total (foreign and mainland) imports.
(5) Total (foreign and mainland) imports (excluding oil).

1.5 demonstrates, exports as such do not form a very large part of the region's total income, although as these figures do not include invisible exports (principally receipts from tourism) they must be interpreted with some caution.

Moreover, the importance placed on dominant export crops produces a distorted view: the identification of the dominant crop and the interests of the plantation owners with the interests of the rest of the agricultural sector and, to a large extent, with the interests of the whole economy. In the case of bananas, the consequences have been so especially negative that we may talk of a "system of *institutional comparative advantage*"—a complex structure of institutions and decision making that reinforces specialization and dependence (Selwyn, 1978: 22).[11] I am referring, particularly, to the heavy demand for water of the banana crop. As Table 1.6 shows, the banana crop consumes more than half of the total water used by agriculture in both provinces.

Even though the critical water situation of these islands provides a prima facie case for shifting agricultural production to crops with lower water consumption, it still could be argued that there is nothing exceptional in this; as long as the profitability of the crop is sufficiently high, its cultivation could be justified or, if one takes *social* costs and benefits into consideration, at least explained. Paradoxically enough, the cultivation of bananas can hardly be justified on the grounds of mere profitability as Table 1.7 illustrates the *total* income generated to the banana plantation owner is lower than that obtained from other products except for potatoes. Note also that wage and owners' income per cubic meter of water is also much lower than it is for other crops.

Moreover, there are also other types of consequences, probably of wider relevance, insofar as the vulnerability and flexibility of the economic system is at stake. Crusol and Crusol (1980: 1027, 1031) have argued that

> Some of the economic characteristics of small island plantation economies generate a particular political structure in which the plantation interest is predominant. This makes their adjustment to the present decline of some of the main traditional plantation crops difficult and painful, since most of their economic policy measures are not long-run policies to ensure competitiveness, but are short-run expedients to save uncompetitive crops. . . . Producers attempt to maintain their revenues by transferring their economic problems to the political market.

The Canary Islands are just a case in point—but one where flexibility is further diminished by the strong control that the plantation owners in

TABLE 1.5   Total Regional Income (RI) and Exports (in millions of pesetas), 1962-1977

Year	RI (1)	Exports Foreign (2)	Exports Foreign (3)	Exports Total (4)	Exports Total (5)	Exports as Proportion of RI (2) (1)	Exports as Proportion of RI (3) (1)	Exports as Proportion of RI (4) (1)	Exports as Proportion of RI (5) (1)
1962	15,660	3,914.0	2,177.1	8,045.4	6,308.5	24.99	13.90	51.37	40.28
1964	27,729	4,324.4	2,397.2	10,104.6	8,117.4	19.02	10.54	44.45	35.71
1967	34,625	3,620.3	2,254.1	12,817.5	7,338.8	10.45	6.51	37.01	21.19
1969	46,736	4,385.8	3,026.5	17,499.7	9,890.8	9.38	6.47	37.44	21.16
1971	66,336	6,483.8	5,180.9	20,973.5	15,004.3	9.77	7.81	31.61	22.61
1973	102,396	7,860.2	5,193.2	23,357.7	15,984.8	7.67	5.07	22.81	15.61
1975	147,746	12,585.6	8,304.4	35,884.4	19,285.2	8.51	5.62	24.28	13.05
1977	237,856	31,236.5	19,326.8	59,274.8	47,365.1	13.13	8.12	24.92	19.91

SOURCE: Renta Nacional y su distribucion provincial del Banco de Bilbao Direccion General de Aduanas, Anuarios de Comercio Exterior.

(1) Regional income.
(2) Foreign exports.
(3) Foreign exports (excluding oil).
(4) Total (foreign and mainland) exports.
(5) Total (foreign and mainland) exports (excluding oil).

TABLE 1.6   Total and Percentage Water Consumption in Agriculture
(Hm^3)

Crop	Las Palmas (1973)		Santa Cruze de Tenerife (1974)	
	Hm^3	%/Total	Hm^3	%/Total
Cereals	3.26	2.49	2.37	1.47
Legumes	0.93	0.07	0.98	0.60
Potatoes	7.96	6.10	27.23	16.94
Flowers	0.29	0.02	4.53	2.81
Vegetables	37.61	28.82	26.36	16.40
Tomatoes	30.48	23.36	22.58	14.05
Cucumber	3.14	2.40	—	—
Others	3.99	3.05	3.78	2.35
Bananas	71.04	54.44	88.38	55.01
Others	9.38	7.18	10.81	6.72
Total	130.47	100.00	160.66	—

SOURCE: Estudio cientifico de los recursos de agua en Las Islas Canarias. Vol. II y
III. M.O.P. Direccion General de Obras Hidraulicas y Unesco, 1975.

general, and banana producers in particular, have over water. Thus contrary to previous historical periods, production shifts within the agricultural sector are much harder to facilitate.[12]

FROM ECONOMICS TO POLITICS

From a theoretical perspective, the fact that the vision of the economic history of the region is centered on the level of circulation instead of production reflects the nature and character of the political programs proposed. The circulationist character of the model in question is based on the previously mentioned fact that it is centered on external trade in general; that is, it is located at the level of visible empirical history, which in turn leads to the periodization of the Canary Islands' history on the basis of the evolution of the main exports. This emphasis on the analysis of the "external" aspect of the social formation, leads to the theoretical primacy of exchange over production relations. As Dobb (1972: 43) explained:

One might think it is harmless enough to make an abstraction of certain aspects of exchange-relations in order to analyze them in isolation from the social relations of production. But what actually

TABLE 1.7 Profitability and Return to Inputs of Different Crops (GRAN CANARIA)

	Bananas	Cucumbers	Potatoes	Tomatoes
(1) Wages per hectare (pesetas) GRAN CANARIA (Total)	103 $(10)^3$ 410 $(10)^6$	445 $(10)^3$ 125 $(10)^6$	60 $(10)^3$ 180 $(10)^6$	154 $(10)^3$ 460 $(10)^6$
(2) Owners income per hectare GRAN CANARIA (Total)	103 $(10)^3$ 426 $(10)^6$	327 $(10)^3$ 92 $(10)^6$	100 $(10)^3$ 300 $(10)^6$	206 $(10)^3$ 620 $(10)^6$
(3) Water consumed (m^3/hectare)	16 $(10)^3$	7 $(10)^3$	6 $(10)^3$	10 $(10)^3$
Wages generated by m^3 of water $\left[\dfrac{(1)}{(3)}\right]$	6.44	63.6	10	15.4
Owners income by m^3 of water $\left[\dfrac{(2)}{(3)}\right]$	6.69	46.7	16.6	20.6
Total income per m^3 of water $\dfrac{(1)+(2)}{(3)}$	13.3	110.3	26.6	36

SOURCE: Estudio científico de los recursos de agua en Las Islas Canarias. Volume: II and III. M.O.P. Direccion General de Obras Hidraulicas y Unesco, 1975.

occurs is that once this abstraction has been made it is given an independent existence as though it represented the essence of reality, instead of one contingent facet of reality.

As a consequence, the "internal" aspect of the reality was not, in general, an object of study, and hence was relegated for all practical purposes to a secondary place. Furthermore, as the fundamental political question (or perhaps contradiction) of the period was the lack of political rights and freedom, mixed with a strong degree of centralism—a smoke screen used cunningly by the local oligarchies—there was no need for a wider economic analysis to be projected and/or used as a means to rationalize the political programs. For the same reason, there were no demands requiring an economic coherence (understanding this in a wide sense) to the political program: The question of freedom and democracy was relocated, to some extent, in the terrain of ethics.

Subsequently, with the termination of the Franco dictatorship by natural death and the "appearance" (almost out of the blue)—following Spanish liberalization—of political parties with a genuine local basis, the lack of understanding of the internal aspects of the Canary Islands' reality—not only economic, but also socially and culturally—explains the initial lack of articulation and clear political content that has characterized the nationalistic position in the islands. Hence the continuous references made to "searching for an identity against the clock," which has materialized in the apogee and acceptance enjoyed by all cultural manifestations of a Canarian character. This reference makes necessary a short detour into the subject of nationalism.

Certainly, strong widespread and politically articulated manifestations of nationalism cannot be found in the history of the Canary Islands. In this sense the situation is different from that of other Spanish regions. It is true also that Africa and the Canary Islands have no similar political history to the extent that while virtually all of Africa used to be a colonial area, the Canary Islands, *strictly speaking,* never were. The islands are politically integral parts of Spain—merely "incorporated" (as the expression went) into the Kingdom of Castile after the conquest—although they are geographically, but not culturally, part of Africa.[13]

To start with, the lack of strongly differentiated local culture or an indigenous language and the very "islandness" of the region are all factors that work against the formation of a nationalist sentiment. In addition, and without necessarily taking Amin's strong economistic position on this point, the consequences of the lack of integration of the economic structure must also be noted:

> What we have here is not a nation, in the economic sense of the word, with an integrated internal market. . . . The weakness of the national cohesion in the third world is often a reflection of this fact [Amin, 1974: 289].

It would be misleading, however, to say that there have been no nationalistic manifestations at all. There have been, if only because certain objective conditions were present: the physical separation from mainland Spain, the historical links with Spanish America, the strong influence exerted by the English from the second half of the nineteenth century up to World War II.[14] In fact, as certain undercurrents[15] of the Canary Islands' history indicate, there are several examples that show that the national feeling was not quite so dormant as official history would lead one to believe. It was only natural that many politicians were surprised at the outburst of nationalism and the appearance of several local nationalist parties and movements following their legalization. As I will address this theme in more detail in the last section of this chapter, it need detain us no longer than it takes to deal with a movement that has wider implications.

Although with tenuous origins stretching as far back as the 1960s, the pro-independence party, MPAIAC,[16] really came to the fore with the "abandonment" of the Sahara by Spain at the beginning of 1976. At this time, MPAIAC became the most *vocal* and well-known independence movement this archipelago has ever had going so far as to ask the Organization for African Unity (OAU) to declare the Canary Islands a territory subject to decolonization. The relative prominence enjoyed by this movement seems only to confirm one of the features that has characterized the different outbursts of nationalism in the Canary Islands: a nationalism in the wake of external circumstances, a contagion spread by the independence of Spanish America, the English influence, and the decolonization of Africa. The influence of the latter is not so much exerted on the basis of a demonstration effect, but is rather the result of the geostrategic significance of the Canary Islands.[17] This significance results, in the first place, from being located astride an important sea lane in the Atlantic: The main ports of the Canary Islands are of worldwide importance. Second, and more important, the government has announced its intention of building a huge naval base on one of the Islands. (Later in the chapter I will refer briefly to the economic implications of this.) Despite government reassurances to the contrary, there is a strong local suspicion that the base could be used by NATO as soon as Spain becomes a member of this organization, an event expected to take place in the near future. The building of a naval base in the Canary Islands, in turn, worries some of the nearby African states. The interplay of all these factors probably explains the support given to the MPAIAC.

In any case, and to return to the point of departure, the clarification of the relationship between extroversion dependency and the structural problems of the economy, or to put it more generally, the internal aspect of the reality of the Canary Islands' socioeconomic system, constitutes the most relevant omission of the model to which I have repeatedly referred. However, to the extent that the external sector—or what is the same from the perspective of the internal production, the monoculture—is based and depends on certain forms of internal organization, these forms must be also object of analysis. How shall we characterize these forms of organization? What is the function played by the social relations of production, the forms and conditions of the reproduction of the labor force, the accumulation of capital and the structure of classes and power? These are some of the aspects of the Canary Islands that have not been properly studied; standing out especially is the absence of a class analysis revealing the relationship and functionality between institutional changes, policy measures, and continuity of the dominant power groups.

Yet the lack of analysis of these themes is not the only cause that justifies the need to study them. The fact that they are the object of my attention in this present work is further explained by their role in my attempt to provide an alternative conceptual framework. In this respect, it is important to underline the difference entailed by the use of the categories like "reproduction of the labor force" and "accumulation of capital" as opposed to sectoral analysis. The difference lies not only in that the former categories have a specific conceptual content, but also that they can act as guiding threads that transcend and unify a reality that has only been empirically sectoralized. A global vision of the totality of the system is thus facilitated. I leave aside, therefore, as my point of departure, the external facade of the different sectors and its commodities and industries, which are subsumed in the former categories. These are the coordinates in which my work is located, and this is the theoretical vacuum that I am trying to fill.

It is in this context—where we believe that questions of vital importance in the present political and economic conjuncture are largely concealed or in a conceptual limbo—that this discussion must be located. Inasmuch as the present moment is characterized by a political conjuncture in which the basis for a new articulation and conformation of the local system of power is being laid, the prime importance of the analysis of class alliances—an analysis that requires the correct identification of the different class interests—should be stressed. What do the alliances and political fractions that have taken place during the period of political transition in Canary Islands represent? What class interests are represented by the different political groups? To underline the importance of these considerations it is sufficient to note, at this stage, that the solutions to some of the structural problems of Canary Islands require a rupture with the dominant power structures, whose continuity as such power groups precisely depends on the continuity of the above problems.

RECENT GROWTH OF THE ECONOMY: AN ANALYSIS

In the short summary of the model included in the first section of this chapter a reference was made to tourism as the last variant of the model, another cycle whose crisis, with the safety valve of emigration closed, implied the exhaustion of the island's economic growth model. This assertion requires a more profound elucidation. First, because having been taken for granted, this question has become a reference point from which to judge the problems of and alternatives to the present situation. Second, it is necessary to explain how and why the recent economic evolution, which has been characterized by high rates of growth, has led to a situation, not of slackening or downturn in the cycle, but of exhaustion.

For these reasons, it would be convenient to start giving some—if only cursory—quantitative evidence of the magnitude of this recent process of growth. During the 1955-1975 period, the annual cumulative growth rate of total net production per capita (in pesetas at 1975 values) was 7.9 percent and 7.3 percent for the provinces of Las Palmas and Santa Cruz de Tenerife, respectively. In the same period, the growth of net total production was 361 percent (Las Palmas) and 373 percent (Santa Cruz de Tenerife). These figures show very crudely the nature of the problem. Put rhetorically: How is it possible that a process of growth of such magnitude did not lead to the required structural transformations, thereby avoiding the present need for a new pattern of growth? To put it differently: What changes in the Canary Islands' social formation have made it possible for the first time for some social groups to support the need for a complete new orientation of the economy? Continuity and change are thus the defining features of the present situation, which I will proceed to analyze from this double perspective.

GENERAL CHARACTERISTICS OF THE 1964-1975 PERIOD: THE MASK OF TOURISM

The fact that the economic boom of this period is generally identified with the growth of tourism needs clarification. Although it is unquestionable that tourism has produced some multiplier effects on the rest of the economy, the authentic agents of change and dynamic elements affecting the accumulation of capital have been the various speculative movements that have accompanied (or been produced by) the building of the infrastructure required by tourism. That is, tourism is only the external facade—the mask of this period that had, let me say it again, its main engine and source of economic surplus in *land speculation*.

This point is essential for a full understanding of the evolution of the period. Although the tourist activity per se has played an important part in the structure of employment, its role as a source of monetary surplus, and hence its capacity to push and/or maintain economic growth in the islands is, to say the least, very limited. So despite the fact that we cannot give a quantitative answer to the question, "How much is left on the islands as a result of tourism?" We do know, nevertheless, that the rise in the number of visitors tailed off in 1977 (the middle of a generalized economic crisis). This shows the limited dynamic function of this sector. Thus the so-called exhaustion of the model of growth of the economy on the basis of the evolution of the tourist sector alone should be questioned or at least qualified in light of the above considerations. With this background we proceed to characterize this period from the double perspective of continuity and change.

CONTINUITY: DEPENDANT EXTROVERSION, LABOR COSTS, AND THE ROLE OF RENT

The first form of continuity and one of the central parameters of the economy of these islands, namely dependent extroversion, has been perpetuated by tourism. To the exports of agricultural products has been added the export of services to meet a demand still conditioned and molded mainly by outside forces and with a very limited internal capacity to influence its own evolution. The function of the island economy within the world economic system continues to be the same; it is similar to that of other zones of the periphery: the production of goods, in this case services, which permit a reduction in the costs of reproduction of the center labor force.

Second, regarding the capacity to compete with other zones (and hence its long-term possibilities), the tourist activity, like other exports, was developed on the basis of low labor costs. This was in part due to the incorporation of women in the statistically registered labor force. With this I do not want to minimize the role that has been played (and can continue to play) by the so-called natural comparative advantages in the development of exports in general, and tourism in particular. But it is also widely accepted that throughout our history that those advantages have not produced a sufficient margin to offset the advantages accrued by lower-wage areas. The case of tourism is still more grave because its own development has damaged the environment, which is part of its material basis, thus leaving the "yearly hours of sun" as the only natural advantage. On the other hand, as is well known, the value of the labor force is strongly linked to (or is a function of) the general development of the economy. As Marx (1976: 275) argued:

> The number and extent of his [the worker's] so-called necessary requirements, as also the manner in which they are satisfied, are themselves products of history of civilization attained by a country; in particular they depend on the conditions in which and consequently on the habits and expectations with which, the class of free workers has been formed.

As a consequence, the margin and possibilities of the tourist industry to compete with other less developed zones—with lower labor costs—is certainly limited.

Third, despite the fact that specialization in tourism leads to a change in the economic structure, especially in the distribution of employment, I have already noted that the authentic engine of the whole process was land and real estate speculation. It will be sufficient at this stage to say that the economic importance of this point lies in the fact that the surplus produced during this process is obtained mainly in the form of rent (and not in the form of profit). This represents a clear element of continuity in the characteristics of the process of capital accumulation in the region. I leave for another section a more detailed analysis of the economic and sociopolitical implications of this point.

CHANGE: WAGE EARNERS, THE LOCAL
MARKET, AND RESOURCES

The three major elements of change that I wish to identify here are the increase in the number of wage earners, the extension of the internal (local) market, and the appearance and strengthening of new contradictions in the use of basic resources, namely, land, water, and energy.

The reallocation of the agrarian active population to the service and the building industry during the 1960-1975 period is not only a change of location and transformation in the general structure of employment. More relevant from an economic point of view is the alteration in the distribution of the number of wage earners, as shown in Table 1.8.

The increase in the percentage of wage earners reflects a change in the forms of employment, which in turn implies a stronger nexus and dependence on the market to satisfy consumption needs. This is correct, of course, to the extent that self-sufficiency in consumption was more important, or was at least more likely, in the former occupations of the neophyte wage earners. This point receives further empirical support from Table 1.8, which shows the reduction of self-employment in agriculture.

In this period the pressure on the "scarce" resources of land, water, and energy and their use as a source of surplus not only increased, but the origin of that pressure was displaced: The interests of the urban residential and tourist zones prevailed over those of the rural zones. The demands of the plantation agricultural sector on water supplies on the basis of a self-imputed priority over other consumers is another case in point.

Before passing to the next section, where I will proceed to a more detailed examination of some of the features of continuity and change, it is necessary to deal with one of the elements of continuity, if only because is so frequently only partially understood (that is, generally taken in a purely literal sense). I am referring to the feature of dependent extroversion, the most generic of all the characteristics I have mentioned, in the sense that its influence can be detected not only at the economic level, but also on the social and cultural levels. In this context, it could be of some interest to be explicit about the way in which I use the concept of dependency. General references to this concept emphasize its external, coactive character; however, I also see dependency as "conditioning the *internal* structure which in turn internalizes the dependency situation according to the structural possibilities of the different economies" (Dos Santos, 1971: 100). That is, the specificity of dependence is not so much

TABLE 1.8 Proportion of Wage Earners in Total Employment

	1955		1964		1975	
	Las Palmas	Santa Cruz de Tenerife	Las Palmas	Santa Cruz de Tenerife	Las Palmas	Santa Cruz de Tenerife
Employment	165.502	167.138	171,124	182,036	193,935	209,122
% Wage Earners	55.57	50.50	61.57	53.90	76.49	66.55
% Nonwage Earners	44.43	49.50	38.43	46.10	23.51	333.45

SOURCE: Renta Nacional de Espana y su distribucion provincial. Serie momogenea 1955-1975. Banco Bilbao.

the external conditioning situation, but the manner in which dependency is internalized by the local socioeconomic structure. This is so to the extent that the form in which external conditioning acts on the national (local) reality is determined by the internal components of that reality.

From this perspective, the impact of tourism ought to be judged by its capacity to deepen the orientation of the socioeconomic system toward the exterior, thus diminishing its flexibility and capacity for a possible internal reorientation. Furthermore, one of the differences of tourism, vis-à-vis previous activities, is its transnational character.

> The transnational system has been eliminating elements that do not fit into it, remnants of earlier sociocultural systems, and has been integrating the remaining elements into a whole having a remarkable consistency. . . . Because of transnationalization, national societies in the capitalist sphere, both "underdeveloped" and "developed," are suffering deep changes in their social structure. In the first place, a process of *disintegration* has set in. This is most obvious in its effect on the economy. . . . At the same time national societies are generating a variety of counter-processes or *reintegration*, with a reassertion of national or subnational values and meanings, which sometimes find political expression, in an attempt to assert the separate identify of the nation or of subnational entities, at all levels, social, cultural, and personal [Fuenzalida and Sunkel, 1976: 5, 6].

Thus the impact of tourism ought to be judged by its capacity to reinforce the external orientation of the socioeconomic system, thereby diminishing its flexibility and capacity for a possible and necessary internal reorientation. The mechanisms and manifestations of the reinforcement of the dependent extroversion have been many and varied. As elements of the process of disintegration I can mention: the rural-urban migration, the partial decline in domestic food production, the domination of foreign capital over internal resources and the subordination of the local dominant classes as the internal links and representatives of external capital, and the preference granted to external transport infrastructures vis-à-vis the internal, and within the latter those related to tourism, while the local transport infrastructure is still insufficient. At the level of new institutions, preference has also been given to the creation of those activities related to tourism.

The effects of tourism illustrate the point that the recent growth process of the Canary Islands (to which reference has already been made) has not been accompanied by a qualitative transformation in the orientation and basic structure of the region's economy. This is why the growth process can lead to "exhaustion" when the initial dynamics based on speculation enter into crisis.

RESPONSES TO CHANGE AND ITS CONDITIONING

It is obvious that in my description of the tourist-speculative process[18] (incomplete and partial because of its complexity), I have had to select those aspects that seemed the most relevant. It is necessary, therefore, to explain the reasons for my selection, and why I have differentiated the elements according to their functionality for continuity or change. To put it briefly, the *forms* of capital accumulation and reproduction of the labor force have been my guiding threads in the study of the effects of the tourism process. Let us see now what specificity these forms have, and their relationship with the configuration of social classes and the Canary Islands' social formation in general.

THE REPRODUCTION OF THE LABOR FORCE

The Canary Islands' social formation has been characterized by the coexistence of the wage relationship with other precapitalist social relations, which permitted a cheap reproduction of the labor force. It has yet to be determined to what extent this coexistence of different forms of employment still fulfills that function nowadays. In some cases, the social relations of production have clear feudal connotations. In other cases, the wage is generally supplemented by other activities—sharing arrangements for the breeding of cattle, plantation workers' right to cultivate subsistence crops in small plots on the plantations, wage laborers working simultaneously on their own plots, and so on. All these, however, have the same economic function: to lower the costs of labor. This in turn implies that if the dynamics and continuity of the economic system depend on maintaining a great part of the active population at very low levels of income, salary—but also consumer income—has an institutional ceiling that it cannot exceed. In other words, the function of wages as a cost limits and dominates its function as income in the formation of effective demand. It is well known that this contradiction between the twin functions of wages is common to all capitalist economies; however, the difference is that in extroverted economies—where the bulk of demand comes from outside— wages can and tend to be as low as the political and social conditions permit, whereas in the autocentric economies, the reduction of the total wage fund beyond certain limits affects the dynamics of the system.

In any event, whatever the actual forms (wage or nonwage work) that employment takes, the conditions for the simultaneous holding of different jobs are more favorable in small than in large economies. As the analytical relevance of this comment may well go beyond the case of the Canary Islands, I shall elaborate on this point. Although some of the literature on island economies has referred to this matter, it has done so from a different angle. Diversity and diversification are not the only result of a security-centered survival algorithm, so that "risk-minimisation is a major principle of modern economic behaviour in underdeveloped regions" (Brookfield, 1975: 56). They may also be explained by the opportunities that small size provides and/or by the economic structure that generally goes with small size and more particularly with island economies. Small size per se (in this case short transport distance) facilitates the simultaneous holding of a rural and an urban job. We may talk of this case as the worker having one leg in the country and the other in the town. The small size also helps rural-urban migrants to maintain their links with the place of origin—these links probably explain why, in the period of crisis after 1976, there was an increase in the active population in the agricultural sector. Moreover, the coexistence of rural and urban jobs is further enhanced by the relatively higher importance of the service sector in this type of economy—a sector that, as is well known, provides a host of opportunities for casual, nonpermanent employment. All these, incidentally, may be quite consistent with maximization principles rather than with risk-minimization.

These forms of reproduction of labor are at the basis of the difficulties that the widening and diversification of the internal local market faces—hence the few possibilities available for the development of an industrial bourgeoisie, which through its association to the market led to the transformation of the system. The lack of protectionist policies, and the ease of importing implicit in the duty free system, complete the group of difficulties preventing the development of new industries. On the other hand, the absence of a large industrial proletariat, the presence of precapitalist forms of social relations of production, together with the fact that "emigration is for the exploited classes of the precapitalist world the main substitute for class struggle" (Rey, 1976: 258) explain the difficulties involved in the constitution of a labor movement with enough strength to exert a sufficient influence on the local power structure.

THE ACCUMULATION OF CAPITAL

In this section, I only want to refer to the implications of the fact that a large part of the surplus is obtained in the form of rent—agricultural (including that resulting from the trade of water) and urban. It would be convenient to remember that "contrary to profits, which in order to be reproduced must be exchanged for productive labor, rent is reproduced regularly as long as the title to the property lasts. In general, by its own nature, rent is largely spent on nonproductive expenditure" (Benetti, 1976: 201).

The existence of this monetary mass obtained in the form of rent and without any productive responsibilities or investment requirements for its reproduction endows both the activities where rent is obtained[19] as well as a large part of the economy of the region with a strong speculative (and unproductive) component. The importance of rent in the total surplus is one of the main reasons for the speculative character of the Canary Islands' economic system.

The following consequences of the speculative component just described can be mentioned. In the first place, the high rates of profit obtained in speculative activities does not simply continually raise the average expectations of the market; these rates are hardly obtainable in "normal" productive activities. This explains the tendency to deviate economic resources to this (speculative) type of activity.[20] Second, to the extent that rent is a substitute for profit, the social classes who depend on it tend to retard social progress. To the difficulties implied by land ownership, we have to add in this case the rights of property over water. Special mention is made of the structure of banana prices inasmuch as the institutionalization of different prices for this crop represents a laboratory case of the practical implications of the Ricardian model of differential rents. Although I cannot enter into a detailed examination of all these points, it would be useful to specify some of the implications of the existence of differential rents in the agricultural sector. As Gutelman (1978: 98-100) argues:

> The producer enjoying the best conditions (A) will always have—for a given volume of demand for agricultural products—an interest in the existence of producers situated in bad conditions. (C) . . . (A) will defend the existence of C, because to a large extent on C's existence depends the volume of the extra-profit A will be able to obtain. . . . (A) will be in favour of policies to maintain agricultural prices that will allow the subsistence of marginal producers and,

simultaneously, maintain their extra-profit at a high level. But, although (A) agrees on the survival of (C), he would like to do it as a marginal producer. Indeed, if (C) would improve (by investment, for example) his condition of production, it is obvious that the extra-profit of (A) would diminish. In consequence, although (A) desires the existence of (C), he would never propose any practical measure that would in fact permit (C) to improve his position. (A) would not accept anything other than selective aid measures.

CHANGES IN THE FORM OF REPRODUCTION
OF THE LABOR FORCE

The role and importance played by precapitalist social relations in the cheap reproduction of the labor force and the implications for the rest of the system (especially in its limiting effects on the internal market) have been modified in the last fifteen years. In this respect, the first thing to be stressed is that tourism has generated appeasing effects. On the one hand, as the hotel industry started and developed with a need to maintain low labor costs, precapitalist social relations (or other means to supplement wages, such as the simultaneous holding of jobs in both the tourist industry and the agricultural sector) became functional to the tourist industry. The opposite tendency is the change in the location of population from rural to urban zones, and the increase in the number of wage earners or the proletarianization of the labor force. The latter in turn has also been associated with the extension of the capitalist mode of production in the agricultural sector of the region. [21] Table 1.9, where the growing share of costs and amortization in the final product is shown, can be taken as partial empirical evidence of that extension—much more so if we also consider the reduction in the numbers of the self-employed in agriculture.

One of the consequences of the increase in the number of wage earners and the reallocation to urban centres is the deficiency of infrastructural services such as housing, education, and health care. Rural-urban migration is generally used to explain that shortage. And although these infrastructural deficiencies are common to the rest of Spain, the question remains: How can we explain why the Canary Islands is one of the most backward regions in terms of social infrastructure? It is our contention that migration is only the *external* form of a process; the ultimate cause of these deficiencies is the extremely short time during which the rural exodus[22] led to a change in the reproduction of the labor force from

TABLE 1.9 Proportion of Costs and Amortization in Final Production in Agriculture (in millions of pesetas)

	1962		1973		1975	
	Las Palmas	Santa Cruz de Tenerife	Las Palmas	Santa Cruz de Tenerife	Las Palmas	Santa Cruz de Tenerife
Costs and Amortization (1)	550.7	254.8	1,818.2	1,837	2,689	2,526.7
Final Production (2)	3,550	2,671.9	7,807.6	7,527.2	8,194.8	9,456.2
$\frac{(1)}{(2)} \times 100$	15.5%	9.5%	23.2%	24.4%	32.8%	26.7%

SOURCE: Renta Nacional de Espana y su distribucion provincial. Serie momogenea 1955-1975. Banco Bilbao.

precapitalist to capitalist forms—where part of the elements of this reproduction are supplied by the state.

Another effect of the increase in the number of wage earners and
urbanization of the population is the widening of the internal market. The
increase in the aggregate demands of goods supplied by the market is
quantitative—to the extent that the buying capacity increases—and qualitative—as a consequence of the different patterns of rural and urban
consumption. If we add to these effects, the "pull-in" demand of tourism,
we can understand the extent to which the basis of the internal market has
been modified. In this way, the conditions for change in the extroversion
of the region's economy have improved, moving toward an internally
oriented economic structure that in turn will allow a stronger convergence
between resource use and internal demand (Thomas, 1974: chap. 4).

Against this background, two strategies (or two groups of interests)
determining the future orientation of the economy can be detected. On
one side, we find the group that obstinately tries to continue the extroversion of the economy, with a fraction of them closely linked to the
speculative sections of the economic system. On the other side, we have
the group that questions the duty free status; although these industrial
interests seem to be numerically and economically weaker, they have been
able to obtain a concrete materialization of their strategy by obtaining
some protective measures.[23] These interests, incidentally, find additional
support in that there are (military) strategic reasons for widening the
self-sufficiency of the economic system as much as possible.

Continuity and change, exhaustion and renovation of the economic
model, are not, therefore, idealistic positions based on any abstract definition of the right strategy for the economy. They are, on the contrary, the
reflection of interests whose material basis can be found in the economic
processes so far described.

THE LIMITATIONS AND POSSIBILITIES OF A NEW STRATEGY

The increase and diversification of aggregate demand is not a sufficient
condition for a change toward a more internally oriented economy. The
question that must be answered is to what extent the present conditions of
the socioeconomic structure of the region permit an increase in the supply
of goods that are (or could be) produced locally. The background of this
question, it must be noted, is the old and always latent polemic of free
trade versus protectionism. Unfortunately, the economic technicalities in
which this discussion is always wrapped leave aside the gist of the argu-

ment. The truth is that the "science of economics" cannot lend definitive support to either of the sides; the decisive element is, as always, power, and alliances of the classes whose interests are at stake. As Seers (1971: 250-251) noted:

> One of the most fascinating phases in the history of ideas has been the way in which the balance of opinion shifted, as between American and British economists. The former were originally protectionist, but as American industry overtook British, the tabernacle of the faith moved across the Atlantic. Now it has crossed the sea once more and can be found in Bonn.

Yet on the basis of economic theory and history something can be said about this point, especially if the experience of countries that have followed a path of industrialization through import substitution (ISI) is taken into consideration. The Latin American economists describe this as the change from *desarrollo hacia afuera* (an outward-oriented development path) to *desarrollo hacia adentro* (an inward-looking development path). Elements like resource endowments, economies of scale, and market size are important questions that must be considered—although we must take care not to fall into a sort of economic determinism.

As regards the lessons from experience (and to summarize a long story), we can say it has not been very satisfactory, but this has been more the result of the economic policies implemented than of the consequences of ISI in itself. "It appears that the much advertised noncompetitiveness of Latin American industry may be rooted more in the failure to modify institutions than in any inability to bring down real costs" (Hirshman, 1968: 28). The change from an outward- to an inward-oriented path has increased, paradoxically enough, the economies' dependence in general and on imports in particular. The orientation of the economy has changed, but the dependency of the economic system has been preserved by means of dependent industrialization, with technology and transnational firms as the fundamental mechanisms of that dependency. At the same time, the market structure resulting from ISI has been characterized by oligopoly or monopoly in industries in which the underutilization of capacity has been the norm rather than the exception (Little et al., 1970). As for the effects on employment, it is sufficient to quote a standard text on economic development:

> In fact, the failure of modern industries to generate a significant number of employment opportunities is one of the most obvious

failures of the development process over the past two decades . . .
for many developing countries the growth of manufacturing output
has exceeded the growth of employment by a factor of three or four
to one [Todaro, 1977: 172].

Yet the majority of the consequences of ISI have been more or less
directly the result of what we previously said was the determining factor:
the structure of power and class alliances.

In this sense, the oligarchic and industrial interests, although maintaining their specificity, are juxtaposed and complemented to each
other. This leads to a series of conflicts that, although not concealing
their antagonism, are limited to a situation of compromise: the basis
on which the oligarchic-bourgeois system of these countries is built.
The birth of the Latin American industrial bourgeoisie is marked by
the limitations and compromises with the dominant oligarchic
classes. And, although there are several cases in Latin America where
it is possible to make this socioeconomic distinction within. the
productive sectors, the distinction cannot be applied to agents [indi-
viduals] who very frequently are one and the same [Bambirra, 1975:
47].

To conclude, it seems clear that the identification of social classes in
this region is, to say the least, problematic. The agents also have their
interests located in different sectors; the conflicts between rent and profit
are transcended by means of a permanent symbiosis that in turn leads to a
continuity of the local power structure; what else could explain the
longstanding persistence of this region's structural problems? Thus class
alliances (and loyalties) in the Canary Islands are characterized by a
considerable degree of fluidity. Moreover, historically the local dominant
classes have been caught in the middle of the following contradiction. On
the one hand, they depend on the central government for protectionist
policy measures (credits and concessions, like the protection of the banana
market). On the other hand, their basis of accumulation or their sources of
profits are located internally, which is also the basis of their existence.
Thus their ambivalent position, which sometimes manifests itself as sharing
the power in the local and in the national systems and at other times,
shows itself when there is a conflict between the two power systems—but
always attempting to hide the dependence of the local system on the
national system. Hence the dominant ideology is directed to permit the
coexistence of the two systems, the local and the national. However, to
push for an inward-oriented path of development could imply a strength-

ening of the local bourgeoisie and a fortiori an incentive for rogue capitalists to play the nationalist card.

In any case, the processes so far described have laid the foundations for a rupture, if only partial, in the continuity of the local power structure, and the nascent industrial bourgeoisie supported by the "popular interests" may gather enough strength to implement its program. For others, this support has no justification insofar as, according to Frank's contention, the immediate enemy is the local bloc of power and not the external bloc, or imperialism, as some would say. But it is not my intention to bet on possible winners. There is no doubt on my part, however, that the role popular interests can play will be determined by a strategy that ought to take into consideration some, if not at all, of the arguments I have developed in this chapter.

NOTES

1. There is some dispute about the magnitude of the genocide committed by the Spaniards. The total disappearance of the language is a partial proof that the Guanches were thoroughly exterminated. However, a number of ethnological studies have amply shown the persistence among the Canary Islanders of many distinctive features, such as blood groups and cranial forms.

2. Consider, for example, the negative effects of tourism or the military implications of the strategic situation of the archipelago.

3. Worth noting in this respect is that water is privately owned and traded as is any other commodity; it is also the object of strong speculative manipulations.

4. The term "model" is used for purely expository purposes as the historical interpretation here included does not have such a formal objective. It is also a fair summary of the historical picture provided by previous research about the Canary Islands, and I shall refer to it later to establish the implications of its use.

5. Closed, because emigration has become harder and less acceptable as a solution by local inhabitants.

6. Even the dates of the different cycles are mere approximations. There have been cases where a deep crisis in 1680 was followed by a marked upsurge in the next century (i.e., wine).

7. In fact, although the production of these two crops has had several downturns, it is only in the 1970s that the situation has really deteriorated.

8. We are referring to studies undertaken in the 1950-1976 period; a good example of them is Bergasa and Gonzalez Vietez (1969).

9. I am well aware that the use of this term for the Canary Islands might be controversial, especially on the basis of some (and only some) of the statistical indices generally used as a measure of development. To deal with this point properly would be the subject of another essay. At this point, it is sufficient to note that my concern here is with the explanatory power of certain analytical tools and approaches

as against others. In this respect I hope my analytical stance is made clear in the text.

10. In the input-output table for 1977, only water presents significant forward and backward linkages.

11. An appropriate term to use in this case, if only because Canary Island bananas enjoy full protection in the Spanish market, as no other bananas are permitted to enter.

12. In fact, and to further confirm what I have been saying so far, growing water scarcity has led the government to grant large credit facilities to introduce drip irrigation in the banana sector—rather than subsidize the shift from bananas to other, less-water-intensive crops.

13. As a matter of fact, the Canary Islands has always lived with its back to Africa, and it is only in the late 1960s that this region began to come to terms with this purely geographical fact. In transcending the schizophrenia of being politically part of Europe but geographically part of Africa, some body of opinion stresses the Atlantic character of the islands: Being at the crossroads of three continents, the cultural result is a melting pot of all three.

14. In fact, during this period the economic links between the Canary Islands and England were stronger than the link the islands maintained with Spain.

15. The use of the term is quite intentional. Official history has always played down (or silenced) any cultural or political events that would indicate the existence of nationalist movements. Thus the claim from some local young historians arguing that there is a considerable vacuum in this respect. To this extent part, if not all, of the "national" history must be rewritten. In fact, the evidence to show the relevance of this point is not hard to find, from the more rigorous, which shows how the word "colony" was at times used in official writings to the central government to the more folkloric, yet representative, local saying that notes that the two biggest historical errors of the Canaries have been to defeat Nelson and to permit Franco to leave the islands and start the Spanish Civil War. It must be noted, however, that none of the groups that have supported nationalistic ideas have offered anything like a complete and coherent body of ideas or political program.

16. This organization, called the Movimiento para la Autodeterminacion e Independencia del Archipielago Canario (MPAIAC), was supported by Algeria. From that country, the leader of the movement, A. Cubillo, had an hourly radio broadcast in which he called for the independence and the recognition of the "Africanism" of the Canary Islands. This support has been largely imputed to Algeria's exclusion from the treaty between Morocco, Mauritania, and Spain over the Spanish Sahara. As a countermeasure Algeria played the card of the Africanism of the Canary Islands inside the OAU; to avoid such a declaration, Spanish diplomats had to move swiftly and bargain for the support of other African states. The voting on this point inside the OAU was finally favorable to Spain.

17. Throughout its history, the Canary Islands have been the object of numerous military attacks (Van der Drake and Nelson among others). During World War II each side was preoccupied with an eventual occupation of the Canary Islands by the enemy. The military plans ("Felix-Isabella" and "Pilgrim") made by the Germans and English, respectively, contemplated this possibility (Morales-Lezcano, 1980: 70-74, 157-163, 145-215). Indeed, it is their strategic significance that led another author to argue that "the Canary Islands are condemned by their geography" to be the continuous object of attention of the "Great Powers" (Barrenechea, 1978). (It is

extremely interesting to note, that contrary to the local publicity enjoyed by most works on the Canaries, this latter book passed almost unnoticed.)

18. The term "process" is unavoidable in this context in order to encompass the different activities and effects that go with tourism.

19. Worth mentioning is the fact the "speculative" agriculture is a widely used local term for export crops.

20. In the 1964-1975 period manufacturing industry's share within the industrial sector (manufacturing plus mines, building, water and electricity) declined from 90 percent to 65 percent.

21. For example, the recent labor conflicts in the cultivation of tomatoes caused by the attempt to change the legal norms regulating the use of labor can be considered in the context of the extension and deepening of the capitalist mode of production: the transformation from absolute to relative surplus value, the need to control the labor process, and so on.

22. Notwithstanding the possible coexistence of rural and urban jobs, between 1960 and 1975 the share of the active population in agriculture declined by almost 50 percent.

23. The so-called special tariff by which some foreign products have a duty levied on them.

REFERENCES

ALTHUSSER, L. (1974) Ideología y aparatos ideológicos del estado. Madrid: Ediciones Nueva Visión.

ALVAREZ, M., J. A. RODRIGUEZ MARTIN, and M. SANCHEZ PADRON (1977) "Economía Canaria 76. Desarrollo del subdesarrollo: especulación y necesidades." Guadernos Canarios de Ciencias Sociales 12, 4. (Centro de Investigación Económica y Social de la Caja Insular de Ahorros de Gran Canaria.)

AMIN, S. (1974) Accumulation on a World Scale: Critique of the Theory of Underdevelopment. Brighton: Harvester.

BAMBIRRA, V. (1975) El capitalismo dependiente latinoamericano. Madrid: Siglo XXI.

BARRENECHEA, E. (1978) Objetivo Canarias (Cubillo al desnudo). Las Palmas: Dopesa.

BENETTI, C. (1976) La acumulación en los países capitalistas subdesarrollados. Mexico City: Fondo de Cultura Económica.

BERGASA, O. y and A. GONZALEZ VIEITEZ (1969) Desarrollo y subdesarrollo de la economía canaria. Las Palmas: Guadiana de Publicaciones.

BROOKFIELD, H. C. (1975) "Multum in parvo: questions about diversity and diversification in small developing countries," pp. 54-76 in P. Selwyn (ed.) Development Policy in Small Countries. Sussex: England: Institute of Development Studies.

CRUSOL, J. and L. CRUSOL (1980) "A programme for agriculture in islands plantation economies. World Development 8, 12: 1027-1033.

DOBB, M. (1972) "The trend in modern economics," pp. 39-82 in E. K. Hunt and J. G. Schwartz (eds) A Critique of Economic Theory. Harmondsworth, England: Penguin.

DOS SANTOS, T. (1971) "Dependencia y cambio social." Información Comercial Española no. 160: 93-103.

FUENZALIDA, E. and O. SUNKEL (1976) An Interdisciplinary Research Programme on the Transnationalization of Capitalism and National Development. Sussex, England: Institute of Development Studies.

GUTELMAN, M. (1978) Estructuras y reformas agrarias. Madrid: Ed. Fontamara.

HIRSCHMAN, A. O. (1968) "The political economy of import substituting industrialization." Quarterly Journal of Economics (February): 1-33.

LITTLE, I., T. SCITOVSKY, and M. SCOTT (1970) Industry and Trade in Some Developing Countries. London: Oxford University Press.

MARX, K. (1976) Capital, Vol. 1. Harmondsworth, England: Penguin.

MORALES-LEZCANO, V. (1980) Historia de la no beligerancia española durante la segunda guerra mundial, Vol. 4 (1940), Vol. 5 (1943). Exma. mancomunidad de Cabildos de Las Palmas. Las Palmas: Plan Cultural.

REY, P. P. (1976) La alianza de clases. Madrid: Siglo XXI.

RODRIGUEZ MARTIN, J. A. y and M. SANCHEZ PADRON (1978) "La economia canaria. Notas para un intento de interpretación global," pp. 12-39 in Información Commercial Española no. 543, Madrid.

SANCHEZ, F. (1981) "El cielo de Canarias como recurso natural de reconocido interes científico para Canarias," pp. 403-419 in Universidad de La Laguna: Canarias ante el cambio.

SEERS, D. (1971) "The role of industry in development: some fallacies," pp. 250-255 in I. Livingstone (ed.) Economic Policy for Development. Harmondsworth, England: Penguin.

SELWYN, P. (1978) "Small, poor and remote: islands at a geographical disadvantage." Discussion Paper 123. Sussex, England: Institute of Development Studies.

THOMAS, C. Y. (1974) Dependence and Transformation: The Economics of the Transition to Socialism. New York: Monthly Review Press.

TODARO, M. P. (1977) Economic Development in the Third World. London: Longman.

2

FROM COLONIALISM TO CONFEDERATION: THE GAMBIAN EXPERIENCE OF INDEPENDENCE, 1965-1982

ARNOLD HUGHES
University of Birmingham

The receding tide of European imperialism has left many exotic and fragile political life-forms stranded on the foreshore of nationhood in the Third World. Whereas, a few decades ago, many of these new states would have been regarded as incapable of attaining independence, the haste with which colonies have been abandoned and the disregard for earlier strict criteria of economic and political viability have resulted in the creation of an unusually large number of very small or micro states. A combination of limited territory, small population, and restricted economic resources places enormous burdens on the governments of these countries in their attempts to create stable and autonomous political systems and to bring about economic development. The severity of their problems is widely recognized in the academic literature (Benedict, 1967; Rapaport et al., 1971), which, on the whole, and regardless of political persuasion, is skeptical about the long-term prospects of most of these Lilliputian states. No longer can we assume a natural progression from colonial dependence to full and equal membership in the community of nations: Instead, the future of these states may be as clients of larger countries, not necessarily their former colonial overlords; or they may even be swallowed up by their neighbors or otherwise dissolve their separate existence in some form of regional union.

Take 1 million inhabitants as an admittedly arbitrary definition of micro statehood; there are eleven states with smaller populations located on the African continent or off its shores. One of these is the Republic of The Gambia, on the West Coast of Africa. At the time it obtained its independence from Britain in February 1965, The Gambia's population was only 315,000 and its annual revenues £1,700,000. Its surface area of 4003 square miles makes it the smallest mainland state in Africa. It is further handicapped by its elongated shape—a narrow and long finger of territory virtually entirely surrounded by neighboring Senegal (see Maps 2.1 and 2.2). Its near-enclave situation, as much as its small size, creates formidable problems for its long-term political and economic development. Its principal national asset, the river Gambia, is shared by two other countries, Senegal and Guinea, while its "intrusion" into Senegal has posed a number of delicate issues over the years.

In the early 1960s, the prospects for this last remaining British colony in West Africa seemed so dismal that a number of alternatives to independence were proposed. There was talk of a link-up with the nearest former British dependency, Sierra Leone; it was even proposed that a permanent association with Britain, similar to the Channel Islands, take place; but the most widely canvassed option was integration with Senegal. The British administration favored it; so did the newly independent Senegalese state; and many influential Gambians were also persuaded of the impossibility of political survival by themselves. Yet despite a series of moves in the early sixties, including government-to-government talks, a study commissioned from the United Nations (Van Mook et al., 1964), and proposals for a federation, in the end The Gambia opted for independence.

Remarkably, in view of the generally pessimistic forecasts made at the time, The Gambia survived, neither degenerating into a British client state, nor allowing itself to be swallowed up by Senegal. It is all the more astonishing that this tiny state should have come to acquire an unsurpassed reputation for political tolerance and stability, and even a measure of economic prosperity, at a time when many of its better-endowed neighbors were succumbing to despotic governments or actually breaking apart. It seemed that The Gambian experience refuted the conventional academic and popular views on the capacity for survival of small states.

Unfortunately, The Gambia's impressive performance could not be sustained. After nearly two decades of harmonious existence the country underwent an uncharacteristic political trauma in mid-1981. Self-styled leftist opponents of the government attempted to seize power through a coup d'état. They were joined by numerous members of the security

The Gambia

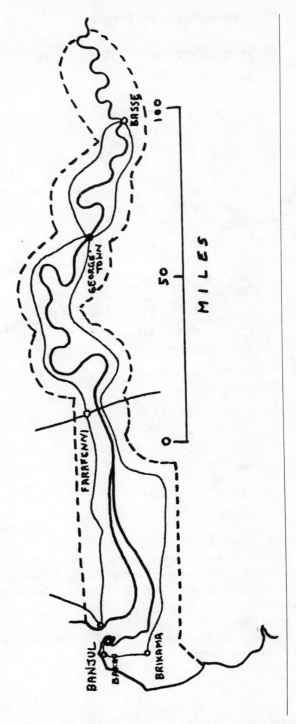

Senegambia Region

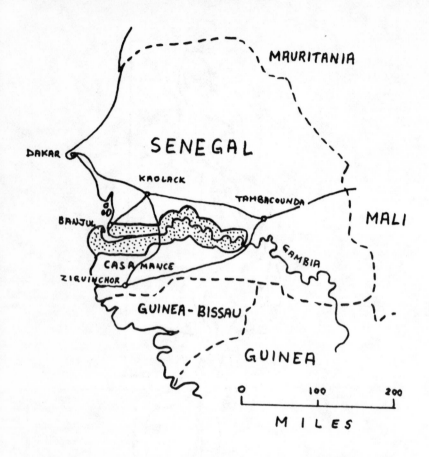

forces, and order was finally restored only by a large-scale military intervention by the Senegalese. The attempted coup not only damaged The
Gambia's proud reputation as one of the few upholders of parliamentary
democracy in Africa; it also undermined its sovereignty. The Senegalese
military presence remained, and in early 1982 a confederation came into
being between The Gambia and Senegal. There can be little doubt that
Senegal is the dominant partner in The Senegambian Confederation, and
the unequal distribution of power between the two governments raises the
question of how long the Gambians can retain their national autonomy. Is

TABLE 2.1   Major Gambian Ethnic Groups (1973)

Group	Number	Percentage of Population
Mandinka	208,000	42.3
Fula	90,000	18.2
Wolof	77,000	15.7
Jola	47,000	9.5
Serahuli	43,000	8.7
Serere	10,000	2.1
Aku	5,000	1.0
Others	13,000	2.6
Total	493,000	

SOURCE: 1973 Population Census returns.

The Gambia destined to end up as Senegal's "eighth region," or can it establish a *modus vivendi* with its putative protector?

This chapter seeks to explain the circumstances under which The Gambia, despite its unpromising start, stood against the tide of political instability on the African continent for nearly two decades. Second, it examines the reasons for the dramatic deterioration in its domestic political situation in 1980-1981 leading to the summoning of Senegalese military assistance. Finally, it reviews the position of The Gambia in the wake of the abortive uprising.

GAMBIAN POLITICS BEFORE 1980

Despite its small population (about 620,000), The Gambia is as much a plural society as are much larger African countries. Its political boundaries disregard both ethnic and geographical realities. To succeed, political arrangements must take account of both ancient cultural divisions and cleavages deriving from the more recent colonial past. Present-day ethnic labels conceal a considerable amount of cultural assimilation between the various groups and suggest a depth of historical identity that is misleading (see Table 2.1). In the nineteenth century there was much more social fluidity and fragmentation among the Gambian peoples. Internal migrations, wars, and local attempts at state building combined to present a very different cultural and political map. The Mandinka were fragmented into fifteen separate chiefdoms; the Wolof split among several small states straddling the northern boundary of The Gambia; the seven Fula clans were scattered across a wider area than what is present-day Gambia; and the Jolas of the southwest were a socially atomized people found as far east as Guinea Bissau. With the exception of the Aku, descendants of settlers from Sierra Leone, all the peoples of the country were also found in Senegal, if not further afield.

The politicization of ethnicity occurred during the late colonial period during the struggle to determine who would take over from the departing British. Ethnicity was revived by political parties in their efforts to build up a following on a territorial basis. British administration gave more importance to the division between the area around the capital, Banjul (then Bathurst), known as the "Colony," and the greater part of the dependency in the interior, referred to as the "Protectorate." These distinctions resulted from the slow pace of British advance up the river valley. In the colonial capital, Wolof migrants from the French coastal settlements to the north and Sierra Leonians from the east responded to the educational, religious, and economic opportunities provided by British rule. From among them, particularly the Aku, emerged a prosperous and educated element that found a subordinate niche in the colonial administration and acquired restricted political rights. In time, protonationalist movements grew under their control, and they came to view themselves as the natural successors to the British. In contrast, the Protectorate was governed under the system of indirect rule, with a handful of British field officers, several dozen chiefs, and hundreds of village headmen maintaining the authority of the government. It was only after World War II that the franchise was extended to the Protectorate, even though the wealth of the dependency had derived from taxes levied on groundnuts grown by farmers in the interior. To add insult to economic injury, the urban politicians claimed to speak for all Gambians, tending to resist and ridicule provincial efforts at political organization.

By the early fifties, three Colony-based political parties were active—the Democratic Party, the United Party (UP), and the Muslim Congress Party. Each tried to establish a foothold in the Protectorate as the franchise was extended, but their urban origins and concerns provoked a "green uprising" among the predominantly Mandinka rural populace. Under the leadership of a rural petty bourgeoisie drawn from school teachers, clerks and other minor officials, and small traders, internal divisions among the Mandinka were overcome so that by 1959 a rival political movement, claiming to represent the countryside (but more specifically, the Mandinka and Jola), came into being. The People's Progressive party (PPP) made up in numbers what it lacked in political experience. Though it failed to win a commanding majority in the first general elections in The Gambia, held in 1960, it won the subsequent ones in 1962, thus enabling it to lead the country to internal self-government and then independence in 1965 (Nyang, 1974; Hughes, 1975; Fletcher, 1978).

The promotion of communal solidarity by the UP and PPP (the former portraying itself as the champion of the urban populace and the Wolof, Fula, and Serahuli in the interior, and the latter appealing to all provincials to unite against their economic and political subordination to the city politicians) threatened to create the kind of communal antagonism and strife common elsewhere in Africa. Feelings ran high and wild rumours circulated in Banjul about what the PPP extremists would do once they took power. Thus in addition to the problems of smallness and poverty, a potentially ruinous and violent division within the community cast further doubt about The Gambia's viability. The danger was contained by a shift in approach by the PPP, from a party of revenge to one of conciliation. The system of politics that evolved closely approximated the "consociational democracy" (Lijphart, 1968, 1969, 1977) found in the small plural states of Western Europe.

In essence, "consociational democracy means government by elite cartel designed to turn a democracy with a fragmented political culture into a stable democracy" (Lijphart, 1969: 97). The coming together of communal elites from each cultural section of society would allow for an orderly sharing of political power and economic resources, instead of a destructive confrontation. Such an arrangement fitted in reasonably well with Gambian realities, at a time when communal conflict was still within bounds. Here, the very smallness of The Gambia proved helpful. Despite their differences, accentuated by contemporary political rivalries, the peoples of The Gambia had much in common and lived in quite close proximity to each other. Most of them had a similar social system based on Islam and a caste system; they shared notions of consensus in decision making; a great deal of economic interdependency existed; and the sharp division between Colony and Protectorate was softened by the practice of urban families "adopting" rural boys in order to educate them. Dawda Jawara benefited from such an arrangement and went on to marry the daughter of a leading Aku. Communalism in The Gambia was largely free of the hatred and ignorance characteristic of it elsewhere in Africa.

Not only were there social factors conducive to the emergence of consociational government; there were also a number of political ones. Since they were not a national majority, the Mandinka could not form a stable administration by themselves. From the outset, the PPP had to compromise to capture power. Opening its ranks and senior positions to communal groups other than the Mandinka undermined the UP claim to protect the other tribes from Mandinka domination. But the PPP needed more than the support of other rural communities; it also needed the participation of educated and experienced townspeople, particularly those that manned the state bureaucracy and ran the police force. Previously these had tended to be sympathetic to the UP, but by resisting interference in their internal affairs and refusing to swamp the civil service with Mandinka job seekers, the PPP obtained the neutrality and loyalty, if not the active support, of the "bureaucratic bourgeoisie." And at a time when the military were seizing power elsewhere in Africa, the allegiance of the leaders of the small paramility Field Force was secured.

For these reasons, and one should not forget the genuine desire of individuals such as Jawara to create a national consensus, the PPP underwent a transformation between its founding in 1959 and independence in 1965. The political advantages that accrued were very real. Nationally, communal tension declined rapidly as each ethnic elite "policed" their own communal constituency and engaged in orderly bargaining at the political center. Rural development projects assumed greater importance and, until the mid-1970s, rural society gained from increased groundnut prices as well as from such infrastructural improvements as road construction and the beginnings of health and educational provisions.

The PPP's parliamentary strength increased substantially between 1960 and 1972. Its share of the popular voted grew by 20 percent, from 27,521 to 66,143, while its parliamentary representation rose more sharply, from 9 to 28 in a chamber of 32 directly elected members. Conversely, UP representation fell steeply from 13 in 1962 to a mere 3 ten years later. By 1978, with the defection of MPs for Banjul South to the PPP, the old opposition party lost its last seat in parliament. Its share of the popular vote also declined from 22.6 percent in 1962 to 15.58 percent in 1972. In the subsequent general elections held in 1977 and 1982, the UP failed to offer more than localized opposition in the Banjul area, and the two seats it retained in 1977 were soon lost.

While the UP leadership lost, its leader, P. S. N'Jie, a Wolof lawyer from Banjul, effectively withdrew from politics after his party's defeat in 1972, former opposition leaders prospered within the PPP. Ministerial appointments and state patronage were extended to several of those who "carpet-crossed" to the ruling party, and they could claim that their constituents also benefited by their actions. The principal beneficiaries, undoubtedly, were the previously antagonistic fractions of the petty bourgeoisie, who now shared rather than fought over the resources of the postcolonial state.

The head of state can also be said to have gained from the operation of the consociational system. As prime minister, and then as president from 1970 to 1975, Sir Dawda Jawara had frequently faced challenges from rival Mandinka leaders within the PPP. By diluting the Mandinka element in the government, he was able more effectively to resist such opposition. Non-Mandinka ministers, on the whole, proved more loyal to the president. The close involvement of the Banjul bureaucratic leadership in government gave Jawara and additional power base. The result was a benign form of "neopatrimonialism" of the kind depicted by Gellar in Senegal.

The Gambia's "elite cartel" presided over by a genuinely liberal head of state and provided the country with an unusually stable and open political system, which soon became the envy of Africa and earned the little country fame and approbation across the world. Nevertheless, the incomplete nature of participation and redistribution in Gambian consociational democracy contributed to the crisis of 1980-1981 (Hughes, 1982a).

Difficulty stemmed from two quarters: one was communal, the other generational and class-based in nature. Although consociational democracy is principally organized to regulate in a nonantagonistic way communal rivalries, its very success in The Gambia promoted opposition from sections of Mandinka society dissatisfied with the extent of the concessions made by the PPP leadership to leaders of other communal blocs. This discontent was evident as early as 1973, but it assumed serious political proportion only in 1975, when the former vice president of the country assumed its leadership. Sheriff Dibba was a founding member of the PPP and a Baddibu Mandinka. He quickly achieved high office but a scandal (the Buttut Affair) involving a brother of his cost him his position in 1973. He came to be seen among some Mandinka as a victim of the president's policy of favoring non-Mandinka and, when he was expelled from the PPP in 1975, allegedly for trying to engineer a revolt against the president in cabinet, he quickly formed a rival movement, the National Convention party (NCP), which gained the support of his disaffected fellow tribesmen.

Dibba did not confine himself to championing Mandinka rights, a politically limiting course of action as events would prove. He also promoted himself as a populist critic of the same government in which he had played such an important part. That he was of the same mold as those he criticized was evident from his lifestyle and political ideology. The NCP's manifesto, the Farafenni Declaration, differed little from that of the PPP, and his critique of the government was mainly confined to personalities rather than to fundamental policies at this stage. Relying primarily on the backing of Baddibu Mandinka and the discontented elements in the vicinity of Banjul, he posed a serious political challenge to the PPP in the general elections of 1977. The NCP put up 30 candidates and backed rump UP candidates in the remaining constituencies. His presence forced the government to reactivate its somewhat moribund village committees and to speed up several rural development projects. PPP counterpropaganda concentrated on portraying Dibba as a Mandinka tribalist and opportunist, threatening to destroy the delicate "grand coalition" so carefully brought together during the past fifteen years. Dibba's defeat in the elections in part represented strong public support for the elite cartel. Non-Mandinka rural communities voted overwhelmingly for the PPP, undoubtedly alarmed by their perception of Dibba's aims. Most Mandinka also remained loyal to the president and "their" party. Only in the Baddibus, where he held his own seat and in the townships around Banjul, did Dibba do well. Overall, the NCP won five seats but over 40,000 votes, 22.7 percent of the total. While replacing the UP as the major opposition party, the NCP could not claim to be a truly national party. Its limited territorial penetration was further revealed in the Area Council elections of 1979. It won 40 percent of the votes east, but only 18 seats, and once again the bulk of its votes came from parts of North Bank Division, Western Division, and the Banjul environs, where its support was concentrated. The containment, if not the destruction of the NCP, saved Jawara and the PPP from internal schism, but a more serious challenge presented itself soon after.

THE POLITICAL CRISIS OF 1980-1981

It would be an exaggeration to claim that there is a substantial socialist element in Gambian politics, but, at the same time, the activities of a couple of small and obscure leftist groups in the Banjul area nearly caused the downfall of the state in the summer of 1981. Their actions, in a way not anticipated by them, also seriously undermined the country's sovereignty, although they claimed to be acting in furtherance of The Gambia's freedom from external control. Since the early seventies, Banjul and nearby settlements—Bakau, Serrekunda, Brikama, and Sukuta in particular—attracted a growing number of young people in search of excitement or relief from toiling on their families' farms in the provinces. By 1973, Serrekunda-Bakau had grown to about 35,000 inhabitants, very near the size of the capital itself. Housing and job opportunities could not keep up with the urban drift, and the squalid compounds incubated revolutionary thoughts among the young.

In the early seventies, a vulgarized form of Marxism and Fanonism, a political radicalism tinged with Black racism, found acceptance among some urban youths and even school children. Several youth societies, *vous*, became radicalized, adopting such names as Black Panthers and Black Scorpions. Kukoi Samba Sanyang, leader of the 1981 coup, was reputed to have been a member of the latter group. In the main, radical youths in the early seventies did not seek confrontation with the state, and the few clashes that occurred were easily contained by the still loyal police. There was a resurgence of radicalism in the late seventies, in part a reaction against not only the PPP and its elite cartel, but also against the NCP. One violently revolutionary underground news sheet denounced all constitutional politicians as "bush pigs," to be exterminated at the right hour. It would appear, from events in July 1981, that the NCP was divided in its attitude toward revolutionary change. While its rhetoric sounded increasingly combative, Dibba remained a constitutionalist. Though detained after the coup's suppression, he was found not guilty when put on trial in the summer of 1982. Hopes of the NCP becoming a vehicle for revolutionary change did not materialize, which explains both the attacks on the leadership of the party and the formation of new and more determinedly militant organizations.

In 1975, a young Banjul lawyer, Pap Cheyassin Secka, formed the National Liberation Party (NLP) to contest the general elections slated for 1977. Secka presented himself as a radical socialist critic of government. Rather than join up with Dibba to form a common opposition to the PPP, he chose to fight alone, although a tenuous electoral alliance with some UP candidates in the provinces was declared. Together they polled only 3350, or 1.0 percent of the total vote. Secka lost his deposit both in the general elections and in a subsequent by-election in Banjul. The NLP was apparently disbanded, but Secka remained in close touch with radical elements and was to be successfully charged, and condemned to death, for taking part in the 1981 coup.

With the NCP lukewarm in its support for revolutionary change and the NLP disbanded, opponents of the PPP regrouped around two obscure movements: the Movement for Justice in Africa–Gambia (MOJA-G) and the Gambia Socialist Revolutionary Party. Both surfaced in 1980 and conducted propaganda campaigns against the government and ruling class, voiced in familiar Marxist terms. Political graffiti suddenly appeared, and two boats belonging to the president were damaged. Public meetings urging revolutionary action were also held. Both organizations, whose numbers probably never exceeded a few hundred, though they could (as later events showed) bank on the sympathy of many more youths, embraced an eclectic and vulgar Marxism combined with pan-Africanism. The Liberian MOJA-G, which had shot to prominence in 1979-1980 following the overthrow of the Tolbert government and the Ghanaian radicals that seized power under Flight Lieutenant Jerry Rawlings in June 1979 undoubtedly influenced the thinking and action of Gambian leftists. It is doubtful if they did more than this.

Greater controversy surrounds the role of Libya in fomenting revolutionary agitation in The Gambia. Initially, cordial relations existed between Gaddafy and the PPP, with the Libyans agreeing to provide funds for rural development as well as for the inevitable mosque construction. By 1980, both the Gambian and Senegalese governments grew alarmed at what they felt to be Libya's subversive intentions in Black Africa. A dispute took place over the recruitment of Gambians for work in Libya; the Gambian government believed that they were receiving military training and being encouraged to return home to wage war against it. In July, the Senegalese government published a report purporting to show how the Libyans were furthering sedition in West Africa in general and, more particularly, in the Senegambian area, where they supported a Senegalese fundamentalist Muslim opponent of the government—Sheikh Ahmed Niasse of Kaolack. Following distrubances in Banjul in late October, the Gambian authorities also retaliated against the Libyans, closing down their embassy in Banjul and deporting its staff. The authorities never published their evidence, but it was officially believed that the Libyan embassy was assisting radical groups in the Banjul area.

The domestic crisis of October 1980 was the first extraconstitutional threat to the Gambian system of government. Even today, the exact details are not known, or have not been disclosed (but see Africa Contemporary Record, 1980-81: B478-B479, for a short summary). The central event was the murder of Emmanuel Mahoney, deputy commander of the Field Force, by a mutinous paramilitary policeman, on October 27. Rumours of a plot among the Field Force were discounted at the time, but the government's decision to call in 150 Senegalese troops, ostensibly as part of a training exercise, indicated the authorities' concern. Their fears would be fully borne out within a few months. The Libyans were sent away and the two revolutionary movements banned on October 30; six members of MOJA-G, including its leader, Koro Sallah, were arrested and given bail on charges of organizing a subversive movement and possessing weapons. Five were subsequently acquitted and the sixth fined a small sum. If the government thought that a combination of leniency and firmness would put an end to subversion, it was to be cruelly disappointed. Within eight months a much more serious subversive outbreak, costing the loss of perhaps 1000 lives, was to occur (Hughes, 1981).

On July 30, taking advantage of President Jawara's absence at the royal wedding in London, a group of leftist civilians teamed up with defectors from the Field Force to attempt the overthrow of the state. Several key points in the vicinity of the capital were seized—the airport, State House, Parliament, Radio Gambia, and the police barracks and armory—and a 12-man revolutionary junta, the "Supreme Council of the Revolution," abolished the constitution and pronounced the birth of a Marxist-Leninist state. Headed by a former NCP parliamentary candidate defeated in the 1977 general elections, Kukoi Samba Sanyang, the rebel leadership was a curious mixture of political nonentities, most of whom were either illiterate or had little formal education. None had any practical experience of administration either, being ordinary Field Force constables, unemployed or in casual or semiskilled employment. Nearly half were Jola, the ethnic group that, it could be argued, had gained the least from the operation of the ethnic grand coalition. Later evidence revealed that the plot had been hatched in Somita in Jola country and had been launched from Talinding Kunjang, a predominantly Jola quarter in Serrekunda, some 12 miles from the capital. Sanyang himself is a Jola.

Credit for the coup was claimed by the Gambia Underground Socialist Revolutionary Party, banned the previous October, but other radical or dissident elements joined the insurrection: MOJA-G, the more militant elements of the NCP, about half the Field Force (some possibly under duress), convicts released by the rebels, and members of the general public, mainly young men from the coastal townships, all joined the original conspirators. There were sporadic incidents up-river, but the uprising was largely confined to Banjul and nearby towns and villages. Later claims by exiled rebels that it was a national revolt against the government are difficult to sustain; of the 1000 or so persons detained in the weeks after the coup, nearly 90 percent came from an area within 40 miles of Banjul. On the other hand, the indifference of much of the population to the imminent fall of the government indicated that it had lost a great deal of popularity in recent years. The willingness of members of the PPP, including a minister and a prominent chief, to make prorebel speeches on the captured state radio (some would claim to have been forced into doing so) provided additional proof of the demoralization of the regime. Lastly, the active participation of so many Field Force lower ranks in the insurrection and the unwillingness of the bulk of the remainder to rally to the government was a particularly painful revelation. Only a few dozen loyalist police could be found, but these, under the command of senior officers not taken prisoner by the insurgents, were able to hold out in the central police station in Banjul until relieved. Several senior ministers were able to join them to maintain the semblance of a government and keep the exiled president informed about events.

Acting on such information, Jawara decided to try and regain power. Appealing to the Senegalese for military assistance for a second time under the provisions of the 1971 defense treaty, he flew to Dakar to help plan his return. The Senegalese, alarmed by the extravagantly revolutionary broadcasts of the insurgents, mounted a military expedition of nearly 3000 men, and, in a week that saw some hard and bloody fighting, put down the insurrection. Sanyang, and a number of other rebels, managed to avoid capture by fleeing to Guinea Bissau.

Given the wide range of groups and individuals taking part in the rebellion, the brevity of the rebel seizure of power, and the confusion surrounding it determining the motives and objectives of the insurgents is not easy. Probably a majority of those who took part did so on an opportunistic and spontaneous basis; the collapse of law and order provided a perfect occasion for settling old scores—for robbery and the looting of commercial premises, both African and expatriate owned. Easy access to weapons stolen from the Field Force armory and heavy drinking undoubtedly contributed to the widespread lawlessness and killings that accompanied the insurrection. Attempts by the rebel leaders to impose their own martial law on the anarchical forces they had unleashed met with only limited success and, faced with so much personal insecurity and economic disruption, initial support for the insurgents among the urban populace waned.

Transcripts of rebel broadcasts made over the captured state radio (Bakarr, 1981) reveal that the inner leadership of the rebellion shared a similar populist-revolutionary ideology to that of the Doe and Rawlings coups in Liberia and Ghana. Rebel propaganda was strong in its denunciations of the Jawara government but vague and reticent about its own plans. Hidden among the thickets of Marxist-derived slogans about a proletarian revolution and solidarity with other freedom struggles were a number of cloudy promises about the total transformation of Gambian society, down to the eradication of witchcraft. The *comprador bourgeois*

PPP government was accused of political repression, corruption, nepotism, tribalism, a range of economic failures, and turning the country into a satellite of Western imperialism. Many of its accusations were rhetorical exaggerations or even falsehoods, but in some respects they echoed popular feelings.

There is little doubt that, after nearly two decades of uninterrupted power, the PPP had grown complacent and insensitive. Too many of its leaders seemed bent on pursuing personal wealth rather than the interests of their followers. Several financial scandals involving ministers and senior officials eroded public confidence in the government. While prepared to dismiss the worst offenders, the president failed to have them prosecuted or make financial restitution. Men previously dismissed for improper conduct were brought back into the government. It did seem to many people that power was too much in the hands of a self-perpetuating elite drawn from the older generation of PPP activists. It was only in 1979 that the PPP held its second national congress; the first took place in 1963, two years before independence. Its deliberations disclosed many grievances among the party rank-and-file, and youths in particular felt insufficiently represented in the upper ranks of the party. Many were critical of the economic performance of the government at a time of worsening conditions.

The economic failures of the government have played an important part in undermining the political system bequeathed from the sixties. The elite cartel was seen as failing both to pass along resources to its communal supporters through patronage networks and to generate adequate resources in the first instance through its management of the economy. More than human failings accounted for this state of affairs. Consociational democracy in The Gambia evolved during a period of economic prosperity and opportunity linked to the Africanization of the state apparatus and the growth in export trade from the mid-1960s. A decade later the economy was going into decline, and opportunities for additional employment in the state and private sectors had narrowed. Economic discontent fueled political disenchantment with the government.

Yet the economic policies of the PPP were cautious and sensible, even if their implementation was less than satisfactory. At independence it had inherited a tiny and improverished economy, resting almost entirely on peasant production of groundnuts for export. With over half the cultivable land devoted to groundnuts and over 90 percent of export earnings derived from the sale of groundnuts, it would have been irresponsible and foolhardy for the government to attempt to change things overnight. Besides, groundnut production and world prices increased steadily in the years following independence. In 1965 output was 91,000 tons, but by 1973 it reached a peak of 136,000 tons. In the same period groundnut prices more than doubled, providing a growth in real income for farmers and increased revenue for the state. Government policy was to develop the economy through integrated rural development programs centered on groundnut cultivation, but with gradual diversification into rice and other foodcrops and increased animal husbandry. Foreign aid was channeled into a range of rural infrastructural projects: improved communications and storage facilities, more agricultural extension services to improve farming techniques and crop yields, loans to farmers, and so on. With such a small and poor domestic market, the government wisely avoided unrealistic industrialization schemes, though it did divert resources to tourism in the seventies. Then came prolonged drought and world inflation and recession, against which the government could do very little.

From 1973 real GDP has been in decline in The Gambia and may be accounted for in part by a collapse in groundnut production as a result of several poor harvests consequent on a series of droughts in the Sahel in the mid-1970s. It is probably more than a coincidence that political unrest reached a pitch when groundnut production slumped to its lowest level in 30 years, 45,000 tons in 1980-1981. The cost of imports has also soared; the trade deficit in 1973 was a manageable U.S. $6,480,000, but by 1980 it had risen to U.S. $80,000,000 (part of which was accountable for by development investment, some 80 percent of which was covered by foreign loans and grants). Groundnut earnings were no longer sufficient to cover vastly inflated fuel and other import costs. Foreign reserves were down to U.S. $5,670,000 by 1980, leading to a squeeze on imports. The government was also obliged to introduce a series of austerity budgets, the one of 1981 coming a few days before the attempted coup.

Rebel propaganda tended to blame the government for all economic reversals and exaggerated the degree of misery produced. The Gambia did not suffer hyperinflation or chronic shortages during the past decade (a telling observation on this is the growth in reexport trade between Banjul and neighboring radical states such as Guinea and Guinea Bissau in these years), but the economic constraints, combined with the accumulation of wealth, sometimes corruptly, by the ruling class, provided ready ammunition for the government's adversaries. Economic difficulties thus helped to undermine the foundations of consociational democracy in The Gambia. While it may be premature to talk of class struggle in Gambian society, there had emerged by the late seventies a growing number of disaffected elements, principally in the urban areas, which constituted an underclass or a lumpenproletariat, rather than a working class. Despite its internal fragmentation and seemingly naive and contradictory ideology, it had the ability to coalesce and to pursue political objectives of a radical, even extremist, nature, and largely free from the control of members of the petty bourgeoisie in power. In an urban environment, traditional mechanisms of control associated with the operation of communal patron clientage are weaker and tend to be rejected as manipulative and exploitative. In the absence of a radical working class, the trade unions denounced the 1981 coup. It has been elements of the lumpenproletariat, albeit in an adventurist and undisciplined manner, that have adopted radical political action in The Gambia.

GAMBIAN POLITICS AFTER THE ATTEMPTED COUP

Two major problems confronted the Gambian government and political system after the suppression of the 1981 coup: On the one hand there was an obvious need to return to the peaceful political situation of the past, while at the same time eliminating some of those shortcomings that had contributed to the recent instability; on the other hand, now that The Gambia was militarily dependent on the Senegalese, a new relationship had to be worked out in the context of this reality.

A precondition for a return to political normality would be the ending of the state of emergency declared after the president's return and the holding of fair and speedy trials of over 1000 detainees arrested under emergency legislation. Such arrests were bound to be regarded as political, even if most of the charges to be preferred were criminal. Non-Gambian judges and prosecutors from other Commonwealth countries were appointed to handle the trials, though initial screening was carried out by two panels of widely respected laypersons chaired by lawyers. The trials began in December, and those of major defendants completed by July 1982. A total of 26 persons were sentenced to death, the majority for treasonable offenses. These included several members of the Supreme Council of the Revolution, as well as Pap Cheyassin Secka, leader of the defunct NLP. A number of others have been released or given custodial sentences or fines, but some 800 other detainees remain to constitute a financial as well as a political embarrassment to the government. The state of emergency, under which they are held, was extended for a further six months in July. A curfew and restrictions on public gatherings continue as well.

Notwithstanding these restrictions, the government decided to hold the general elections due in the spring of 1982. They were of crucial importance in reestablishing the country's reputation as a parliamentary democracy in the world at large, as well as domestically, and would enable the PPP to measure its support among the electorate soon after the traumatic events of the previous summer. In the absence of a separate referendum, the elections would also demonstrate public support for the decision to enter into a confederation with Senegal, which came into effect in February 1982. The PPP spared no effort in seeking a large majority for itself and for its presidential candidate, Sir Dawda Jawara, now to be chosen in a separate direct ballot rather than by elected MPs.

The elections revealed a renewed interest in politics among the populace, even though the turnout was considerably lower than in 1977. Such was the demand to stand for parliament among government supporters that 137 nominations were received for the 35 places. Nearly all the 13 Independent candidates were PPP candidates turned down by the party. The NCP, understandably, fielded only 19 candidates, compared with 31 in 1977. Dibba remained in detention but was allowed to stand for parliament and for the presidency. The detention of other NCP activists suspected of involvement in the 1981 coup also hampered the opposition's election campaign, both in a practical sense and because of the stigma still attaching to the party from the previous year's events.

The results (Hughes, 1982b) showed the PPP, and the president even more so, still to be popular, though Independent candidates, campaigning on local issues such as the poor record of sitting MPs, took five seats away from the government. There was a fall in the PPP's share of the vote of some 8 percent, but it still won 62 percent of the total, to which might be added most of the 16 percent taken by the PPP/Independents. Though expelled from the party for their disobedience, most of them and their supporters still regarded themselves as government supporters. The striking victory of President Jawara in the presidential election, over 72 percent of the vote, bore this out. The PPP could also derive satisfaction from taking two seats from the NCP, including that of Dibba. Despite these two losses, the NCP was down only 1 percent on its 1977 performance. Dibba, who was released from custody in July following his acquittal, still had a party to return to, whereas only a few months previously, many had expected the NCP to collapse and the PPP to declare a one-party state.

The May general and presidential elections renewed links between the elite cartel and its supporters and received favorable notices abroad, not least because opposition forces were able to take part in a fair contest, as demonstrated by the absence of tension and recrimination as well as by the loss of seats by the ruling party. Domestically, it gave President Jawara a massive mandate to lead the country and to continue the close relationship with Senegal.

Those in power appeared to learn something from the events leading up to the coup and from the elections. The PPP ditched eight MPs, felt to be too old or ineffective, in order to allow a greater number of younger and better-educated persons to stand. The need to placate youth and improve the intellectual quality of ministers is reflected in the composition of the new cabinet as well; the new vice president, Bakary Darbo, is a university graduate and an experienced administrator and diplomatist, and yet is only 36. Women, too, have been given an increased voice in government, and what emerges from the reconstitution of parliament and the Cabinet is a recognition that youth and women, as much as ethnic communities, need to be given collective representation in the ruling grand coalition. The prominence of Mandinka in the legislature as well as the government may swing the ethnic balance too far in their direction, but it cuts the ground from under the feet of Mandinka hardliners, whose dissatisfaction in the past helped launch the NCP.

The extreme left in Gambian politics is still reeling from the severe blows dealt it by the Senegalese army and remains constrained by the state of emergency as well. Insurgents not killed or captured have fled, some to Europe, others to Guinea Bissau. Recently, Sanyang is reported to have been deported to Cuba from Guinea Bissau. With several hundred Senegalese soldiers now permanently stationed in The Gambia as part of a confederal defense force and the mutinous Field Force disbanded, there is little likelihood of another populist coup for some time to come. To succeed, the next uprising would have to take place in the Senegalese capital. Perhaps the carnage of last summer has convinced a majority of Gambians that there is little to be gained from political violence. The government and the elite cartel it represents have at least won themselves a breathing space in which to attempt to correct past mistakes. The doubling of the groundnut harvest in 1981-1982 and the generous international assistance received after the ending of the 1981 rebellion also buy the government additional time.

In the meantime, there is the pressing issue of working out a new relationship with the Senegalese. Gambians have an ambivalent attitude toward their closest neighbors, as well they might. While anxious to cooperate with the Senegalese for their mutual gain, anxiety exists over the ultimate aims of the Dakar government. There is an appreciation of the drawbacks, as well as of the advantages, of close ties with Senegal. Since 1980 the military advantage has outweighed any of the drawbacks, at least as far as the Gambian government is concerned. It shares with the Diouf administration a fear of being destabilized by foreign powers such as Libya and the Soviet Union and needs the Senegalese military umbrella today, not only to protect itself from imagined or real external threats, but to give it immediate protection from its own armed forces. Until the Field Force has been purged and reconstituted, Senegalese soldiers are required to ensure internal political order. The joint army under consideration must inevitably be dominated by the Senegalese, who have an estimated defense establishment of 10,000 men. Even before the political crisis, when its loyalty was not suspect, the Field Force never numbered more than 500. The Senegalese forces are not only more numerous but they constitute one of the most formidable armies in Black Africa in terms of experience and equipment. Now that they are established on Gambian soil, will their political paymasters use them as a bargaining factor to extract concessions from the Gambian government?

The Senegalese, while preoccupied with The Gambia providing a back-door entry for political subversion to Senegal itself, also have other interests in their tiny neighbor. It is no secret that elements within the Senegalese government have long favored the total incorporation of The Gambia as Senegal's eighth region. To them, such a move would end the anomalous position of The Gambia in relation to Senegalese communications with the Casamance region to the south. As is frequently pointed out, the most direct route to Ziguinchor, is via the trans-Gambia ferry at Yelitenda. Before confederation, the use of this route raised delicate points about Gambian sovereignty; the present political arrangements avoid them.

The Senegalese have also felt that an independent Gambia presents an economic threat to them. In 1969-1971 the thorny issue of Gambia's reexport trade to Senegal, regarded as smuggling by the Dakar authorities, brought about a diplomatic crisis in the relations between the two countries. Senegalese irritation at the loss of revenues to their own exchequer led to a tightening up of border partrols and the ill-treatment of Gambians suspected of smuggling. Senegalese forces ignored Gambia's sovereignty on several occasions in this period, and later in 1974, to resist, in the notorious phrase of the then finance minister, "economic aggression" on the part of the Gambians. The actual extent of the smuggling and its effects on the Senegalese economy have never been accurately established, but it remains an issue that the Senegalese would like to have eliminated by alterations in The Gambia's import levies so as to make it unprofitable. In the past, The Gambian government has refused to accede to this demand because it would lead to an increase of some 50 percent in the cost of living to its people. Political union would remove this particular obstacle (Hughes: 1974: 13).

It is also apparent that the Senegalese wish to have greater access to the Gambian market. Hughes, looking at trade figures between the two countries for between 1965-1966 and 1971-1972, found a growing imbalance in favor of Senegal, with Senegal providing finished goods and the Gambians supplying raw materials (Hughes, 1974: 14). This trend has accelerated in recent years as Senegal's manufacturing sector has grown, and with it, a search for markets. Table 2.2, based on figures provided by the Gambian Central Statistics Division, summarizes the situation.

Security, the smuggling issue, and trade sum up Senegalese interest in The Gambia, with shortened communications lines to Casamance or to the sea at Banjul and the Gambian river ports as additional concerns. Security is also of prime concern to the Gambian government. The defense agreement allowing for mutual assistance goes back to 1965, but it lay dormant until the first political crisis in 1980. The second need of The Gambia, as an enclave state, is Senegalese (and Guinean) cooperation in the development of the Gambia river basin, particularly an agreed policy on water use so as to ensure an adequate supply downriver for Gambian agricultural purposes. A Senegambian Secretariat was created in 1968 to promote closer functional ties between the two countries. Ten years later the Gambia River Development Organization (to which Guinea acceded later) brought within its remit existing arrangements for joint exploitation of the waterway. The most ambitious joint project is the proposed bridge-barrage scheme at Yelitenda, which, after many years of planning, is expected to

TABLE 2.2   Trade Between The Gambia and Senegal
(1971-1972 through 1980-1981)[a]

	Imports from Senegal	Exports to Senegal	Trade Balance
1971-1972	1,467,294	117,731	−1,349,563
1972-1973	2,439,635	237,194	−2,197,441
1973-1974	2,939,594	241,217	−2,698,377
1974-1975	3,488-802	869,685	−2,619,117
1975-1976	2,765,153	721,399	−2,043,754
1976-1977	1,916,618	283,755	−1,632,863
1977-1978	3,880,271	273,940	−3,606,331
1978-1979	3,824,404	4,897,310[b]	+1,072,906
1979-1980	4,968,569	761,589	−4,206,980
1980-1981	7,161,446	386,396	−6,775,050

a. In million Dalasi.
b. All were groundnuts.

be completed before the end of the Second Development Plan in 1985-1986.

Cooperation between The Gambia and Senegal goes back to preindependence days, but, as a number of commentators have pointed out, Gambians have always been reluctant to make important political and economic sacrifices (Hughes, 1974; Bayo, 1977; Senghor, 1979). Outnumbered nine to one, in the past they have avoided outright political union. Jawara's proposal for a federation in 1964 did not go far enough for the Senegalese, and all that emerged on that occasion were closer functional links and a special relationship, adknowledged in the Treaty of Association, signed in 1967.

The present Treaty of Confederation (reproduced in the Gambia Times, January 16, 1982) goes much further than previous agreements, but still seeks to strike a balance between the Senegalese preference for total union and the Gambian desire to retain significant areas of autonomy. These contradictory objectives are responsible for the ambiguities in the treaty, the most striking of which is that while the "independence and sovereignty" of each state are guaranteed, they are to proceed to the "integration of the armed forces and the security forces" and the "development of an economic and monetary union," a move long sought by the Senegalese to bring Gambian practices in line with their own. While the powers of the Confederal Assembly are vague, Senegal will have a two-thirds membership of it, a permanent majority. The other agreements, joint foreign policymaking and the continuation of technical cooperation, present fewer difficulties from the standpoint of Gambian autonomy.

On balance, in the short run The Gambia gains military protection and hopes of economic growth at a later stage when joint programs for utilizing river resources and the port of Banjul on a regional basis materialize. Against this is the long-term prospect of succumbing to Senegalese economic and political preponderance. At worst, The Gambia could become a client state of Senegal; even a less pessimistic prognostication would see the country exposed to the vagaries and pressures of Senegalese domestic politics and a growing Senegalese presence in the Gambian economy. The Gambia's reputation abroad could also suffer if it becomes identified with Senegal's sometimes assertive and controversial foreign policy. And, behind Senegal, looms France.

Perhaps the way out of the present dilemma—how to obtain security without renouncing sovereignty—lies in a suggestion made by President Jawara in 1974: Other neighboring countries should join Senegal and The Gambia in a regional federation. This would achieve a better political balance between the component units, create additional economic resources, and more truly reflect the geographical realities of the area. Guinea and Guinea Bissau come to mind in this respect. Guinea has enjoyed good relations with Banjul for many years and, more recently, its abandonment of its radical isolationism has brought it closer to Senegal. It already belongs to the River Gambia Development Organization. Guinea Bissau has close economic ties with The Gambia and, despite the Sanyang affair, political relations have always been good between them. A swing to the right in Bissau since 1980 makes its government ideologically less distant from those of the Senegambian Confederation. Economic self-interest may yet overcome the political divisions among the countries of the Senegambia region.

CONCLUSION

What part has "smallness" played in the postcolonial history of The Gambia? One important conclusion suggested by the Gambia experience is that smallness can be advantageous in certain circumstances. We have seen how the small size of the country and its population have made it easier to create a common identity and for the government to penetrate the territory administratively. The Gambia has avoided problems of size, distance, and isolation, which have bedeviled attempts at state building and national integration in such richer African countries as Nigeria or Zaire. Its enclave status, though economically a hindrance, in the past encouraged a sense of pulling together among Gambians living in the shadow of Senegal. Restricted size has also been helpful in external relations. The Gambia poses no aggressive threat to its neighbors and is accepted as an "honest broker" among larger states—the reconciliation of Guinea and Senegal or bridge building between Anglophone and Francophone countries in West Africa. Economically, Gambian difficulties stem from a number of sources, of which size is but one. The natural environment, colonial policy, postcolonial management of the economy—each has affected the material prosperity of the country. It is true that The Gambia is too small to industrialize or to develop its water resources single-handedly, but at the same time, limited resources have discouraged grandiose development projects that have beggared better-off neighbors. Its very smallness, with, of course, its tolerant political system, has won the country much international sympathy and assistance. Since independence, The Gambia has been able to lessen its financial dependence on Britain significantly because so many other countries, of widely different ideological beliefs, have been willing to assist it. Which brings me to my final observation. The quality of political leadership is of crucial importance to small states: The policies vigorously advocated by Sir Dawda Jawara have helped overcome internal divisions at home and earned The Gambia an honorable reputation abroad.

REFERENCES

BAKARR, S. A. (1981) The Gambia Mourns Her Image. Banjul.

BAYO, K. M. (1977) "Mass orientation and regional integration: environmental variations in Gambian orientations toward Senegambia." Ph.D. thesis, Northwestern University.

BENEDICT, B. [ed.] (1967) Problems of Smaller Territories. London: Athlone Press.

FLETCHER, A. J. (1978) "Party politics in the Gambia." Ph.D. Thesis, University of California.

HUGHES, A. (1974) "Senegambia revisited or changing Gambian perceptions of integration with Senegal," pp. 139-179 in R. C. Bridges (ed.) Senegambia. Aberdeen, Scotland: Aberdeen University, African Studies Group.

――― (1975) "From green uprising to national integration: the people's progressive party in The Gambia 1959-1973." Canadian Journal of African Studies 9, 1: 61-74.

――― (1981) "Why the Gambian coup failed." West Africa 26 (October): 2498-2502.

――― (1982a) "The limits of "consociational democracy" in The Gambia." Presented to the IPSA Round Table on Government in the Plural Societies of Black Africa, Brussels, April 5-8.

――― (1982b) "The Gambian general elections." West Africa (May 10): 1241-1242; (May 17): 1305-1307; (May 24): 1361.

LIJPHART, A. (1968) The Politics of Accommodation: Pluralism and Democracy in the Netherlands. Berkeley: University of California Press.

――― (1969) "Consociational democracy." World Politics 21, 9.

――― (1977) Democracy in Plural Societies: A Comparative Exploration. New Haven, CT: Yale University Press.

NYANG, S. S. (1974) "The role of the Gambian political parties in national integration." Ph.D. thesis, University of Virginia.

RAPAPORT, J., et al. (1971) Small States and Territories: Status and Problems. New York: Arno.

SENGHOR, J. C. (1979) "Politics and the functional strategy to international integration: Gambia in Senegambian integration, 1958-1974." Ph.D. thesis, Yale University.

VAN MOOK, H. et al. (1964) Report on the Alternatives for Association Between The Gambia and Senegral. Bathurst: Government Printer.

3

THE STRUCTURE OF TERROR
IN A SMALL STATE:
EQUATORIAL GUINEA

IBRAHIM K. SUNDIATA
University of Illinois at Chicago

The Republic of Equatorial Guinea, a miniscule state in western equatorial Africa, has had a turbulent postcolonial history. After gaining independence from Spain in 1968, the Republic received limited outside attention because of the closed and repressive nature of the government of President for Life Francisco Macias. From 1969 onward, the twin props of Macias's regime were the Juventud on Marcha con Macias ("Youth on the March with Macias") and the National Guard. These two agencies ensured, through expropriation of private property, intimidation, and political murder, that the powers of the head of state were not challenged. It has been said that

> nowhere else in modern times had a tyrant of Macias' magnitude managed to destroy his country and annihilate his own people so extensively and persistently in the full knowledge, if not with the assistance of the nations' former colonizer; of its refugee-crowded neighbors, Nigeria, Cameroon, and Gabon; of its allies and/or aid partners, the U.S.S.R., Cuba, China, France, the U.N. organizations, and the European Economic Community; and of the Vatican, not to mention with the tacit acquiescence of the OAU [Pelissier, 1980: 10].

In the 1969-1979 period, thousands fled their homeland and sought refuge in Cameroon, Gabon, Nigeria, Europe, and America. According to some estimates, about one-third of the approximately 300,000 people of Equatorial Guinea fled abroad (Artucio, 1980: 2). Finally, on August 3, 1979, Macias was overthrown in a palace coup and executed a month later. In 1981 a United Nations investigator concluded that still "the country is in a shambles—economically, politically and socially" (Africa Report, May-June, 1980: 33).

What brought about this state of affairs in Equatorial Guinea? Thus far, little attempt has been made to analyze the factors that gave rise to the repression intermittently mentioned in the outside press. Yet the Republic may very well be a prime illustration of the torturous attempt to build a nation within anomalous boundaries bequeathed to European imperialism.

Equatorial Guinea, the only Hispanophone country in sub-Saharan Africa, has a total area of 10,820 square miles and a population estimated at 318,000 in 1974. The state's two major components are the mainland enclave of Rio Muni (10,039 square miles) and the island of Biyogo (779 square miles). The two significant ethnic categories on the island are the Bubi and the Fernandinos. The latter are the descendants of formerly English-speaking recaptured slaves settled by the British in the nineteenth century. The Fang are the dominant ethnic group in Rio Muni, having migrated to its coast in the 1800s.

Like most present-day African countries, Equatorial Guinea was born of colonial partitioning. For most of the past century, the Spanish presence was, at best, superficial. While nominally ruled by Madrid since the end of the 1700s, the island portion of the republic (formerly Fernando Po) was not entirely explored by Europeans before 1900. The bulk of the coast of Rio Muni was claimed by France until the 1900 Treaty of Paris, which conceded it to Spain. Although the Paris treaty established the frontiers of Spanish Rio Muni and an administration was organized in 1904, most of the territory remained unexplored by the Spanish until the 1920s. It was not until 1926-1927 that control of the border regions of Rio Muni was consolidated, against the intermittent resistance of the fiercely independent Fang (Pelissier, 1968: 17).

Under colonialism, the various ethnic groups in Spanish Guinea fared differently. On the island, the Spanish allowed some of the indigenous Bubi to establish themselves in the professions or enter Spanish employment. Few such benefits were extended to the populations of the mainland. This neglect enabled the people of the Rio Muni to remain more immune to the cultural imperialism of the metropole. And "being on the mainland, they were also far more open to the African nationalist influences which swept through the British and French colonies after World War II. Colonialism had barely established itself in Rio Muni when the rest of Africa began to clamor for independence" (Cronje, 1976).

The "winds of change" blowing in Africa after 1945 affected Equatorial Guinea. Its tentative moves toward independence began in the rapidly changing Africa of the 1950s. Underground nationalist movements were formed in 1954, and the security apparatus of the colonial regime was quick to respond. Two leading nationalists, Enrique Nvo and Acacio Mane, were assassinated, but mainland nationalism could not be contained. From 1959 onward, when the nationalist movement became irreversible, Spain sought other means of controlling the situation. In 1959, the colony, which had been governed by an admiral, was made an integral part of Spain and named the Spanish Equatorial Region. Pressure from the United Nations, coupled with African nationalist agitation, forced some liberalization in Spanish colonial policy. Political prisoners were released, and a few of the liberated prisoners were given responsible posts in the colonial bureaucracy. The distinction made between *indigenas* (natives) and *emancipados* (*evolues*) was formally abolished, and all Africans became technically full citizens of Spain. In 1960 three Africans were sent to the Spanish *Cortes* as representatives of the Equatorial "provinces."

Increasing pressure from nationalist exiles in neighboring Gabon and Cameroon, and from the United Nations, forced further liberalization. In August 1963, Spain announced its intention of giving the two provinces of Spanish Guinea greater autonomy (Klinteberg, 1978: 9). On December 20, 1963, Spain's Equatorial Region was officially renamed Equatorial Guinea. After this date, the two provinces had a joint legislative body and a cabinet consisting of eight African councillors and a president elected by the legislature. The Spanish governor-general was replaced by a high commissioner, and efforts were made to woo political opponents and exiles into accommodating what was left of the Spanish presence.

To further their plans, the Spanish appealed to newly released leaders and a few colonial civil servants. From the inauguration of the "autonomous" regime in 1963 onward, nationalist movements were recognized legally as political parties. By the year of independence (1968) there were five contending parties in Spanish Guinea, all but two advocating independence and strong union between Rio Muni and Fernando Po (Biyogo): MUNGE (Movimiento de Union Nacional de Guinea Ecuatorial),

MONALIGE (Movimiento Nacional de Liberacion de la Guinea Ecuatorial), IPGE (Idea Popular de la Guinea Ecuatorial), Union Democratic Fernandino, and Union Bubi.

Union Democratica Fernandina and Union Bubi, both based on Fernando Po, had separatist platforms. While the latter favored total separation from Rio Muni to protect Bubi interests, the former sought to protect certain powerful interests on Fernando Po through a federal solution that would secure the island from Fang nationalism.

The five-year period between 1963 and 1968 saw intense party rivalry and maneuvers for Spanish endorsement. MUNGE and MONALIGE participated in the autonomous government, but the situation was manipulated by the Spanish authorities, in collaboration with the *casas fuertes* (large Spanish trading houses). The most moderate of the nationalist parties, MUNGE, headed by Bonifacio Ondo Edu, gained the patronage of the Spanish interests and emerged as the principal party in the autonomous government.

During the period of the autonomous government, international opinion, especially within the United Nations, demanded a quickened pace for Spanish decolonization. A visit by the subcommittee of the U.N. Committee of 24 in August of 1966 strengthened the hand of the unionist parties. It insisted upon talking to MONALIGE and IPGE leaders as well as to those of MUNGE. The subcommittee reported to the Committee of 24, which in turn reported to the UN General Assembly that the inhabitants of Spanish Guinea wanted and should have independence no later than 1968. In December of 1967, the UN General Assembly called on Spain to promise that Equatorial Guinea would accede "to independence as a single political and territorial entity not later than July 1968 (Africa Report, February 1968: 36).

The metropole, moving rapidly toward decolonization before the end of 1968, announced on August 21 of that year that presidential and general elections would be held on September 22 and that independence would be granted on October 12. Thus fascist Spain, unlike Portugal, moved to divest itself of its sub-Saharan African holdings before the end of the decade. However, as in many other such situations, a problem revolved around the devolution of power. In a first round of voting, on September 22, no candidate received the required absolute majority: Macias received 36,716 votes; Ondo Edu, 31,941; Atanasio Ndongo (head of the main wing of MONALIGE), 18,232; and Edmundo Bosio Dioco of the Union Bubi, 4,795 (Africa Report, January 1969: 26).

The leader in the voting was Macias, who was a Fang and a coffee planter born in 1924 in Mongomo, Rio Muni. He had been a local government employee under the colonial regime. He had gradually worked his way up in the political alignments preceding independence. Having belonged to all political parties in the country, he rarely played any active role in any of them. After abandoning IPGE, he helped put together MUNGE, under whose autonomous government he served as vice president. The serious rifts in the political parties worked to Macias's advantage. He left MUNGE and joined MONALIGE. Eventually he emerged at the leadership of a coalition formed by IPGE and two dissident factions of MUNGE and MONALIGE to defeat Ondo Edu. Macias's victory was made possible principally through the support of Atanasio Ndongo, head of MONALIGE, and Edmondo Bosio, leader of MUNGE and MONALIGE dissident groups. Macias opposed the draft independence constitution during a constitutional referendum but campaigned during the election for the maintenance of the union between the two segments of Equatorial Guinea and for close ties with the former colonial power. No sooner had he taken power than he started to violate the terms of the coalition platform and to give intimations of megalomania.

When Equatorial Guinea achieved unified independence, a relatively well developed, but dependent, island was attached to a neglected colonial enclave. At independence, the island and the mainland had vastly different economies. The mainstay of the insular economy was high-quality cocoa, with an annual production of about 35,000 tons in 1968. Coffee was the second largest export crop, with an annual production of 20,000 tons in 1968. Rio Muni was much less developed; timber was the only export of any great significance (250,000 tons of okoume wood in 1968). Rio Muni, with a population composed mainly of fishermen and peasants, had an annual per capita income of U.S. $40. Biyogo, together with the island of Annobon (now Pagalu), had an annual per capita income of between $250 and $280 (Legum, 1968-1969: 483, 489). The enclave had a population of approximately 200,000, while the island had 62,612 inhabitants (Pelissier, 1968: 18).

The postindependence crisis was heightened by the tension that existed between the Spanish economic interests on Biyogo and the Fang of Rio Muni. The Fang had proved difficult for the Spanish to control. Soon after Spain occupied the interior of Rio Muni, the Fang had started the *alar ayong* and *mbwiti* movements, which sought to regroup Fang clans and establish Fang nationhood (Fernandez, 1970: 427-457). Throughout the Spanish colonial period and the autonomous government, the Fang resisted attempts to turn them into plantation laborers, preferring to grow cocoa and coffee on their own small plots. Those who could be persuaded to work for Spanish planters proved troublesome employees.

In the late colonial period only 3.4 percent of the mainland enclave was cultivated for cash crops compared with 24.4 percent of the island. On Biyogo, the available land was concentrated in the hands of a few Spanish planters who dealt with the labor question by importing workers from the mainland, notably Nigeria. The sparse Bubi population had made it comparatively easy for Spanish cocoa interests to take over the land. The local Bubi farmers were often persuaded to exchange their plots for less favorable ones to allow the Spaniards to amalgamate the farms into large plantations. In return, the large Spanish combines—the *casa fuertes*—often paid a small annual pension to the Bubi and sometimes provided scholarships for their sons to obtain secondary or higher education in Spain (Cronje, 1976: 8-9). Almost all of the Bubi and Fernandino agriculturists were in debt to large Spanish commercial firms (Pelissier, 1968: 37).

As early as 1930 it had become clear that Spain intended Biyogo for use by European cultivators. The 1960 census data shows that in that year there were 4,170 Europeans out of a total insular population of roughly 63,000. The Bubi were gradually accommodated to Spanish culture and became vital supports of Spanish hegemony on the island. Spanish dominance can be illustrated with statistics on land use: 55 percent of the island's cultivators controlled less than 3 percent of the crop-producing land in 1962, while 2.3 percent of the farmers worked 53 percent of the cultivated land (Pelissier, 1968: 37).

Biyogo's late colonial development was characterized by close collaboration between the Bubi and Fernandino elites and the representatives of metropolitan agrobusiness. Although the Bubi existed in the shadow of European capital, by the 1960s they were estimated to be 90 percent literate and the owners of prosperous agricultural cooperatives (the most notable was at their ancient capital of Moka). Many were characterized as "quasi-literate well housed cocoa farmers proud of their Spanish citizenship" (Howe, 1966: 48). On the eve of independence it was said:

> In contrast to the economic slowdown and tense relationships on the mainland, Fernando Po [Biyogo] is booming with prosperity. The Bubi, who are indirectly benefiting from the flight of Spanish investment from Rio Muni, are disenchanted with continental nationalism. They are now convinced that independence in union with Rio Muni, and the loss of Spanish protection, would open their island to economic and political plunder from a flood of Fang. In the circumstances, this fear is thoroughly justified [Pelissier, 1968: 37).

Biyogo has many of the characteristics of a plantation island:

(1) small size and peripherality; (2) economic dualism [with] an "enclave" export sector . . . ; (3) a segmental society characterized by a rigid class-caste system and reflecting in its structure the predominance of the plantation crop . . . over every aspect of economic and social life; (4) a considerable fragmentation of land in the traditional agricultural sector; a large number of micro-units, which provide an economic base for small cultivators who work on estates to supplement their income; (5) a highly developed institutional system for the service of the plantation; (6) the extraversion of political and economic power [Lamusse, 1980: 103].

The island also possesses some of the secondary characteristics of plantation islands:

(1) casual seasonal employment for a large part of the labor force; (2) limited investment and employment opportunities outside the export sector; hence a lopsided economy; (3) a situation of economic dependency. The most obvious feature of this dependence is the extent to which such countries depend on exports and imports and the very small control which they have on the terms under which this trade is carried out; (4) a pre-industrial social system characterized by relatively impermeable divisions, an introverted mentality on the part of the different groups and low social mobility; (5) great inequalities in the distribution of income and wealth; (6) galloping demography on a relatively static economic base; hence a growing rate of discrepancy between the rate of population increase and the rate of economic growth [Lamusse, 1980: 103].

Biyogo is deviant in one significant aspect. The last characteristic does not apply to it and sets it apart from other plantation islands. It has been noted that "birth rates in the low to mid-30's/1000 characterized Gabon and Equatorial Guinea, but both could be attributed to the pathological conditions which affect large populations in this part of Africa" (Caldwell et al., 1980: 955). Insular Equatorial Guinea does not have an abundant population, nor, until well into the twentieth century, did it have a stable population.

This fact has molded the island's political economy. Until the 1940s the indigenous Bubi were reportedly declining because of the alcoholism and venereal disease. The birthrate was low due to the sterility of 20 percent of the female population (Teran, 1962: 87). It is estimated that they declined by 50 percent between 1904 and 1945 (Pelissier, 1964: 48). Although the decline of the Bubi was arrested in the 1940s, the island continued to depend on labor migration from mainland Africa (notably Nigeria) to sustain its agriculture. Therefore, a most important component of the insular population was Ibo, Efik, and Ibibio.

Clearly, a major source of conflict in Equatorial Guinea is the physical separation and economic division between the island and mainland Rio Muni, which was conspicuously the poorer. In 1960, exports from then Spanish Guinea (of which Biyogo was the mainstay) totaled more than U.S. $33 million, the highest level of exports per capita in Africa ($135). Some 90 percent of the products of Equatorial Guinea were shipped to Spain, which paid higher than world prices for them. The colony's balance of trade was favorable; the year before the autonomous government was proclaimed, it reached 823 million pesetas (Spanish Information Service, 1964: 52). In 1968 Biyogo was not only an exporter of cocoa, coffee, and bananas, but also possessed some processing industries, such as chocolate and soap factories and palm oil works. The future seemed bright; three petroleum companies were prospecting for offshore oil.

According to the colonial regime the subsidies and paternalistic nurturance given to Equatorial Guinea (particularly Biyogo) during the 1960s led "to the conclusion that the foreign trade of Fernando Po and Rio Muni depends to a great extent on the rest of Spain, and that any drastic change in the present system of exchange would have serious consequences for both territories" (Spanish Information Service, 1964: 51). The "prosperity" of Biyogo was specious. It was subsidized for the benefit of certain Catalan trading houses. The insular economy was an example of extreme dependence—a dependence that was interrupted by the political events of 1968-1969.

Spanish economic interests were opposed to the liquidation of their holdings encouraged separatist tendencies among the Bubi. This was done with financial and other inducements. As economic conditions deteriorated on the mainland, the Bubi-Spanish alliance became stronger. As their interests clashed with Fang nationalism, Macias, on assuming power, determined to eliminate their opposition, which stood in the way of his obviously unfolding designs of personal rule.

Barely four months after independence, which had been superficially smooth, a grave crisis arose that signaled the total removal of all the obstacles in Macias's way. To counter the Bubi-Spanish alliance, Macias had brought over some 7000 Fang to the capital Santa Isabel (the present

Malabo). He demanded that Spain remove its remaining garrisons from the new state and persisted in anti-Spanish speeches. While an exodus of Spaniards began, Foreign Minister Atanasio Ndongo and the Equatorian delegate to the United Nations, Saturino Ibongo, were asked by Spanish officials to stop inflammatory broadcasts. After Macias refused to heed them, the two attempted a coup. Ndongo briefly took over the presidency, but was soon routed. He and Ibongo were captured. The followers of the ill-fated *putsch* fled to the forest, while the president ordered the arrest of a number of political leaders.

Repression in Equatorial Guinea may have been perceived to have had an integrative function. Given the fissiparous tendencies that surfaced in the first year of independence, force may have been viewed as the only way to keep the enclave and the island together. Terror cowed the recalcitrant insular population and, at the same time, promised rewards to the dominant Fang.

The "plunder" of the insular portion of the Republic and the increased use of repression after 1969 did not equally affect all portions of the population. In the opening years of the regime, much violence could be directed by the leader at groups who were conspicuously richer and politically dissident. As the regime continued, the circle of repression widened to include greater numbers of all groups beyond the president's coterie. Eventually the circle included intimates from his own terror apparatus. Initially repression and terror may have served as "social cement" in a situation of extreme geographic and ethnic fragmentation. It also served to divert resources to the leaders of the hitherto disadvantaged mainland majority. They could, no doubt, identify with the triumph of "their" leaders. This identification was aided by the manipulation of traditional Fang religious practices.

Political opponents were among the first to feel the vengeance of the regime. Of the 46 politicians who attended the Madrid Constitutional Conference in 1967-1968, not more than 10 were alive at the time of Macias's fall in 1979. Outside of a few who had died of natural causes, the vast majority had been put to death. The same holds true for the first Legislative Assembly; over two-thirds of its members died violently or disappeared (Artucio, 1980: 44).

As the regime proceeded, it adopted increasingly draconian measures. These stemmed both from the increasing capriciousness of the leader and from economic dislocation.[1] Whole villages and groups were victims of the president's wrath or indifference. Macias was accused of ordering the burning of two villages for reasons of political revenge (Artucio, 1980:

44). The village of the former director of the national bank was destroyed in 1976 and its inhabitants liquidated after the director had been executed following considerable torture, including the burning out of the victim's eyes (Klinteberg, 1978).

The longevity of the Macias regime has surprised certain observers. Looked at in context, the terror in Equatorial Guinea may share common features with other recent African regimes (in 1979 Idi Amin, Jean-Abdel Bokassa, and Macias were deposed after years of despotic rule). Some would place such despots within a broad and frightening "warrior tradition" in Africa: "a tradition which has at times collapsed in exhaustion under the terrors of white hegemony, but which has also had its moments of resurrection." In such a tradition violence "sometimes assumes a disproportionate air of sacredness and mystique. Manhood becomes equated with capacity for ruthlessness, as well as with potential for virility" (Mazrui, 1979: 84).

In a classic work on state power and state terror, E. V. Walter observes that terror is instrumental—it operates to ensure compliance with the wishes of the individual (the "terroristic despot") directing the state. Terror as a process demands a "source of violence, a victim, and a target." In Walters's "dramaturgic model" of terror, "The victim perishes, but the target reacts to the spectacle or the news of that destruction with some manner of submission or accommodation that is, by withdrawing his resistance or by inhibiting his potential resistence" (Walter, 1969: 9) Terror systems create "forced choice" in which "the individuals must choose between two evils, both of which would be rejected in an 'open' situation." Such systems create a situation in which the individual must inform or be informed upon. Avoidance of the noxious alternative puts the individual in collaboration with the system of terror and breaks down solidarity among those outside the terror apparatus.

Some see the rise of Macias's terroristic despotism as the product of the psychopathology. It cannot be denied that Macias exhibited extremely erratic behavior during his tenure in office. A psychological profile of the President for Life refers to "his frequent use of drugs (*bhang* and *iboga*), his pervasive inferiority complex, his failure as a family man, and his association with cults and witchcraft" (Pelissier, 1980: 11). The head of state's inability to reproduce has been noted and may be related to general theories of sexual inadequacy and the brutal quest for power (Mazrui, 1979: 75).

It can be argued that Macias was "insane." But this leaves us to account for the "miraculous duration" of his rule (Pelissier, 1980: 11). Walters notes that the "despot" commanding the state need not be "rational." State terror may exist over fairly long periods of time under "psychotic" rulers, provided certain conditions are met:

> In some cases, the chain of events in a process of terror may being with an emotionally disturbed overlord living in the midst of political tensions, who commands his agents to perform acts of violence which induce the fear reaction which in turn yields social effects upon which the political system depends. Some political conditions call forth continuous behavior of the sort encouraging a king of institutionalized rage, or supporting psychotic behavior. The image and definition of the overlord as a dangerous person may enable the power system to function in a set pattern that could not persist in other circumstances. . . . That the consequences may not be intended by the directors or agents of violence is irrelevant. The "useful" social effects of irrational violence may or may not be perceived and approved after they emerge from the terror process [Walter, 1969: 8].

Despotism and terror are not confined to Africa, as the history of twentieth-century Europe amply demonstrates. There are several prerequisites for a functioning terroristic regime: (1) a shared ideology that justifies violence and clearly labels the victims as evildoers, (2) victims whose liquidation will not cause a major dysfunction in the society, and (3) disassociation of the agents of violence and the victims from ordinary social life (victims may be defined as "unpersons"). The agent of violence are organized as executioners, alien mercenaries, secret police, and so on. In addition, (4) the regime must retain incentives to collaboration with itself, and (5) the traditional social bonds must survive the terror—or new relationships must be substituted (Walter, 1969: 340).

Macias's regime had the characteristics of a "terroristic despotism." The violence of the President for Life was sacralized, while those accused of offenses against the security of the state were specifically stated to have no rights (Review of the International Commission of Jurists, 1974). The National Guard and the Juventud en Marcha con Macias were bound by no law except the will of the president. Macias appointed all judges and public prosecutors. The citizen's sense of isolation was reinforced by rigid postal censorship, the abolition of passports, and the eventual destruction of canoe traffic from the insular portion of the country. Collaboration with the regime was aided by the very vagueness of the often capital charge of being a *descontento*.

Terror in Equatorial Guinea was largely extraconstitutional. Since the President for Life was the fount of all rewards and sanctions and since no act committed in the president's name could be called into question, the court system tended to be bypassed in favor of a direct system of punishments administered by Macias' security apparatus.[2] Trials were rare.[3] Suspected miscreants were likely to be imprisoned without due process. The security apparatus was headed by the President for Life, who controlled a chain of command that ran through the National Director-General of Security and the provincial governors, down to the district heads of the militia (district representatives of the Juventud en Marcha con Macias). At the village level there were local *jefes de seguridad* who often relied on denunciations brought in by village youngsters (Klinteberg, 1978: 32). Suspects were arrested and interrogated, often under torture. The accused's conduct was reviewed by the Director-General of Security and other officials. When this process was finished, the case was placed before the President for Life. There was no trial, no definite sentence, and no defense.

In Equatorial Guinea political prisoners fared worse than common criminals. The system acted so as to define the former as beyond the pale of law. The aim was to destroy political prisoners either physically or morally "since their death was of no account" (Artucio, 1980: 2). No jailer "was accountable for dead prisoners and quite often guards were ordered to kill them, for which they were rewarded."[4]

Macias used the party and traditional religion to create an ideology that justified violence against the real or imagined enemies of the regime. In the Equatorian context these can only be understood against the backdrop of the intensive Hispanization that characterized the last years of Spanish rule. In the mid-1960s it was observed that:

> more than 90% of all children of school-going age in Guinea actually attend school and nowhere else does one find governmental services and the Catholic Church working in such close liaison. Native cults and aboriginal beliefs are harried with all the vigor of the sixteenth century. African customs are suspect and are harassed or suppressed altogether in favor of the only true values of triumphant Hispanism: love the Spanish mother country, the Caudillo and the Church. The new urban centers built since the end of the war therefore bear such names as San Fernando, Mongomo de Guadalupe, Sevilla de Niefang and Valladolid de los Bimbiles. Schools, chapels, hospitals are built alongside "plazas de toros." In other words, an attempt is being made to bring about a thoroughgoing cultural and political assimilation before it is too late [Pelissier, 1965: 255].

It was against this cultural imperialism that Macias reacted. He instituted his own form of *authenticite* to destroy once and for all heavy-handed Hispanization. Macias attempted to create a state cult by relying on both the slogans of mass political mobilization and the forms of indigenous religion.

The task was not easy. Between 90 and 95 percent of the population was nominally Catholic, and certain clerics, like Monsignor Rafael Nzue Abuy, had prestige that made them likely foci of resistance to the regime (Pelissier, 1980: 11). Macias harped upon the close collaboration between the church and colonialism on the one hand and attempted to use aspects of Fang religion to bolster his regime on the other. In 1973, the ruling party was enjoined to pass a resolution at its Third National Congress that said that "the Catholic Church, during its presence in the Republic of Equatorial Guinea, has always been a faithful instrument at the service of colonialism, plotting machinations which apparently were considered religious, and had knowledge of the constant campaign developed clandestinely against the President for Life of the Republic." In 1973, Macias de-Europeanized most of the place names in the country, thus depriving them of both colonial and Catholic connotations (e.g., Santa Isabel became Malabo). The following year a decree ordered priests and pastors to open their sermons with the words "Nothing without Macias, everything for Macias, down with colonialism and the ambitious." In Bata in 1975 the head of state informed his audience that "false priests" were "thieves, swindlers, exploiters and colonialists" (Artucio, 1980: 2). The populace was warned that contact with Catholic clergy would be severely punished. Catholic schools were effectively shut down by a decree that banned all private education (West Africa, 1975: 1198).[5]

Macias sought not only to disestablish the colonial religious order but to create a new one centering on himself. This new "cult of personality" could contain elements of the discredited colonial faith. The head of state was proclaimed the "sole miracle" of Equatorial Guinea. Church services were made to include sycophantic adulation of the President for Life. Political rhetoric evoked the image of the leader as a miraculous figure, eclipsing the discredited roster of Roman Catholic saints:

Slowly like enormous octopuses they [the colonialists] went about slowly enrolling our Nation in their tentacles of death—"Equatorial Guinea is Suffocated, Equatorial Guinea is not able to breathe," . . . in the precise instant in which all appeared lost, there appeared, as in a dream, the Liberator—Father of our constructive revolution. At his side, the National Force, guide for security. "Juventud en marcha con Macias"—and all the [Equatorial] Guinean population rose as if one man to the magnetic nationalist cry of "En Marcha con Macias" [Ngomo, 1970.]

Besides grafting the cult of personality onto the existing practice of Christianity, the regime revivified and used traditional religion. Among the Fang, the Mbwiti movement was both a focus of anticolonial sentiment and a means of interpreting the colonial experience. The Spanish had attempted to eradicate the movement, after accusing it of human sacrifice and anthrophagy (cannibalism). Macias, the son of a Mbwiti leader, found in the movement a manifestation of African authenticity. At his home village he surrounded himself with considerable magicoreligious power. The President for Life's position was sacralized. Rumors that his power had been secured through the effusion of blood heightened his aura of invincibility. As in other contexts, "the collective fantasy about the omnipotence of the great destroyer-provider legitimated his violence" (Walter, 1969: 340; Pelissier, 1980: 11; and West Africa, 1980: 1731).

The regime maintained itself not only through a system of repression, but also through a system of rewards. In the "plunder economy" established after 1969, the agents of terror (e.g., Juventud en Marcha con Macias) were able to both repress insular dissent and plunder the insular economy. Of course, as the economy foundered, the need for repression increased and the agents of terror began to see diminishing returns. Unlike the Fang (or the Zulu) of the nineteenth century, the regime was not able to expand the area plundered. Terror was also difficult to delimit. The insular portion of the republic's wealth depended on migrant Nigerian labor, which was extremely recalcitrant in the face of Macias's repression.

At independence the mass exodus of many Spanish *hacendados* had threatened the economy with collapse. Plantation work was disrupted and many workers (reportedly 15,000 on Biyogo) lost their jobs. The satisfaction of the demands of the laborers (a force which, on the island, outnumbered the Bubi, Fang, and Fernandinos) was essential. In 1970, the Equatorial Guinean government was asked by Nigeria whether or not it would revise the labor laws enacted by the colonial government. Macias promised his government would promulgate a new labor ordinance that would remove all oppressive legislation. In December, the Equatorian Ambassador to Nigeria visited the Nigerian Commissioner for Labour and Information about preliminary negotiations for a new labor accord. The situation did not improve; on the contrary, it was exacerbated by the departure of from 15,000 to 20,000 Nigerian plantation workers, out of an original total of 40,000 (Legum, 1971-1972: 504).

The end of the Biafran war in 1970 gave impetus to the return of workers to their homeland. But, more important, the slowdown in the whole cocoa economy resulted in the nonpayment and disaffection of workers.·The Equatorial Guinean Ambassador in Nigeria lamented at the end of 1971 that cocoa production had fallen off because "hundreds" of Nigerians had not recontracted. He attributed this state of affairs to the dilatory way in which Nigeria contemplated ratifying a new labor agreement. This new agreement increased wages; provided free housing, medical attention, and food; and instituted rigid regulation of working hours.

Equatorial Guinea found itself in the position of a miniscule republic that could only be kept alive by transfusions of labor from a larger and more powerful neighbor. The postindependence series of labor treaties signed between Equatorial Guinea and Nigeria had fallen into desuetude by the middle seventies. The ruling party congress held in Bata (July 9-13, 1973) condemned the continued decline in cocoa production and encouraged Guineanos to increase production through patriotic effort. In a revised prognostication, published in June, the 1972-1973 production of cocoa was estimated to be 15,000 tons. The figure had fallen to half of the 1970-1971 level of 30,000 and far short of the 1971-1972 estimate of 22,000 tons (Legum, 1972-1973: 545-546).

Relations between migrant workers and the government became extremely tense in 1972 when approximately fifty Nigerian workers were killed after demonstrating over the arrest of fellow laborers. This action highlighted a signal problem of the Equatorial Guinean rulers. Internally terror might coerce compliance with the dictates of the regime. However, it could not be a truly effective weapon of economic mobilization. A migrant work force can attempt to return home. Force, when employed against praedial labor, was counterproductive. Having crushed insubordination among its own nationals, it was loath to grant immunity to the large alien population in its midst. Following the 1972 incident, workers again began to desert the island. Only about 12,000 workers were recruited for the cocoa plantations by the end of the year and friction between migrant and local workers was reported. A group of Nigerians returning to Calabar claimed they had narrowly escaped death and had been forced to abandon their property (Legum, 1972-1973: 545-546).

The following year arrests and expulsions of Nigerians from Equatorial Guinea caused the Nigerian government to suspend further recruitment. After the expiration of the bilateral labor agreement between the two states in February 1972, a Nigerian labor official visited Malabo and was disappointed to find that the terms of previous labor agreements had not been lived up to. In July the Nigerian government refused to send 1000

workers recruited in Calabar pending a full investigation and the arrangement of a new agreement (Legum, 1973-1974: 597). In the spring of
1975, the Nigerian government airlifted over a thousand of its nationals
out of Equatorial Guinea. The exodus gave the *coup de grace* to an already
desperately ill economy.

As early as 1973 Macias's party proposed to remedy the labor crisis
through the recruitment of 60,000 Guineanos (Partido Unico de Trabajadores, 1973: 4). The following year the party noted that these workers
had not been recruited and urged renewed efforts at production for export
(Partido Unico de Trabajadores, 1974: 12). Agriculture continued to run
down, especially in the face of the exodus of Nigerian labor. An African
journalist reported that "in the countryside, cash crops have been replaced
by fields of indian hemp and opium as the regime's answer to economic
paralysis" (West Africa, 1975: 198). In 1976 the President for Life
decreed compulsory labor for all citizens over fifteen. A year later the
number of unpaid workers was put at 45,000 (including dependents), a
figure that represented about one-fifth of the population remaining in the
country (Pelissier, 1980: 11).[6]

The desperate measures taken by the Macias regime did not overcome
the downward slide of the economy. As the economy unraveled, few
statistics were kept (most statisticians had fled or fallen afoul of the
regime). It is estimated, however, that cocoa production fell from 40,000
tons at independence to approximately 3,000 tons in 1978. Except for
coffee (a few hundred tons), the export economy had collapsed by early
1979 (Pelissier, 1980: 11). Economic distress exacerbated demographic
problems. Infant mortality almost doubled between 1965 and 1975, and
the number of miscarriages increased (Amadou, 1975: 51).[7]

The devolution of the economy also affected monetary policy. The
continuing labor crisis wrecked the export sector of the economy and this
in turn affected all other sectors. It has been noted that in micro states
"the question arises whether the currency law should recognize [the
extreme openness of the economy] by establishing the currency of a
major country or sole legal tender . . . or by requiring that the amount of
currency issued by the monetary authority . . . be covered to a specified
percentage by foreign assets" (Khatkhate and Short, 1980: 1024).

The Spanish unsuccessfully tried to convince Macias to enter a permanent monetary union with Spain similiar to the one between France and
her former colonies. Macias was, however, persuaded that a national
currency could be built on the foreign exchange accumulated from cocoa
or by creating a national currency guaranteed by the World Bank (Gard,

1974: 33, 24). Macias's decision to proceed with the issuance of his own national currency flew in the face of economic reality. The state could not earn the requisite foreign exchange. Terror discouraged the migratory labor system and, without this system, any idea of economic viability, much less an independent monetary system, became illusory. By the time of Macias's fall, Equatorial Guinea had a largely barter economy. Its money was nonconvertible, and no rules existed for investment, economic policies, or commercial practices. Although Macias received aid from the Eastern bloc, the mercurial nature of his rule made any consistent application of socialism impossible. Early in his dictatorship his government specifically rejected Marxism in favor of a vague African humanism (Mbonio, 1970). Before the collapse of the cocoa economy, a coterie of European adventurers and financial advisers persuaded him to substitute Iberian agricultural capital with large-scale European (especially French) finance capital (Gard, 1974: 15-16). Although Macias asserted that he knew "that capitalists never invest on shifting sands or smouldering embers; for this reason we will do all in our power to guarantee political stability in the country," the extreme capriciousness of his rule militated against the growth of investor confidence (Legum, 1971-1972: 504).

By the late 1970s, Equatorial Guinea was a plunder economy with nothing left to plunder. Forced labor affected increasing segments of the population. The 1976 labor decree called for the recruitment of 20,000 workers from Rio Muni (Pelissier, 1980: 11). The recruits' remuneration consisted solely of subsistence a ration of rice, palm oil, and fish and made no allowance for the needs of dependents. In addition to a twelve-hour word day, the laborers were subjected to a regimen that included beatings, capricious brutality, and the withholding of food rations. Military personnel and public officials were also made to submit to part-time labor service (Artucio, 1980: 8).

The system survived by continuing to provide the coterie around the President for Life with benefits. The lower-level agents of terror may have felt a diminution in the rewards falling to them, but Macias "had all the key positions in the security field in the hands of close relatives, like the traditional Fang leader who handed favor only to his Esengui clansmen and a few trusted or thoroughly compromised people" (Pelissier, 1980: 13).

However, by the spring of 1979, terror in Equatorial Guinea had come to include members of this coterie itself. Macias had members of his bodyguard executed in Mongomo. These men were reportedly members of his own clan. In this way the President for Life "cut the mystical link between the leader and the faithful" (Pelissier, 1980: 13). In June of 1979 Macias struck at his inner circle by liquidating five military officers, one of whom was the brother of his successor, Lieutenant Colonel Obiang Nguema Mgasogo. It may have been evident to Obiang, as well as to others, that the terror apparatus was being turned in on itself. If terror had been "functional" in 1969, it was definitely dysfunctional by 1979. The number of individuals who benefited from the terror had dwindled to almost a minority of one.

For eleven years Macias ruled a state that was both a geographical and economic anomaly. Terror played an important part in keeping this anomaly together. However, because of the state's dependence on foreign labor for the production of its major export crop, terror was ultimately dysfunctional. It served to keep the state together, but it could not ensure the proper use of labor. In the long run, force could not insure the stability of the regime, since it could not insure the stability of the labor force. As the economic "pie" dwindled, dissaffection, even among the Fang associates of the president, increased. Ultimately, as the amount of wealth squeezed from the system decreased, threats to the regime multiplied. At that point the instruments of terror devised by the regime were turned against their creator.

NOTES

1. In 1971, insulting the president became a serious offense and foreigners working "against the territorial integrity" of Equatorial Guinea were threatened with twenty to thirty years in prison or death (the same penalties imposed on nationals). Later, the number of punishable offenses was greatly expanded. It came to include donating to missions, not appearing for demonstrations in praise of the leader, and the much vaguer crime of being a *decontento* (Klinteberg, 1978: 32). Correspondence with the outside world was severely punished. A school teacher, Isabel Ipuwa, reputedly had her arm amputated for maintaining correspondence with her parents who had fled abroad (Amadou, 1975: 5).

2. By the time of Macias's fall, the judiciary consisted of the Secretary-General of the Ministry of Defense, Lt. Colonel Theodoro Obiang Nguema Mbasogo, and the Vice President, Bonifacio Nguema Esono, both relatives of the president.

3. One of the few occurred in Bata in 1974; 102 prisoners in the Bata jail were accused of plotting rebellion. The case was tried by a People's Military Tribunal composed of military officers directly appointed by the president. The prisoners, who were members of an organization called "Crusade for the Liberation of Equatorial Guinea by Christ," were given an extremely brief trial. Twelve of the 102 prisoners were publicly executed by firing squad (Artucio, 1980: 43).

4. Prisoners were placed in three categories. "Brigade A" contained political prisoners, those who plotted to overthrow the system or those who were considered to have the potential for overthrowing the system. Brigade B contained individuals who had criticized the regime or who had had difficulties with the Juventud. Like Brigade A, they were liable to compulsory labor. Brigade C included common criminals who were in many ways treated better than were those in the other two categories, although members of Brigade C could also be called to compulsory labor (Artucio, 1980).

5. The campaign against the Christian churches did not go unnoticed. A publication of the World Council of Churches warned that "President Macias is the new God." It noted the restrictions on the churches and specifically complained that "Church leaders have been prevented from traveling abroad, the Presbyterian Church was unable to be represented at the recent assembly of the All Africa Conference of Churches, and internal church meetings of all kinds must receive the specific approval of the authorities, which has to be sought several months in advance" (World Council of Churches, 1974: 9). Exile sources in Spain also published accounts of the continued persecution of priests and the mandatory denunciation of imperialism and Christianity at the opening of religious services (see West Africa, October 6, 1975: 1198).

6. According to Artucio, the number of actual workers recruited in 1977 was 25,000. He gives the number of dependents as 15,000 (1980: 8).

7. The Republic has three functioning pharmacies and ten doctors (only two of whom were indigenous).

REFERENCES

Africa Report (1968, 1969, 1980).

AMADOU, F. (1975) "Le tigre, la guelle ouverte." Afrique-Asie (March).

ARTUCIO, A. (1980) The Trial of Macias in Equatorial Guinea: The Story of a Dictatorship. Geneva: International Commission of Jurists and International University Exchange Fund.

CALDWELL, J. C., G. E. HARRISON, and P. OUIGGAN, (1980) "The demography of micro states." World Development 8, 12.

CRONJE, S. (1976) Equatorial Guinea: The Forgotten Dictatorship. Research Report 2. London: Anti-Slavery Society.

FERNANDEZ, J. W. (1970) "The affirmation of things past: Alar Ayong and Bwiti as movements of protest in central and northern Gabon," pp. 427-457 in R. I. Rotberg and A. Mazrui (eds.) Power and Protest in Black Africa. New York: Oxford University Press.

GARD, R. (1974) Equatorial Guinea: Machinations in Founding a National Bank. Munger Africana Library Notes, Issue 27. Pasadena: California Institute of Technology.

HOWE, R. W. (1966) "Spain's equatorial island." Africa Report (June).

KHATKHATE, D. and B. K. SHORT, (1980) "Monetary and central banking problems of mini-states." World Development 8, 12.

KLINTEBERG, R. (1978) Equatorial Guinea–Marcias Country: The Forgotten Refugees. Geneva: International University Exchange Fund Field Study.

LAMUSSE, R. (1980) "Labour policy in the plantation islands." World Development 8, 12.

LEGUM, C. [ed.] (1968-1969). African Contemporary Record, Vol. I. London: Rex Collings.

——— (1971-1972) African Contemporary Record, Vol. IV. London: Rex Collings.

——— (1972-1973) African Contemporary Record, Vol. V. London: Rex Collings.

——— (1973-1974) African Contemporary Record, Vol. VI. London: Rex Collings.

MAZRUI, A. (1979) "The resurrection of the warrier tradition in African political culture." Journal of Modern African Studies 8 (March).

MBONIO, P. N. (1970) "Relaciones entre la educación y el desarrollo economico." Organo Informativo de Ministerio de Educación Nacional de Guinea Ecuatorial VII (March).

NGOMO, B. O. (1970) "Nacimiento de la libertad de Guinea Ecuatorial." Organo Informativo de Ministerio de Educación Nacional de Guinea Ecuatorial VII (March).

Partido Unico de Trabajadores (1973) Resoluciones génerales de tercer congreso nacional de partido único nacional de trabajadores de la Republica de Guinea Ecuatorial. Bata.

——— (1974). Comite-Central. Primero congreso nacional extraordinario de PUNT. Decisiones adaptados. Bata.

PELISSIER, R. (1964) Los Territorio Españoles de Africa. Madrid: Instituto de Estudios Africanos.

——— (1965) "Spain's discreet decolonisation." Foreign Affairs 44 (April).

——— (1968) "Uncertainty in Spanish Guinea." Africa Report 13 (March).

——— (1980) "Autopsy of a miracle." Africa Report 25 (May-June).

Review of the International Commission of Jurists (1974) Vol. 13 (December).

Spanish Information Service (1964) Spain in Equatorial Africa. Political Documents 2. Madrid: Spanish Information Service.

TERAN, M. de (1962) Síntesis Geográfica de Fernando Poo. Madrid: Instituto de Estudios Africanos e Instituto Juan Sebastino Elcano.

WALTER, E. V. (1969) Terror and Resistance: A Study of Political Violence with Some Case Studies of Some Primitive African Communities. London: Oxford University Press.

West Africa (1975, 1980)

World Council of Churches (1974) "Terror grips Equatorial Guinea." One World 1 (November).

4

CABINDA:
THE POLITICS OF OIL
IN ANGOLA'S ENCLAVE

DANIEL DOS SANTOS
Department of Sociology, Université de Montréal

IS CABINDA A PROBLEM?

The Angolan enclave of Cabinda is not only one of the richest regions of this young African republic, but also one that traditionally causes a good deal of political trouble to the ruling MPLA/Workers party and to the central government. Located in the northwestern extreme of Angola, Cabinda is in fact geographically separated from the main country, by the river Congo, the Republic of Zaire, and the People's Republic of Congo. Historically, its situation is the result of European colonialism. One might compare it to Alsace-Lorraine in France, as it has not always belonged to Angola, or to Oriental Prussia in that that territory was nevertheless a German province from 1918 to 1940, even if it was geographically separated from Germany.

Until the fifteenth century the enclave was shared by three kingdoms— Kakongo, Ngoye, and Loango. The Portuguese arrived there in 1482 and were joined by the British and French, mainly for the trade of merchandise and slaves. Commerce was supported by the traditional ideological work of the European church—the sending of missionaries to preach Christianity. The Portuguese established themselves on the free port of Tchiowa, later known as Cabinda, which became the aim of the other European colonial powers. The French occupied this port in 1783 and had to face attacks from the Dutch and British.

The dispute and the rivalries amongst the European powers allowed the Cabinda kingdoms to survive. It was not until the end of the nineteenth century that the Portuguese were able to sign three treaties—Chinfuma in 1883, Chicamba in 1884, and Simulambuco in 1885—by which the three kingdoms recognized Portuguese sovereignty in exchange for protection of their cultural traditions, their authority, and the integrity of their territory. While Cabinda became a Portuguese protectorate, Angola was defined as a Portuguese colony by the Berlin Conference in 1884-1885.

The first quarter of the twentieth century in Portugal was the scene of a social and political conflict that placed liberals and republicans in opposition to monarchists and conservatives. The country was facing economic disaster. Salazar, called to the government as minister of finance, seized power and installed a fascist regime with the support of the Portuguese Catholic church. In the 1933 Constitution defining the *Estado Novo,* Cabinda and Angola were still considered distinct and separate parts of Portugal. However, in 1956, amendments were introduced in the Colonial Law and the Overseas Organic Law changing Cabinda's status. It became a "district" of the Portuguese "overseas province" of Angola, under the same colonial authority, that is to say the General-Governor of Angola.

This was not a simple administrative move, as Portugal considered Cabinda to be a colonial protectorate and not an international one. This situation was made quite clear in the New Constitutional Law of Portugal in 1974, adopted after the military coup that disposed of the fascist regime, and in the Alvor Agreement (1975) between Portugal and the Angolan liberation movements, the MPLA, the FNLA, and UNITA. This agreement stipulated the process of decolonization and defined the roles of the three Angolan organizations and Portugal itself in the transition to independence.

It was during this period that Alvor's political settlement, despite different efforts to tie up the three movements in a sort of government of national unity, failed to fulfil its aims. FNLA and UNITA troops and ministers fled the capital, Luanda. While the South African army invaded the south, Zaïrean troops occupied the north with the help of mercenaries engaged by the American CIA (Stockwell, 1978). The MPLA alone declared the independence of Angola "from Cabinda to Cunene" and asked for Cuban help. Cabinda's status did not basically change. The colonial heritage was taken, in this case, by MPLA leaders without any further questioning. Cabinda is one of the provinces of the newly independent state of Angola.

However, the historical problem remains: The state apparatus the MPLA took possession of at the moment of independence, as a colonial legacy left to Angolans, is an artificial one, as it was built along the lines of European bourgeois interests whose ultimate aims were to support economic exploitation and protect metropolitan profits. This difficulty in dealing with both ethnic problems and colonial borders deriving from the dismembering of former societies and civilizations by the imposition of the capitalist mode of production, is reflected in the MPLA's own position as it is stated in Article 47 of the Angolan Constitutional Law (1975: 32): "The local administration shall be guided by the combined principles of unity, decentralization and local initiative." One cannot deny the existence of a Cabindan identity, shown by the land and cultural traditions, but also the language Fiotee. But clearly not every ethnic group that once formed a society pretend to independence. There are hundreds of other groups in the same situation throughout the whole African continent.

So, if the MPLA is to surpass the traditional role of the colonial and capitalist state—an important question if one is to understand the meaning of transition to a socialist society—and thus look for a positive integration of Cabinda into the Angolan nation, the answer should lie in the balance of power between central government control and regional decentralization. This must mean support for local Fabindan initiatives. But the application of such politics is not as easy as it appears at first sight.

Cabinda is vital for Angola not only for economic reasons; it also remains the political target and prey of the ambitions of neighboring states and individuals who carry on sabotage and other actions against Angola, forcing it to concentrate a large proportion of its resources on military and repressive operations to protect and preserve the links between Angola and Cabinda. Such a situation reinforces the power of central government and constrains the MPLA in dealing effectively with social and economic problems not only in Cabinda, but in the whole country. One must not forget that Angola, as a southern African country, survives in a rather hostile environment. Not only does it face the hard problem of Cabinda, but it suffers the combined attack—as a permanent threat—of the South African army and UNITA and FNLA guerillas supported by some Western countries, particularly the United States of America.

All this implies that the application of Article 47 of the Constitutional Law represents a quite delicate matter. Every time the question arises, the MPLA leadership overreacts. On the eve of Angolan independence a group of intellectuals and militants, considered to be in the left of this leadership, published a manifesto called "Active Revolt." The manifesto recognized not only a Cabinda identity but a specific character to the Angolan state—namely, the fact that Angola was built on the existence of several peoples and cultures disarticulated by colonial capitalism. The unity of the nation could only be achieved through the recognition of this principle and its concrete application (Manifesto, 1974). The MPLA leadership accused the Manifesto group of being a proimperialist faction that wanted to sell Cabinda to foreign capital. The debate was not opened and repression soon followed this declaration. At the same time and outside the MPLA, in Cabinda itself but also in Zaïre, Congo-Brazzaville, Portugal, and France, political opposition to the MPLA was being organized, calling for the independence of Cabinda and the separation from Angola.

THE POLITICAL QUESTION

The opposition to Angola, especially to the MPLA, in Cabinda is not a recent event. The movement for the liberation of Cabinda led by Luis Ranque Franque was born in 1959, while the Action Committee for the National Union of Cabindans led by Henrique Tiago N'Zita was founded in 1962. Together with the Mayombe Alliance they founded the Liberation Front of Cabinda's Enclave in 1963. Several other organizations appeared later, such as the Democratic Union of the Peoples of Cabinda, and the People's Movement of Cabinda. Most of these organizations have collaborated with the Portuguese. They were criticized by the more radical political movement, the Liberation Front of Cabinda, which presented itself as progressive and anti-imperialist.

Nevertheless, when studying these organizations and their political behavior, one is struck by the numerous contradictions they represent. This is mostly due to the fact that they do not represent the people of Cabinda, but only the personal ambition of their leaders and the state interests behind them.

At the beginning, FLEC was supported by Abbé Youlou, first president of Congo-Brazzaville, whose dream was to integrate Cabinda in the Congolese state. When he was overthrown by Massemba-Debat, who supported the MPLA, FLEC was ordered to leave Congo-Brazzaville. A long period of silence was to follow, till 1974. At that time, FLEC came to life once again, this time in Kinshasa. The MPLA had some internal contradictions to solve: on the right, the dissidence of Daniel Chipenda, a member of the steering committee, who claimed to be the leader of the largest Angolan ethnic group, the Umbundu; on the left, the intellectuals and militants who accused Neto and the steering committee of dictatorship and an unwillingness to accept a people's democracy.

A meeting of the Cabindan movements was organized in Pointe-Noire (Congo-Brazzaville) during the summer of 1974. The new FLEC no longer spoke of an "enclave" but a "state" (*Estado*). Luis Franque, the businessman from Kinshasa became "honorable" president; Alexandre Tchioufou, an assistant director-general of ELF-Congo, was the president. Tchioufou was based in Brazzaville. Tiago N'Zita as vice president, remained in Cabinda. The race between Congo and Zaïre for Cabinda was further complicated as Holden Roberto of FNLA, supported by Mobutu, did not enjoy a love affair with Franque. As for the MPLA, it declared that Cabinda was Angolan territory. In Brazzaville, Neto criticized Tchioufou, whom he looked upon with suspicion because of the links he had with a French oil company.

In 1975, the MPLA, FNLA, and UNITA met at Mombassa, Kenya, and agreed on a common position on the Cabinda issue: The enclave was and would remain Angolan territory. The situation became rather grotesque: Congo-Brazzaville supported the MPLA but if favored the self-determination of Cabinda and allowed FLEC to operate in its territory. Pointe-Noire was used as a port for the landing of Cuban arms and munitions for the MPLA that might be used against FLEC. But the Congo also supported Tchioufou, who was an ally of Chipenda, the rightist dissident of the MPLA. So, the Congo effectively supported the MPLA's enemies. Zaïre and the Americans both supported Franque, and at the same time Holden Roberto, while Gabon and France supported N'Zita. In the meantime the MPLA had complete control of Cabinda, as the Portuguese withdraw their support for FLEC.

By then, FLEC's links with suspicious individuals became clear. These included Jean Kay, a mercenary comprised in a swindling affair against Dassault; Marc Varant, Kay's lawyer, who worked for FLEC in Paris; Jean da Costa, formerly of the French and Congolese armies and at one point Franque's minister of defense. He had connections with a Parisian named Bory, who had quite a record with the French Minister of Justice.

From 1976 until the present, while FLEC continued its contradictory existence, other Cabindan organizations disappeared as quickly as they were born. After the MPLA accused France and Zaïre of backing "Cabinda reactionary groups," French economic interests in Angola put pressure on the Zaïre government, and FLEC moved to Brussels and Lisbon. Pressure was mounted by Western countries on Mobutu to reach an agreement with Angola. Mobutu thus put an end to FNLA and FLEC actions from Zaïre, while Neto was able to halt support for the MNLC. From there on, Cabindan political groups lacked any credibility, as nobody knew for sure how many governments in exile existed or how many presidents Cabinda had.

The anticommunist sentiments of these groups was outweighed by the personal ambition of their leaders to transform Cabinda into a "neutral African Switzerland" or an "African Kuwait." This program was, however, not considered sufficiently viable by multinationals or Western capitalist states for them to destabilize the MPLA's regime. Cabindan political groups opposing the MPLA were thus viewed as an instrument that could be useful in a certain political context—compromising the independence of Angola—but they no longer serve any purpose to foreign interests. Politically, they have fallen into disgrace. Not even the most neocolonized African countries (with the exception of Gabon whose opposition to the MPLA is well known) paid any attention to the legal claims made by a Parisian lawyer on behalf of FLEC. This document asserted the right of Cabinda to independence and accused the Portuguese of deliberately offering Cabinda to the MPLA in violation of the Simulambuco Treaty of 1885 (Anonymous, 1977). Economically, a FLEC administration of Cabinda does not offer any serious guarantee to the people of Cabinda, and as long as foreign capital can negotiate with the MPLA, multinationals have little further interest in the future of Cabindan people.

THE ECONOMIC QUESTION

Oil is the main resource of Cabinda. In 1973, 89.7 percent of the total production of oil in Angola came from the enclave (Dilolwa, 1978: 265). Cabinda also represents the most important wood production region of Angola, as the forest of Mayombe covers two-thirds of its territory. Other products of less importance are coffee, cocoa, manganese, and potassium. Most of its 100,000 inhabitants are in primary sector activities, mainly agriculture. The soil is fertile, and production can be self-sufficient. About 25,000 residents live in the province's capital, Cabinda.

The search for oil in Angola and Cabinda started as early as the beginning of this century (Da Costa, 1908), but it was only in 1957 that the Cabinda Gulf Oil Company was founded, after a concession was obtained by a subsidiary of the American Gulf Oil Corporation. The agreement with the Portuguese government gave the right to the company to prospect and exploit onshore and offshore Cabinda oil for fifty years, renewable for another twenty years after negotiations. Cabinda Gulf did not have to comply with certain requirements usually asked by the Portuguese authorities, such as having the main business office in Portuguese territory, having a majority of Portuguese nationals on the board of directors, or transferring 20 percent of the capital stock to the colony of Angola. The company was free to decide the level of production as well as the storage and sale of whatever it found in its concession zone. However, the company did not have the right to build a refinery. In 1970, the colonial government of Angola owned 12,000 shares of the company's stock at U.S. $25 each, received royalties of 12.5 percent on the total value of the company sales, and had a prior right to purchase a maximum of 37.5 percent of the annual production of crude oil. As a guarantee, Cabinda Gulf had to deposit 25 million escudos with the Bank of Portugal.[1] Regarding taxes, the company had to pay up to 50 percent of the profits of the oil sales, but at the same time it was free from liability for custom duties or taxes on capital, titles, and shares, so long as they remained the property of Gulf Oil Corporation or of one of its subsidiaries (Eurafrica, 1975: 53-61).

One of the big "seven sisters," Gulf Oil Corporation, is controlled by the Mellon Group (of the United States) through a package of controlling shares and the financial concentration of the enterprises it controls: Aluminum Company of America (ALCOA) is the first aluminum trust in the world; Koppers Company is the main industrial gas producer in the United States. Through Westinghouse Electric, it controls three steel trusts in Pittsburgh. With Gulf & Western, it controls an important share of the world film market. As a multinational, Gulf has its own financial institutions that allow it both to gain ready access to financing and to help the circulation of capital to conduct international and domestic operations. The Mellon National Bank & Trust of Pittsburgh, F. Mellon & Sons, Milban Corporation, the National Union Fire Insurance Company, the General Reinsurance Corporation, and the North Star Reinsurance Company are all company offshoots.

It is not my purpose to describe Gulf's economic empire. By mentioning some of the elements of its network, I wanted rather to illustrate the importance of this corporation. One should notice that oil is not all Gulf is interested in. However, either by direct control, as in the case of Cabinda Gulf Oil Company, or in association with other corporations or state capital, the presence of Gulf Oil is spread all over the world, both in the Third World and in industrial countries. In addition, Gulf was the only multinational company operating in Cabinda. But Petrofina (Belgium), C.F.P. (France), Total (France), Texaco (USA), Sacor (Portugal), Mobil

Oil (USA), and Shell (Great Britain and Holland) had concessions and were operating in Angola.

Since 1968, the traditional image of Cabinda has completely changed. The wood houses have been replaced by concrete buildings; hotels and supermarkets have appeared like mushrooms. Artisan workshops have been able to compete with the new industries, and Cabinda has become no longer a small town, but a new urban center in Angola. Cabinda Gulf Oil Company was a sure source of revenue not only for the fascist regime in Portugal, but also for the colonial government in Angola. New roads were built and repaired; new schools and health centers were used as propaganda material against the actions of the MPLA in Cabinda. Investments were made to implement coffee and cocoa production and support the growth of the wood production industry. A migratory wave of Angolans seeking to work in Cabinda took place.

In 1974, with seven platforms working off shore, the Cabinda Gulf produced 8 million tons and paid U.S. $550 million in royalties, representing 70 percent of Angola's foreign trade income. Angola was to become the fourth African producer of oil, after Nigeria, Libya, and Algeria (Brieux, 1980: 78-79).[2]

ECONOMY, WAR, AND STRATEGIC CONSIDERATIONS

The military coup in Portugal sounded like the bell calling the fighters to the battle ring. Competition among multinationals to enter Angola or to establish a position, the ideological contradictions among the Angolan political movements, and the intervention first of Zambia, Zaïre, and Africa and then of Cuba served to internationalize the Angolan question, with the United States and Soviet Union supporting actions of their allies. The question behind this struggle for power was not purely ideological but rather economic. Transitional government was inoperative; relations between the three liberation movements were so hostile that they often finished in bloody quarrels if not cold assassinations. Without popular support in the capital, FNLA and UNITA troops were easily driven from there. FNLA went up north and UNITA down south, until South Africa decided to invade Angola from the south, and Zaïre through the north. UNITA troops joined those from South Africa, whereas the FNLA linked up with the Zaïrian army, which was supported by CIA's mercenaries.

One strategic point, which most observers seemed to ignore at the time remains crucial. Economically, the South African invasion concerned the Cunene River Dam, the importance of which was similar to that of the Cabora Bassa Dam in Mozambique. Second, UNITA and South African troops occupied one of the most important agricultural regions of the country, damaging the food distribution network and thus putting the MPLA in a difficult position. Third, the fighting in the south also stopped the most important railroad in Angola, linking the port of Lobito to Zaïre and Zambia, in this way cutting one of the main sources of revenue for Angola. Finally, the conflict also spread to the iron strip zone and the port used for its export. Nevertheless, the MPLA managed to resist the occupation of Lobito, a key strategic area.

With respect to the combined invasion of Zaïrean troops and mercenaries joined by FNLA, the purpose was identical. The northeastern region of Angola contains the most important zone of diamond extraction, where DIAMANG—an international consortium controlled by De Beers, a South African subsidiary of Anglo-American Co.—was operating. Here, the MPLA also successfully resisted the incursion. The same forces were joined by FLEC and tried to invade Cabinda but were driven back by MPLA troops after several weeks of hard fighting.

The final strategic point was the control of the capital Luanda, mainly because it was the political center of the country, but also because it represented half the urban population and contained 50 percent of all of Angola's industries. In addition, Luanda was the main entry by sea and by air to Angola. As independence day approached, Luanda represented more and more the center of legitimate political power. This was quite well understood by the invasion forces who tried to reach the capital. The South African army and UNITA troops were stopped at the central region, while FNLA and Zaïrean troops reached as close as fifty kilometers to the capital. On November 11, 1975, MPLA declared the independence of Angola to the sounds of FNLA guns.

During this period, contradictions between U.S. government policy toward the MPLA[3] and American big business corporations operating and trading with Angola appeared. Gulf had to pay U.S. $500 million in royalties to the transitional government of Angola, which no longer existed, as only the MPLA and Portuguese ministers remained in Luanda. Two months before independence, Gulf Oil paid the third installment of $100 million to the Bank of Angola in the name of the colony's government. The other installments were due to be deposited in December 1975 and January 1976. Kissinger and the CIA working group on Angola pressured Gulf to stop operations in Angola, as they did not want the MPLA to take possession of that amount of of money. For its part, the CIA was acting against the MPLA with a budget of 31.7 million.

But by defeating the Cabinda invasion, the MPLA had real and effective control of the oilfields. At the moment of independence, Neto's movement took over control of the Bank of Angola and possessed the contracts file concerning Gulf Oil. At this point, the MPLA urged Gulf Oil to resume operations and declared that it would guarantee the safety of the company's staff and protect the company installations and equipment. Put under pressure by its own government, which tried to block the payments due to Angola, Gulf Oil accepted a final compromise with the U.S. State Department and deposited the fourth installment in an escrow bank account.

Angola had bought two 737 Boeing jets before independence. Even though the planes were already paid for, Kissinger revoked Boeing's export licenses. Angolan pilots were already being trained at Seattle. It was only in March 1976, when the American administration and CIA admitted the failure of their policy toward Angola and the MPLA threatened to negotiate new contracts with other rival multinationals in Europe, who were eager to come to Angola, that Boeing got permission to deliver the planes and install radar systems in the Angolan airports. It was also at that time that Gulf Oil paid the royalties to MPLA's government and started its operations again. All this happened without some "rocambolesque" episodes, as the one at Rome's Fiumicino airport, when a senior officer of E.N.I., the Italian state-owned oil company, was detained by CIA agents at the moment he was leaving for Angola to negotiate possible agreements.

So the MPLA's strategy of controlling such zones as Luanda (the capital), Cabinda (oil fields), and Luanda (diamonds) was quite decisive. For American companies, and in particular Gulf Oil, the question was to remain in Angola as long as it could be profitable for them, in spite of the political regime. But for some other companies, mostly European, the problem was how to get into Cabinda or Angola, at the very moment Gulf was having trouble and the MPLA, on the eve of independence, seemed to be losing its commanding military position.

As the outcome of the Angolan conflict was uncertain, the internationalization of the problem, under the cover of ideology (U.S./Soviet) was the result of specific economic and political interests of financial capital in Europe and in the United States. However, this was not the only reason. U.S. and European capitalist states did not have a true Angolan policy. Their view was quite simple: Regarding the economic exploitation of Angolan raw materials, they relied on Portuguese fascism and colonialism in exchange of some political support in the international arena. For "safety reasons" and ideological ones, they supported the most conservative and corrupt of the nationalist movements in Angola. They had always thought that they would best preserve their interests in so doing. This is the reason why they were so confused and surprised at the exercise of force by the MPLA and at the popular support given to this organization.

Again, they intensified their support to FNLA, UNITA, and FLEC, partly because they wanted to wipe out the MPLA, whom they considered too socialist. For their part, people like Kissinger were saying (Africa Report, 1976: 13-15) that the question had nothing to do with American or European economic interests in Angola or even with the ideology of Angolan political organizations. The problem was the Soviet Union and its expansion. So as Cuba and Soviet Union supported the MPLA, the United States should automatically back the FNLA and UNITA and all anti-communist organizations or movements opposed to the MPLA. In this way, they thought, the Soviet Union would be contained.

At the same time, competition among multinationals became fierce, and contradictions amidst the financial bourgeoisies of industrial countries emerged, as the attempt to Balkanize the country showed. In the meantime, American multinationals were preoccupied with the State Department, as they were afraid it would damage their relations with Angola, and especially with the possibility of favorable negotiations with the MPLA government after independence. Besides, the Europeans distanced themselves from American policy toward Angola, as *Time* (1976: 24) noted:

> French, British and West German experts generally agree, however, that Angola lies outside the realm of vital western interests, and they questioned whether Luanda Marxist President Agostinho Neto will be a subservient Russian client. By and large, the Western Europeans criticize Washington for clumsily backing a sure loser—the corrupt, inept and unpopular FNLA leader Holden Roberto—and alienating moderate Africans by not protesting South Africa's intervention in the war.

In Cabinda, both the MPLA government and Gulf expressed satisfaction when the company began operating there again. For the latter, Cabinda represented important oil reserves. For MPLA and Angola, it is the main source of revenue and foreign currency. However, Cabinda was, and still is, quite vulnerable to outside forces, as Zaïre still covets Cabinda and helps FLEC and the FNLA, though in a more discreet way. Even if this is not a real threat to Angola's central government control of the enclave, it forces Luanda to spend an important part of its state budget on military and defense tasks, as South Africa and UNITA attacks on southern and eastern Angola continue. This continuing pressure on Angola represents a heavy burden and the main obstacle to the implementation of Angolan economic and social development programs. A large amount of the financial, technical, and human resources of Angolan society are permanently mobilized for defense purposes.

SOCIALISM AND OIL

The Angolan economy is vulnerable, as it still bears the marks of five centuries of the colonial presence that shaped and defined the characters of a peripheral capitalist area, first as a supplier of cheap labor (slavery and forced labor), and then of raw materials (agriculture and mining), for the industrialization of Europe. In 1975, one could have said that it was an underdeveloped economy, characterized by "distortion" as it was integrated to the world capitalist system. By distortion I mean a disarticulated economy in which the different sectors have no solid and no complementary link between them, in contrast to an industrialized economy, normally articulated and self-centered. I also mean that each sector or branch of the Angolan economy was producing for export and not for internal consumption. The notion of a national market is thus of limited significance.

The growth of the Angolan economy was conditioned by that of the industrialized countries, as they in turn dominated Portugal's economy. Even if Angola, as a colony, financed the development of the bourgeoisie in Portugal, and particularly the financial capital represented by fourteen families (Mello, Espirito Santo, Cupertino de Miranda, Champalimaud, Quina, and others), Portugal was one among other markets for Angolan raw materials. With regard to capital investment, countries like Great Britain, Belgium, the United States, Germany, and France played major roles, in particular after 1960. Quite often, the Portuguese bourgeoisie searched for foreign partners to invest in Angola. Though there was growing investment in the tertiary sector in the 1970s, Angola remained an agricultural producer and mineral-exporting country. By producing export-oriented goods, Angola tranferred the surplus value expropriated from the workers—either by the forced labor system (*contratados*) or by miserable wages fixed by the colonial government (Dos Santos, 1979: 34-42)—to Portugal and other European countries and the United States. The level of capital accumulation in Angola was low, as most of it found its way into European and American pockets. The other weakness of the Angolan economy was the absence of a national bourgeoisie. For obvious reasons, the Portuguese bourgeoisie could not allow the development of such social class in Angola, as it already had to compete with the wealthier European and American bourgeoisie. The colonial bourgeoisie would invest only a part of their profits in Angola; the rest was normally invested in Portugal.

Turning to the primary sector, and particularly to agriculture, which employed 77 percent of the active population (1970) and represented only 26 percent of the GNP value, most of its products were for export, as they were financed by foreign and direct investments. In other words, Angola's rural economy operated from the foreign demand point of view, as it was created by foreign capital.[4]

Angolan mineral wealth is considerable. But before 1975, it was completely in the hands of Portuguese and international capital. German Krupp invested in iron mines; South African De Beers, together with Société Générale de Belgique (Belgium), Morgan Trust Bank (USA), Banque de l'Union Parisienne (France), and others formed a diamond consortium in Angola, at the turn of the century. Gulf Oil from the United States had a heavy presence in Angola, together with Petrofina (Belgium), Texaco (USA), Mobil Oil (USA), and Shell (Great Britain and Holland). But here, too, most products of the extractive industry were exported: diamond production was totally exported, 80 percent of the oil went abroad, and more than 60 percent of the iron produced in Angola was also exported (Dos Santos, 1979: 34-42).

Manufactures and tertiary activities started to develop mainly in the 1960s, when the colonial bourgeoisie contested the Colonial Pact rules that protected Portugal's production and forced Angola to import cloth, shoes, wine, light equipment, and other similar products. So as an underdeveloped economy (Amin, 1971: 9-47), Angola before independence was characterized by an unequal sectoral distribution of productivity, meaning that investments were more important in the extractive industry, where the profits were higher. In an autonomous, self-centered economy, the benefits of economic growth are diffused by the adjustment of prices, wages, and profits, so that the distances separating the sectors may be reduced.

However, most of the exchanges were done with the outside world. There were almost no exchanges between sectors or between regions. As a result, Angola was dependent on relations with Portugal and a few other countries, and foreign trade income was based mainly on four products (oil, coffee, diamonds, and iron). Angola's customers and suppliers were a restricted number of industrialized countries: Portugal, the United States, Germany, France, Great Britain, and South Africa were the most important.[5] When the MPLA declared independence, the economic situation was compounded by Portuguese settlers who destroyed everything they could when they left the country; technicians ran away, leaving the economy completely paralyzed.

The construction of a socialist society from a peripheral capitalist economy meant for postindependence Angola the possibility of creating a situation, step by step, in which it could separate from the world capitalist system and build a national economy (that is to say, stop the transfer of surplus value or at least reduce it to such proportions that Angola could start a self-centered process of capital accumulation). From this point of view, the question of national revenue is quite important (how it is realized and how it is distributed).

In the 1977 Congress (Jornal de Angola, 1977: 5), it was decided that national revenue would be used for two purposes: to create an accumulation and a consumption fund, the latter divided into private and social consumption. The priority was put on the accumulation fund as the way to build an independent and national economy. This meant that production was geared to avoiding the dependence on foreign capital for purchasing equipment, goods, and technology abroad. Without an increase in production, private consumption will grow at the expense of capital accumulation, forcing the country to become more and more dependent as it increases its financial debt to international capital. This would create a vicious circle, as, in order to service the debts, it will have to produce more and more, not for internal consumption, but for export. But private consumption also has implications for social consumption, defined as the services created and distributed by the state to its citizens (education, health care, social services, public transport, and so forth).

Agriculture became the top priority of the development plan, while industry is the basis. The government aimed to restore production to the 1973 level by 1980. A law was passed on discipline at work, to force workers to produce. Some privileges were banned and some class barriers reduced. But by the target year no branch or sector had reached the 1973 level, except for oil (Gulf) and more recently tobacco. Coffee production went down dramatically, as did diamond extraction.

Meanwhile, the government nationalized a number of sectors: 61 percent of diamonds, 100 percent of textiles, 100 percent of sugar, 100 percent of wood, 80 percent of boat construction, 100 percent of electricity, 100 percent of banking. Commercial distribution was placed under state control. However, the black market flourished with the scarcity of goods, and is mainly controlled by civil servants. Production levels are still low. Oil becomes more and more the primary good. In 1977, a quarter of the state budget was being spent on importing food stuffs in which the country was self-sufficient in 1973 (Africa, 1977: 66-67).

In May 1976, a top-ranking team from Sonatrach, the Algerian state-owned company, visited Angola to talk with Angolan authorities. They agreed to put their expertise and advice at the disposal of Angola, and arranged to train Angolan technicians in Algeria. At the same time, Angola created Sonangol, as a state company, and the Oil National Institute to train technicians and workers. The state company is responsible for all activities concerning oil (research, production, transport, refinery, storage, and distribution). It has the right to create new companies, owning them completely or in association with private interests. In this way, Sonangol is associated with Gulf (51 percent), with Petrangol-Petrofina (30 percent), with Texaco (60 percent). New contracts have been concluded, in particular with ENI (Italy) and CFP and Total (France).

The new investment code, imposes 51 percent Angolan participation in any foreign investment. In certain cases, this participation is reduced, depending on the importance the Angola government gives to the sector or branch concerned. The transfer of profits abroad is allowed, but such transfers need ministerial permission, which is given after the taxes and royalties or other kind of revenue due to the state of Angola have been paid.

Oil has become Angola's oxygen. This creates a dangerous situation, because contrary to what has been planned and put forward by Angola's government, oil means dependence, especially because Angola gets its main source of revenue from one product while it is not able to increase production in other sectors.

I have argued that continuing pressure from South Africa and UNITA and from FNLA and FLEC forces the MPLA to concentrate on military and defense activities, wasting the very few resources left to put forward the economic and social program as defined by the two last congresses. This means that Kissinger's objectives, which were initially frustrated, may become a threat through the indirect political and social erosion caused by external pressures. The Angolan independence struggle was a difficult one, but as Lucio Lara put it recently, "The third liberation struggle is about to begin."

NOTES

1. In 1966, that meant less than U.S. $1 million.

2. On the eve of independence, Cabinda Gulf Oil Company employed 420 technicians of whom 17 were Americans; 10 percent of Gulf Oil Corporation's foreign crude supply was provided by its oilfields in Angola.

3. I refer here to Kissinger's position and CIA actions against the MPLA, in support of FNLA, UNITA, FLEC, and Zaïre.

4. I do not include here the food production of peasants for self-consumption as it is realized outside the sphere of circulation of the capitalist mode of production.

5. They represented in 1974 about 67 percent of Angolan imports and 70 percent of exports.

REFERENCES

Africa (1977) "Angola since the Nitista 'Putsch.' " Vol. 76 (December): 66-67.

Africa Report (1976) "Special Angola." Vol. 2 (January-February): 2-17.

Afrique Asie (1978) "Special Angola." 164 (July 9): 1-54.

AMIN, S. (1971) L'accumulation à l'échelle mondiale. Paris: Anthropos.

Angolan Constitutional Law (1975) Luanda: Ministry of Information.

Anonymous (1977) A Independencia de Cabinda. Queluz (Portugal): Ediçao Literal.

Brieux (1980) Angola An III. Paris. Editions Rupture.

DA COSTA, J. C. (1908) A riqueza petrolifera d'Angola. Lisboa: Sociedade de Geografia de Lisboa.

DILOLWA, C. R. (1978) Contribuicao à História Ecónomica de Angola. Luanda: Imprensa Nacional Angolana.

DOS SANTOS, D. (1979) "Angola, colonialisme et dévelóppement." M.Sc. thesis, Université de Montréal.

Eurafrica (1975) "Les sociétés multinationales en Angola." February: 53-61.

GJERSTAD, O. (1977) The People in Power. Oakland, CA: L.S.M. Information Center.

Guardian (1981) "Angola. a special report." March 2: 11-18.

HEIMER, F. W. (1979) The Decolonization Conflict in Angola 1974-76. Genève: Institut Universitaire des Hautes Etudes Internationales.

Jornal (1982) "Caderno Especial/Angola." 372 (April 22: 1-44.

Jornal de Angola (1977) "Linhas Mestras do desenvolvimento económico e social até 1980." November 23: 5.

LEITAO, C. (1929) A Questao da Cabinda. Lisboa: Author's Edition.

Manifesto (1974) Apelo a todos os militantes e quadros do MPLA. Revolta Activa (Angola).

MEDVIN, N. (1974) The Energy Cartel. New York: Vintage.

MURRAY, R. (1979) "Angola: nationalization and the role of foreign capital." African Business (September): 27-28.

Novembro (1980) "Transformar o petróleo no paô de todos os dias." 4 (October): 38-39.

STOCKWELL, J. (1978) In Search of Enemies. A CIA Story. New York: W. W. Norton.

Time (1976) "Angola: an easy rout – and an olive branch." (February 23): 22-25.

5

ST. HELENA:
WELFARE COLONIALISM
IN PRACTICE

ROBIN COHEN
University of Warwick

The small island of St. Helena is located in the South Atlantic Ocean at latitude 16°S and longitude 5°45′W. It is somewhat over 1600 km west of its nearest mainland, Angola, but this is of little significance as no regular lines of communication or travel exist between Angola and the island. As St. Helena has no airport, the only regular means of reaching the island is to undertake the two-week journey from Britain (7240 km.), which normally calls at Ascension St. Helena's "dependency" (1131 km NW of the island), or to travel by sea from Cape Town (2726 km.). The geographical isolation of the island and the difficulties of traveling there signify its collapse into obscurity.

This was not always the case. During the sixteenth and seventeenth century, the Portuguese, Dutch, and British occupied the island, the Dutch abandoning their claims when they settled the Cape of Good Hope. With the exception of Ireland, St. Helena is Britain's oldest colony and looks very likely as if it will be its last. The English East India Company effectively administered the island for 182 years after the granting of a charter to the company in 1659. St. Helena was used to repair and provision the many ships that called on the way to and from the East. The large garrison stationed on the island during the period of Napoleon's captivity (1815-1821) also produced great prosperity for the island. So vital was the island to the sea routes that until 1869, when the Suez Canal was opened, the island was often considered probably the most important of all the colonies (Hughes, 1958: 3).

Though the depredations of goats introduced by the settlers and the casual treatment of the land by colonists soon took their toll, when the island was discovered in 1502, Mellis claims that "rich vegetation clothed its surface, the interior being described as an entire forest, with Gumwood and other indigenous trees overhanging some of the sea precipices" (Mellis, 1875: 1). The contrast with St. Helena in the mid-1970s, when this author undertook fieldwork on the island, could not be more stark. The island survives virtually entirely on budgetary support and development aid provided by the British government. Since the collapse of their flax industry in the mid-1960s, due to competition from artificial fibers, the islanders have been unable to develop any form of export. Large areas of the arable land (only about one-third of the total surface area of forty-seven square miles) are still covered with the carefully planted, but now useless, crop. A promising attempt to use the green bark of flax for cattle fodder has been abandoned, while clearing the flax for pasturage or cultivation has only been undertaken fitfully. What land remains, comprises, for the most part, precipitous slopes and thinly covered pastures incapable of supporting sufficient stock to meet the local demand for animal protein. Frozen meat and even poultry are imported in large quantities. Fresh vegetables and fruit are grown on a private basis on small acreages or in backyard plots, but of the score or so full-time farmers, only a handful operate at a profit and without a supplement from a wage income. The difficulties in sustaining independent primary production are threefold: the rainfall has been unreliable, particularly in recent years; the use of irrigation has been minimal; and finally, farmers have to compete with the heavily subsidized Agricultural and Forestry (A&F) department. In April 1975 a new Agricultural Development Authority (ADA) was created, replacing the A & F's combined functions of research and the production of at least some vegetables and meat for the local market. As many islanders comment, it is remarkable that an island that once produced enough to provision 800 sailing ships calling annually in the eighteenth century can now produce only a small fraction of the food consumed by the 5000 members of the local population.

Other than agriculture, the major natural resource is fishing. Here too the picture is dismal. Only nine boats go out regularly and these are small rowing boats usually fitted with low-powered and (as this author found to his cost one day) unreliable outboard motors. Fishermen cannot fish the untried deeper grounds and have to huddle in the leeward side of the island. Despite the vagaries of this precarious form of fishing, substantial catches of tunny and edible small fish are brought in, if on a rather sporadic basis. The major problem in using fish as part of the regular protein diet of the islanders lies in questions of storage and distribution.

The economy of the island can be simply summarized. No exports, minimal production for local needs, a low level of savings, and an overwhelming dependence on imports for consumption—the level of which is determined by the quantity of British aid. The roots of this appalling economic record lie deep in St. Helena's history. The opening of the Suez Canal, the invention of the steamship, which allowed ships to bypass the island, and the recall of the garrison for Napoleon all knocked the props from under the island's economy. But this common interpretation of the island's history—as a series of unfortunate accidents of fate—is analytically superficial. The island's decline was conditioned by the dominant form of capital found there, namely merchant capital. In Kay's (1975: 103) words, "The conditions which merchant capital had created throughout the underdeveloped world by the middle of the 19th century, were absolutely unconducive to the full development of capitalism." In the case of St. Helena, the land was stripped bare and the major mercantile firm, Solomons & Company, left almost no basis for local capital accumulation and investment. Instead, the profits of trade were invested in gold and diamond mines in South Africa where the Solomons's family became prominent magnates, politicians, and judges. The English East India Company also abanoned its no longer useful colony, dumping it back into the hands of Whitehall and a local colonial administration, who, since the mid-nineteenth century, have administered it with a patient, but far from munificent spirit.

The timing of the author's research on the island happened to coincide with two major attempts to revitalize the island's development. The first was an attempt—which ultimately was to be officially stopped—led by an outside entrepreneur who saw the development of the island in terms of the classical prescriptions of stimulating local initiative through the injection of capital and the development of the productive forces. The second was the introduction of St. Helena's first integrated development plan by the colonial government, which is characterized here as a new phase of "welfare colonialism." But before examining these two alternative strategies it is necessary to describe in greater detail the social and political conditions presently existing on the island.

SOCIAL CONDITIONS ON ST. HELENA

The island has made only limited progress in terms of constitutional development. The governor, together with the executive council (key appointed officials plus some representatives from the legislative council [Legco]), effectively takes local decisions within the framework of policy and aid established by the Foreign & Commonwealth Office. Direct representation is limited to a 12-member legislative council, established in 1968. The exercising of a democratic voice is thus a recent phenomenon, but participation in elections has been sufficiently high to belie the views of those who have berated the St. Helenians for their passivity.

This assumed passivity has often been generalized and commented on by outside observers. Cledwyn Hughes, a British parliamentarian who visited the island in 1958 commented that "several factors have combined to produce a subservience and shyness in their nature and tardiness to complain or appeal for help. The great majority suffer distress in silence and really outspoken St. Helenians can be numbered on the fingers of one hand." Hughes goes on to speculate that memories of slavery, fear of victimization at work, the monopoly of business by one company, and "the aloof and often unimaginative rule of the Colonial Administration over the years" have combined to produce the attitudes he claimed to observe (Hughes, 1958: 2).

My own findings based on a period of residence and a sample survey conducted in 1975 (N = 110, see below) suggest a more complex reading of the island "character," attitudes being conditioned by a compound of affection and loyalty for Britain (many islanders are partly descended from British stock, nearly all expressed sentiments of patriotism and identification), cynicism and hostility directed to colonial officials, acute suspicion of certain visitors and "experts," and a sense of resentment and helplessness in the face of the adverse circumstances that confront them.

What then are these circumstances? It is difficult to obtain an accurate gauge of living standards, or one that would provide a meaningful point of comparison with the standards of, say, a Western industrial society. Private housing is modest, though far from squalid. Public housing in Jamestown, the capital, is functional, but badly sited and aesthetically uninviting. Tenants complained of noise, lack of space, and expensive fuel costs. Many homes on the island are fitted with "chip" boilers burning virtually free wood or shavings, but, as for some reason this was not considered appropriate for new public housing, the tenants have to burn expensively generated electricity or (imported) bottled gas. Outside Jamestown, whose

Main Street boasts Georgian frontages, but rather less prepossessing interiors, houses comprise simple breeze block rectangular constructions, with asbestos or tin roofing. A few more affluent country properties occupied by settlers or well-established families hark back to the days of the East India Company.

Other indices of living standards, like family income, must also be treated with care. At the time of the survey, wages were low (£10 a week was the common remuneration for unskilled government employees) especially in relation to the cost of imported foodstuffs: at a rough estimation 8 to 12 percent above 1975 British prices. On the other hand, rents on government-owned properties are minimal, electricity is subsidized, and education and medical care are provided by the state at a nominal cost. Welfare payments included such items as food vouchers to the needy and outdoor relief work. Since September 1973, supplementary benefits, at the rate of £3.50 per couple per week plus 50p for each additional dependent, generally replaced these forms of welfare. Some private charitable work is also undertaken, particularly by the Salvation Army, which provides meals-on-wheels to 400 islanders. Remittances from relatives abroad, however, constitute the most important supplement to the income of families remaining on St. Helena. Such income is not revealed to the authorities (it may jeopardize welfare entitlements), but interview data suggests that it sometimes constitutes from 30 to 50 percent of a household's total income. The social welfare and health departments are also responsible for the running of an old people's home, a children's home, and a Dickensian mental hostel, which was undergoing some physical improvements to its blackened and fly-blown kitchen. The education system comprises eight primary, three secondary and one senior selective school, and though the buildings are generally adequate, the system has failed to achieve even a modest success in examinations and has failed too to live up to the department's own stated goals of ensuring that children are "less-dependent minded" and more adequately prepared for life on the island and abroad. Instead, in a separate study carried out by the present author, the educational system has been described as "education for dependence" (Cohen, forthcoming). The general impression is one of a down-at-heel welfare state.

The traditional solution by the islanders to their lack of economic opportunity has been emigration, overwhelmingly to South Africa and to the United Kingdom. The rate of emigration has slowed considerably with the passing of discriminatory legislation in those two countries. In the case of South Africa, most St. Helenians are classified as "Coloured" since

1948 hardly the most comfortable of denotations. In the United Kingdom, the Commonwealth Immigrants Act was enforced, probably in violation of an ancient Royal Charter that promised St. Helenians full rights of citizenship "as if they had been abiding and borne within this our realme of England" (Jackson, 1903: 22). After 1981, with the passing of the Nationality Act, St. Helenians were classified as citizens of the "dependent territories" and their historic rights to full British citizenship will again have been ignored. The application of immigration controls has adversely affected a common form of mobility, particularly among girls—domestic service for a couple of years, followed by permanent settlement in the United Kingdom. In addition to such restrictions on mobility, passages are expensive and scarce—until 1978 the only regular means of communication were two cargo ships, spaced three to four weeks apart, running between the South African ports and Southampton. The ships carried only twelve cabin passengers, and many of the passages were taken up by government officials. Since 1978, a 78-passenger ship, the RMS *St. Helena* has been purchased, partly by the St. Helena Government. Though the ship only makes the journey from Avonmouth (Bristol) to Cape Town once every two months, this service has undoubtedly been a boon to the island. The continuing immigration restrictions mean that employment opportunities abroad are very limited, however.

Considerable numbers of young men do, nonetheless, travel to the island of Ascension to work as contract labourers for Pan Am, Cable & Wireless, the BBC, and a few smaller concerns, which have bases on the island. The comparatively high wages earned on Ascension are an attractive bait to the "Saints," as the islanders abroad are called, but employment in Ascension provides only a partial and diminishing solution to unemployment in St. Helena.

Short of discovering a new El Dorado on St. Helena, the possibilities for self-sustaining economic development appeared in the 1970s to be negligible. The island was too far off the beaten track to sustain a large tourist trade and technical difficulties, as well as the low volume of anticipated traffic, mitigated against the construction of an airfield. In the early 1970s, the prospects for a shift in the island's trajectory of development became possible with the injection of some external capital, while the colonial government, for its part, embarked on a five-year development plan. These two strategies, while not intrinsically incompatible, soon showed themselves to be pulling the island in divergent directions.

THE FAILURE OF CAPITALIST DEVELOPMENT

The injection of foreign capital into the island was first heralded in 1968 when a majority shareholding in the island's major private enterprise, the old mercantile company of Solomons & Company, was purchased by the South Atlantic Trading and Investment Company (SATIC), which was headed by a British-born, but South African-based, businessman, Tony Thornton. When news of this reached the island, fears of a South African government takeover, even the introduction of apartheid, were generated on the island. Such a scenario was inherently absurd. Even the most hardened member of South Africa's Race Classification Board would despair at trying to construct a racial typology of St. Helena's citizens. The islanders are blended together from people of European, Chinese, African and even Polynesian origins in what must be a rare example of racial tolerance (as one urbane islander remarked, "We are a selection of liquor-ice all sorts"). Moreover, the South African government could hardly have found a more inappropriate Trojan Horse. Thornton has liberal political views; his wife was banned in South Africa for her anti-apartheid activities.

In an island where no independent news medium exists, rumour is the only effective means of communication, and the colonial government was sufficiently alarmed to intervene. It bought 32 percent of the shares, leaving SATIC with 30 percent and the rest divided among small shareholders. An agreement signed in London in 1968 also allowed the government to purchase, in the national interest, SATIC's share—anytime it chose to do so. In April 1974, this is what it did.

By this time other issues obtruded. Thornton proved to be an energetic director. He revitalized Solomons's multifarious activities—the company is the major importer and owns stores, pubs, a hotel, and the biggest slice of nongovernment farming land. His dynamism attracted a fierce loyalty from his own staff and many islanders who saw in him the epitome of innovativeness and resolution that, so they suggested, was sadly lacking in the government's own conduct of its affairs. One typical response to a questionnaire (see later) on the development plan included the comment, "This island is far behind the times. We did had a good start, by Mr. Thornton; it would have developed the island and [given] a good improvement to many. Maybe you don't know, but the little that is done is built on Mr. Thornton foundation, but it won't carry on . . . because all the development money [will] be down the drain." Another islander pointed out that while there was little accountability in government-supported schemes, private investors at least had their own money to lose. In a clear reference to the Thornton affair, this respondent commented:

> A private Company was taken over by the Government against the wishes of the people. If the man come to the island with a grant-in-aid if he don't produce any food no-one say anything about it, but if that same chap had his own money, he would make a better show because it would be his money he would be wasting. . . . If any one who comes to the island makes an improvement he is soon sent off.

Such pro-Thornton responses were found among a number of islanders in government or Solomons's employ, young and old, in Jamestown, other settlements, or the country. There was a slight tendency for pro-Thornton supporters to be younger and better educated and with working experience overseas.

On the other hand, the strength of the opposition to Mr. Thornton was considerable. The opposition stemmed from three quarters. The government itself, the legislative council (in the critical debate eleven out of twelve opposed Thornton), and some island opinion—organized essentially around the St. Helena General Workers' Union (GWU). The GWU attitude is perhaps most difficult to understand as Thornton initially paid better wages than the government did. As in much else on the island, the answer lay in the particularities of island politics. The previous GWU secretary was an adherent, indeed one of the inspirations, of the Thorntons-as-South African-neo-Imperialist-agents theory. His successor, also incidentally a Legco member, was one of a group that saw a danger to the island in Thornton's manner of financing company expansion—running one company—Solomons—into debt to SATIC. The legislative council's attitude also partly reflected the fear that the arrival of the new management of Solomons would disrupt the traditionally stable relations between the islanders and the two dozen white settlers, who held five of the twelve seats in the Legislative Council. Mr. and Mrs. Thornton were themselves convinced that this was at the root of the moves against them. In an interview with a British newspaper Mrs. Thornton maintained:

> The local establishment have been upset because my husband has promoted the islanders to positions of authority in the company and has doubled the wages of the workers. This cuts the settlers' standard of living. The settlers have come for a tax haven and the low cost of living. They are not a group of socialists who want to take

over a company on behalf of the people. These are a most reactionary people, some of whom have come to St. Helena from Zambia
and Rhodesia. They are Smith supporters [Guardian, April 15,
1974].

As to the government itself, there is little doubt that they resented
Thornton's steamrolling tactics and his practice of not sharing major
decisions with the government-appointed director on Solomons's board. In
their arguments advocating the purchase of SATIC's share, government
officials also pointed out that the company had not paid dividends since
Thornton's control and that its cash difficulties could only be resolved by
further indebtedness to SATIC.

Political and social life on the island became organized on factional
lines—pro- and anti-Thornton. Few on the island succeeded in maintaining
an indifferent or neutral stance. The battle was joined with petition and
counterpetition, public meetings, demonstrations, and court cases that
were ostensibly about something else. Among the British officials and
some of the small settler element, Mr. Thornton and his family were
subject to a degree of social ostracism that in a community of St. Helena's
size and isolation can only be described as ludicrous. The critical decision—
to buy out SATIC's remaining shares—went to the anti-Thornton group,
whose position was ultimately approved by Callaghan, then minister at the
Foreign Office. Despite the fact that Thornton was successfully able to
rally 1139 islanders who demanded a referendum on the issue (a number,
incidentally, well in excess of the 826 people who voted in the legislative
council elections), the Foreign & Commonwealth Office supported the
advice of the governor that the government should exercise its option to
buy out Thornton's share in Solomons. There is little doubt that the
ground for the politicians' acquiescence was well prepared by the prevailing views of the responsible civil servants in Britain. One official from the
West Indian & Atlantic Department of the Foreign & Commonwealth
Office, for example, made some highly damaging remarks about Thornton's alleged conduct in an internal memorandum:

> His most notorious trait is to regard local institutions—particularly
> the Legco—with contempt, and to look upon Government's proper
> insistence that he, as well as everybody else, should conform to local
> legislation, as parish-pump meddling. This is particularly noticeable
> in regard to planning permission and the ownership of property,
> where he appears to see normal legal and administrative require-
> ments as applicable only to lesser mortals. When he is reminded of

his obligations in this respect he is prone to regard this as unreason-
able interference by interfering busy-bodies.

Once his major commercial interest was subjected to compulsory purchase, Thornton left the island, but attempted to rally support for his
position by helping to found a new political party, the St. Helena Labour
Party. The manifesto of the party (St. Helena Labour Party, 1975) is a
sustained attack on the colonial government's neglect of the island and a
critique of the new development plan it proposed to implement. The next
election for the legislative council was not due until 1976, and the party
was ultimately to command little support at the polls. But by this time the
government had moved more decisively against Thornton. The launching
of the party in 1974 and a statement that Thornton intended to start an
independent newspaper appeared to be the events that triggered the
governor's decision to issue an exclusion order in September 1975 formally banishing Thornton from the island. Thornton's interests, other than
Solomons, included a fishing company, which now became inoperative. A
fifty-ton freezer plant, which would have helped in the important area of
fish storage, lay rusting in an open shed. The government now held in its
possession all the major assets on the island and, according to the Labour
Party manifesto, controlled 95 percent of the land and 95 percent of the
employment on the island (St. Helena Labour Party, 1975: 29). As there
were no other contenders in the field, development had perforce to rest
with the government's own efforts.

Depending on one's interpretation of the events described, the people
have been protected from a malign foreign enterprise, or outside capital
has been prevented from contributing to the development of the island.
Whatever the rights and wrongs, the already adverse commercial opportunities for external capital have been damaged by the Thornton case.
Potential foreign investors can hardly read the government's attitude
sympathetically, while the government, for its part, is afraid of "another
Thornton." That the government's attitude to foreign enterprise is less
than encouraging is argued forcibly by one islander who claimed:

The St. Helena Government must encourage private enterprise and
not drive it away from St. Helena such as they have been doing—in
the last year I've seen an Englishman come here and wanted to start
a poultry farm, another wanted to re-establish coffee, another a civil
engineer, was going to buy a private piece of land and employ some
islanders. All was turned away.

Although this author was not able to verify the cases of the civil engineer and proposed coffee grower, that these charges were not without foundation can be seen in the case of Robin Castells of Middlesex, who did indeed make a detailed proposal for a deep-litter poultry to make the island self-sufficient in table poultry and eggs (the island imported 5,937 chickens and 59,400 eggs annually). The proposal involved growing sorghum locally on 60 acres and Castells was prepared to invest £12,000 of his own money. Though the proposal to use so much scarce land would have been difficult to comply with, Castells complained bitterly that his proposal was not even given serious consideration. In a private letter to the government secretary, shown to the present author, Mr. Castells remonstrated: "I'm offering my own money and I can't even get on a boat.... You will no doubt need a few assistants in the archives as it seems to me that everything will end up there—perhaps before being read."

How then do we summarize the reasons for the failure of private entrepreneurship on the island? As has been argued, the structural constraints on the domestic productive forces were deeply embedded in the underdeveloping effects of mercantile capital. This left very little room for domestic savings. The savings/income ratio is extremely low, and there is little incentive for the islanders to accumulate wealth. Indeed in the absence of a banking system, the only institutional form of savings was in the Post Office which, in 1975, paid the paltry interest of 3 percent. So if private investment were to form a part of the island's economic development, it would have to come from outside. In this respect, the rejection of Thornton's initiatives and the coolness shown to other potential investors suggests that the government, despite some public protestations to the contrary, was extremely wary of permitting the importation of outside capital. Part of their caution is to be explained by the particular experience of dealing with one persistent and challenging entrepreneur, who had little inhibition in politicizing his case in London or on the island. But, as will be argued in greater detail later, part of the answer lay in the static nature of colonial government itself. The absence of any significant nationalist opinion, the fact that the islanders were faced with government monopoly of their employment prospects, and the tendency of the small but powerful settler community to social stasis all reinforced the caution exhibited by colonial officers on the ground. Their position was generally reinforced in the Foreign & Commonwealth Office in Whitehall, which was committed to the shedding of all remaining colonial responsibilities, which were generally seen as burdensome and irrelevant anachronisms. St. Helena was, however, a special case in that it was self-evidently unable to govern itself or maintain an even marginally viable economy, even by the minimal standards established, for example, for the micro states of the Caribbean. At least one senior official in the Overseas Development Ministry was prepared to contemplate mass emigration as a solution. Others in the Foreign and Commonwealth Office caught up in the new rhetoric of "development," alarmed by the turn of events in St. Helena, concerned at the fate of their colonial charges, or, less generally, apprehensive of international disappropriation (the UN decolonization committee maintains an interest in the island) decided to press for an integrated development plan for the island. It is to an analysis of this development plan that we turn next.

WELFARE COLONIALISM: THE DEVELOPMENT PLAN

The St. Helena Development Plan was based on a series of reports by visiting experts and advisers commissioned by the Foreign and Commonwealth Office and the Overseas Development Administration in 1973. The major report was divided into a General Survey (Part One) and a set of specialized reports on employment, agriculture, fisheries and the prospects for civil aviation (Part Two). It was presented to the governor in February 1974 and to the secretary of state for foreign and commonwealth affairs at the same time. The latter approved the recommendations in principle in June 1974. From the beginning, the plan was conceived as statement of principles and a set of policies to be directed from the top downward. This can be seen, for example, by the fact that the plan was presented to the legislative council only in July 1974, after the secretary of state had approved its recommendations. Even then, no debate was expected, the council having simply been asked to approve a notion that it "welcomes and supports the Development Plan for St. Helena and requests that an expression of its appreciation be conveyed to Her Majesty's Government." This motion was passed with desultory discussion. Though a public document, the plan itself was not published in Jamestown until eight months after its commencement. Only 100 copies were produced and no attempts were made at the time to ensure public discussion of the document. The major capital expenditure involved approximately £1.5 million over the plan period from 1974 to 1979. The distribution between sectors is listed in Table 5.1.

With the grant-in-aid added, the British taxpayer was committed to provide some £5.5 million to support the administration of the island over the plan period, making St. Helenians, at £220 per capita per year, one of

TABLE 5.1   Capital Expenditure, 1974-1979

	In Thousands of Pounds
Natural Resources	329
Economic Infrastructure	450
Social Services	243
Loan and Grants	100
Unidentified	358
Total	£1,480

SOURCE: St. Helena (1975, Part One: ii).

the largest beneficiaries per head of British aid. Of course, the distribution of this revenue is heavily skewed toward the costs of the administration itself, while the per capita measure gives a poor idea of the real incomes of the islanders themselves. Nonetheless, with such a relatively large per capita expenditure, it is instructive to examine what the guiding principles of the planners were. These are clearly enunciated in a number of key statements in Part One of the plan.

(1) There can be no alternative to grant-in-aid unless and until fresh industry is able to revive the economy. The aim must therefore be to direct capital expenditure towards those sectors which serve to reduce the island's present dependence on imports of even the most essential foodstuffs, and which will increase the island's attraction for outside investors.

(2) The main strategy for investment is therefore to develop those sectors of the economy which support the objective of greater self-reliance, as fast as possible, and to give lower priority to the development of sectors which do not meet this objective.

(3) The two extreme alternatives would be to decide the island would never regain a measure of importance, strategic or otherwise, and to initiate a policy of active depopulation, or else to accept that the island will ever remain a perpetual and ever more costly pensioner tied to the UK standard of living. Neither of these positions is likely to be acceptable to Britain or to the majority of St. Helenians. A compromise must be found whereby the islanders may be led out of the low productivity trap into which they have fallen and to provide the community with objectives for an exciting challenge and a sense of purpose. The basic strategy of development therefore must be to enable the islanders as far as possible to determine their welfare and their future by their own efforts [St. Helena, 1975, Part One: ii, 1, 2-3].

TABLE 5.2   Imports and Exports, 1971-1972

	(in pounds)
Exports	
Frozen fish (40 tons)	4,000
Hides and fleeces	400
Total	4,400
Imports	
Food, drink and tobacco	185,587
Raw materials and largely unmanufactured articles	8,743
Manufactured or mainly manufactured articles	209,594
Miscellaneous and unclassified	8
Total	403,832

SOURCE: U.K. Government (1973: 13, 14).

Let us examine these objectives in turn to see what likelihood the development plan has of shifting the pattern of St. Helena's dependence. With respect to the overwhelming dependence of the island on imports, the planners did indeed confront a formidable challenge. The pattern of exports and imports in the financial year before the plan was commissioned can be seen in Table 5.2.

The list of imports includes many goods for which, on the surface, islanders may reasonably be expected to produce local substitutes or at least reduce their needs for the imported items concerned. The same source shows that, these goods included, with their values indicated, Canned Meats (£13,758), Beer and Stout (£17,815), Confectionary (£8,607), Milk and Milk Powder (£11,129), Margarine (£4,658), Tobacco and Cigarettes (£11,164), Biscuits (£4,869), Lard (£4,796), Cheese (£3,872), Butter (£2,651), Spirits and Liqueurs (£1,043), Wines (£2,651), Soaps (£1,769), and Fruit and Vegetable Juices (£2,254). What evidence is there, then, that the planners were able to suggest areas where the island might develop a reduced dependence on such imports? At a total level, the achievement of greater self-reliance does not in fact appear to have guided the allocation of the projected expenditure. A stark illustration of this is provided not in the sectoral breakdowns, but in the estimates one can calculate for the ratio of revenue to aid (defined as all income coming from Whitehall). Here an already adverse ratio of 1:2.3 (1974-1975) was projected to *increase* to 1:1.9 in 1978-1979. Seen in purely economic terms, the notion of "development" acquired a rather curious meaning for what was acknowledged to be a planned form of increased dependency.

If we turn to the more specific area of food production, where the import bill amounted to £155,000 in 1971, the plan argued that many foodstuffs "could be substituted by island production" and acknowledged that the main problem in persuading islanders to engage in agriculture was that, since the 1960s, the government agricultural department had driven out independent production by "keeping down the cost of its products to below the cost of production" (St. Helena, 1975, Part One: 3). As the agricultural adviser himself noted: "There is little enthusiasm among the islanders for agriculture as an occupation. This no doubt arises from the fact that it has not been, and is still not, a very profitable occupation. None of the three large landowners claim to make a profit from their farming activities and indeed the government, which farms more than half the arable land on the island, shows a substantial loss on its production enterprises" (St. Helena, 1975, Part Two: 17). Yet despite this gloomy account of the government's own record in agricultural production, the takeover of Solomons & Company placed 90 percent of the pastures (as opposed to 80 percent previously) directly under government control. Moreover, the section of the development plan concerned with agriculture devoted much attention to organizational matters—in particular to the creation of the Agricultural Development Authority—yet had no satisfactory account of how, where, and by what amount agricultural, livestock, and dairy production was meant to change over the plan period. There was, in short, no reason to assume that the levels of agricultural production under state control were likely to increase at all. The one area where denationalization was suggested was in the "eventual" creation of "farming units which could be handed over to medium scale tenant farmers" (St. Helena, 1975, Part Two, 27). Yet despite the adviser's argument that these rented units should provide a comparable income potential to other occupations, the Labour Party's manifesto justly points out that the smallholders would, in essence be asked to pay off the ADA's development costs, pay a commercial rental to the authority, and then try to compete with ADA's production subsidy of £150,000 (St. Helena Labour Party, 1975: 16). That this skeptical view is not merely advanced for political ends can be seen in the response of one 31-year-old islander who had worked as a merchant seaman and was keen to start an agricultural enterprise on the island:

> The Development Plan states under ADA, farm units will be lease to the people. Do Government expect a man who gets a regular income to take over a farm unit where he has watch the same land been own by Government for years and they can not produce anything with

their tractor, and men and thousands of pounds—and the man in the street don't make enough to keep his family let alone save enough to gamble on taking over a farm unit.

The increasingly adverse ratio of aid to income, together with the doubtful benefits of agricultural reorganization, in short, suggest that the planners are unlikely to achieve their goal of reducing the level of imports. Nor does the government have any clear idea of which imports it wishes to identify as capable of being replaced or reduced by local production. As this author pointed out in a lengthy letter to the acting governor in March 1975, the plan in fact encouraged the consumption of imported goods and built in no effective protection or positive policy to stimulate local production:

> Initially one can see this on a trivial level. Canned fruit is a preferred item, even though equivalent quantities of locally grown fruit are readily available, approximately one quarter of the price and certainly healthier, given the already high levels of sugar intake. Though trivial, such an example can be magnified throughout the economic system. By raising living standards without an increase in productive capacity, an aid programme simply feeds consumer tastes alien to the community, raises demand for imported "sophisticated" items and further accentuates a sense of relative deprivation amongst those who have been exposed to consumer fads but have no means of satisfying their new demands. Where there exists an island substitute, efforts should be made to encourage the consumption of local goods. . . . There seems to be little reason why locally-produced fruit, preserved and bottled jams and fruit, and eventually a full range of garden vegetables shouldn't be produced locally for local consumption.

The letter continued by arguing that selected import duties should be imposed, that the government needed to promote local produce by other measures, and that the symbolic value in producing something locally would have an important effect in stimulating other efforts at self-reliance. Though the author's views on this question have often been echoed by island opinion, nothing credible has been done to selectively reduce food imports. As to increasing the island's "attraction for outside investors," we have already seen that such a prospect appears to present as much of a threat as an opportunity to those who administer the island's affairs.

If we consider the final quoted aim of the planners—namely, to provide the community with a sense of purpose, to build self-reliance and allow them to determine their own future—one can perhaps see these remarks as a rhetorical moral flourish, not meant to be taken at their face value. But there are some virtues in so doing, because the dynamics of the administration of colonial St. Helena and the way in which the plan was implemented are thereby revealed. But let us start first with a logical objection to the planners' aim. If the community is to be involved in its own development there is also no clear distinction or hierarchy drawn between the roles of government, the role of foreign capital, and the role of the community—all three of which are equally and undiscriminatingly applauded. There is also a rather revealing inconsistency in on the one hand invoking the islanders' involvement and participation in their own future "by their own efforts" and, on the other hand, suggesting that they will have to "be *led* out of the low productivity trap into which they have fallen." Have they fallen, or were they pushed? Who are they to be led by? If the islanders are to be the decisive actors in the determination of their own fates, how are they to be involved and what do they think of the plans drawn up on their behalf? It is to the discussion of these issues, that the next section of this chapter is addressed.

RESPONSES TO THE DEVELOPMENT PLAN

It has already been shown that the plan was drawn up entirely by visiting experts and advisers. No public meetings were held by these advisers, and consultation took place virtually entirely with government officials on the ground and in Whitehall. The plan was to be implemented entirely "from the top," little publicity was given to it, and no attempt made to build in participatory groups in the implementation of monitoring of the plan. The legislative council members were, in effect, notified after the event and made a ritual obeisance to Her Majesty's government for its kind endeavors.

It was in these circumstances that the author decided to undertake three tests of opinion. First, he contacted in person, or by letter, all twelve Legco members. Second, he conducted selective in-depth interviews with a cross-section of islanders and officials, supplemented by visits to community projects, the schools, government departments, and the mental asylum. Finally, he surveyed 200 members of the electorate by means of a mailed questionnaire (the response rate was 55 percent).

The Legco questionnaire elicited only a written response from three members, though others talked to the author informally. Only one councillor had contacted his constituents by letter concerning the development plan, though he was not able to organize a constituency meeting. Two other councillors had organized meetings, though attendance had been disappointingly small, at 15 to 20 people and 40 people, respectively. Another councillor organized a meeting subsequently to being contacted and perhaps as a response to the interest shown in whether any consultation with his constituents had taken place. When asked "what features of the plan do you approve of," one councillor argued in vague terms that "it is necessary to the growth and maturity of the island"; another approved of the broad agricultural strategy, the loans policy for house building, and the proposals for water storage and sewage; a third argued that the committees of Legco "decide the projects to be undertaken, thus giving the people a direct say in expenditure." The last comment is of some interest as the budget heads and major projects had all been tightly allocated prior to the plan reaching the Legco. It also clearly indicated that the councillor concerned conceived the democratic will in representative, rather than participatory or mandatory, terms.

When asked whether "there are any features of the Plan that you personally disapprove of," it is interesting that the same councillor who saw direct democracy at work commented that he thought it a waste of time that all project plans had to be submitted to the United Kingdom for approval. Perhaps the most startling response, however, came from one councillor who thought that "the priorities of the plan are questionable." He also strongly attacked the lack of an economist's report in the specialized reports of Part Two of the Plan (this had been excised from the printed version as some recommendations did not square with the overall arguments of the planners). "We have no guidance whether a project would be economical over a reasonable period, or not," he complained. Yet this fairly fundamental disagreement with the plan by an elected member was never, to this author's knowledge, referred to in official memoranda by those in the administration responsible for the plan's implementation.

When asked 'What role, if any, can a councillor play in activating public support for the development plan," the answers were generally evasive or vague. Only one councillor had a strong position to proclaim. She insisted that councillors could improve relations between the government and people, seeing the former as "amazingly divorced from the day-to-day needs of the people." Councillors should also prevent blunders, keep up faith and morale, investigate grievances, and "can break their hearts, their backs and their spirit trying to achieve a more productive attitude on the one hand and some concrete proof of development on the other." Despite this one idealistic statement, most councillors seemed to reflect a patrician, paternal view and represented their constituents as having negative, indifferent, or cynical views toward the plan.

This author was, by contrast, surprised at the level of interest generated by his own inquiries. The sample survey was constructed by taking approximately every fifth name from the 1972 Register of Electors, which listed 1073 names (St. Helena, 1972). To ensure geographical representativeness, the sample was slightly biased in favor of the small constituencies of Levelwood, Longwood East, and Longwood West and corrected also for sexual bias. Using the cheap local post with a stamped addressed reply envelope proved an effective means of reaching the respondents, who despite St. Helena's small size are widely scattered, sometimes in settlements that are difficult to reach. The response rate was unusually high, respondents often thanking the author effusively for his interest and returning the questionnaire in person, by slipping it under the door of his residence or by covert means. The fact that so large a number of responses were elicited and the manner of their return suggest both that such a level of consultation was a novel experience and that the islanders are less indifferent to their fate than has sometimes been adduced.

Findings

As can be seen from Table 5.3, the returns were particularly good from those in the 30-40 age group, those with working or travel experience abroad, while slightly more returns were made from men rather than women. The last bias is, however, somewhat misleading as the women tended to respond more fully and frankly. A somewhat disproportionate number of replies came from outside Jamestown, the capital, perhaps suggesting that people in the outlying areas were more attracted by the novelty of having their views sought. The basic attitudes to, and knowledge of, the plan by the respondents are summarized in Table 5.4.

The responses listed in Table 5.4 are somewhat difficult to interpret. It's clear, first, that with a sample drawn from the electorate and respondents who might be expected to be better informed, the government has been unsuccessful in providing even the most basic knowledge of the plan, 76 percent claiming, sometimes indignantly, that they knew little or nothing of its contents. This finding confirms the basically elitist character of the plan, awareness of which seems to have hardly filtered down to the population. The poor level of governmental initiative in this respect is compounded by the lack of any independent medium of communication, other than an occasional *Parish News,* issued by an Anglican minister. The

TABLE 5.3   Profile of Respondents

Demographic Variable	Percentage
Sex	
Male	58
Female	42 (N = 110)
Age	
20-30	25
30-40	50
40-50	12
50+	13 (N = 101)
Travel Experience	
Left for period over 2 years	23
Left for short periods	43
Never left island	34 (N = 95)
Employment Abroad	
Contract worker (Ascension)	65
Employment abroad	27
Merchant seamen	8 (N = 58)
Residence	
Jamestown (capital)	34
Rural	66 (N = 110)

radio station (controlled by the government) did apparently broadcast some discussions of the plan, but its main output comprises a constant diet of popular music, interspersed with the odd sports commentary. The *St. Helena News Review,* the official government weekly, carried some bald announcements of the plan's provisions, but these apparently were not widely read. It is not without justice that some islanders have nicknamed this slim publication "The Two Minute Silence." The fact that the over-whelming majority of respondents claimed little or no knowledge of the plan did not, however, prevent some of this group from commenting on its good and bad points. This explains the discrepancy between the smaller number who answered Part A affirmatively and those who were prepared to comment in Parts B, C, and D of Table 5.4.

Of those who expressed their views on the plan, the majority were clearly unimpressed with the work of the development advisor and his team of experts. Several, indeed, were hostile to the advisers. Respondents described episodes when the visitors had revealed their ignorance and complained that they were not asked for their views. Other epithets

TABLE 5.4   Knowledge of Development Plan

QUESTION: What do you know of the Development Plan? What are its good points? And its bad points?	(Percentage)
A. Knows nothing/little	76
Knows basic provisions	13
Provides informed comment	11 (N = 110)
B. Those finding "good points"	12
Those finding "bad points"	88 (N = 32)
C. "Good points" identified (by rank)	
General improvement	75
Loans for private housing	50
More frequent ships to island	50
Better education	25
More employment	25
Better communications	25 (N = 4)
D. "Bad points" identified (by rank)	
The government will do little/nothing	79
Not enough done to provide water	61
Not enough done to provide housing	39
Specific projects are "waste of money"	32
Not enough done to provide help for poor	25
Communications not improved	25
Miscellaneous	29 (N = 28)

directed to the planners included "frauds" and "idiots." Those who saw some good in the exercise nonetheless engaged in some wish fulfillment. The plan is, at best, ambiguous on the questions of improving shipping, communications, and employment prospects, and only the promise of improved loans to those who wanted to build houses seems both to have gained unqualified approval and conformed to the planners' intentions. Two respondents provided detailed evidence of the slow pace of government house construction in support of their views that this endeavor was best left to private initiative. Perhaps more significant is that none of the people who held a positive view of the plan actually identified the major areas of investment promoted by the planners, namely, agriculture and fisheries.

Those who were skeptical of, or hostile to, the government's plans were far more articulate and often impressive in their command of the possibilities for alternative improvements other than those mentioned in the plan.

The prevailing mood of the responses was, however, that the government, its advisers, and agencies were incompetent or stingy or indifferent to the islanders' fate. Only a few islanders expressed their indignation in what could be recognized as a protonationalist response. One 31-year-old male with a lengthy working experience abroad, for example, stated:

> It's my opinion that the people who come to St. Helena wants it to be the poor place it is, because for the islanders it's hell to live with, but to the Englishmen who come it's "A White Man's Paradise." For years we saw the same thing happening.... Don't think the St. Helenian people are happy with the set up here.... What point is there in being a voter if our suggestions is just pushed aside. If St. Helenians was violent people blood would flow here many a time, but maybe it would be the only answer.

The majority of respondents with negative views of the plan were far more muted. Many comments reflected a disbelief that the development plan represented anything but "talk" with little chance of practical success. Other criticisms concerned the government's record in housing and water supplies and the provision of aid to the needy, themes that reoccurred strongly in an open question asking for what improvements the islanders themselves wanted (see below). Finally, a number of respondents attacked specific provisions of the plan. Several were directed to the lease proposals for farm units, some of the proposals on communication, while one islander argued that leveling Francis Plain for a cost of £5,000 was a "waste of money."

The last set of responses were directed to the question, "What do *you* think should be done to improve life for yourself and your family?" This question triggered a vigorous set of responses covering a wide field, the variety of the responses not easily reduced to tabular data. A number of islanders used the opportunity to complain about life in general "being hard," but the specific suggestions for improvement can be grouped into four categories—improvement of water supplies, improvement of houses, improvement of roads, and additional financial assistance. In nearly all cases the proposals were modest, reasonable, and not unduly costly—yet these grass-roots demands gained little attention in the planners' proposals. The flavor of these responses is best conveyed by direct quotation. On the question of water supplies, one 33-year-old male living in a country area stated:

> We have a spring which never been run dry. We would be very grateful if they would prompt water to our houses which would help

me a lot, as I work in a garden, and if we have water actually we would have something growing in the dry weather, which would help as I say.

Two respondents were more concerned with having to carry water over long distances that then became stale. Though the man advocated the simple provision of "Jerry-Cans," the woman felt they would be too heavy. The male respondent wrote:

This man all now one by himself with a weekly small wage of £3 a week. And this is another problem concerning water business. I am living up on a hill and have to fetch this water a very long distance. . . . Hard to fetch this water in lard tins. Then some poor people haven't a donkey and no cans and some people have in less than a week the drums gone bad and cannot make of the water only use for garden use. Why not help these poor people with some Jerry cans with no payment?

On the question of housing, a number of islanders seemed to be more interested in having access to small loans to improve their own houses than in some of the more grandiose schemes of the planners. One 73-year-old woman who had never left the island commented:

As for my home, it is not in a good condition. One room has no window, the weather beats in through the curtain and my bedroom window has no boards nail to it, so that shows the room is very dark. I have written to the Government for a loan, but it seems they not appreciating me and the wind has blown my verandah away. It's not a Government place it is my own home and it is not [within] my means to buy materials.

The state of the local roads also attracted many suggestions for improvement, despite the planners' comment that "there is little that urgently needs to be done at this stage on road development on the island" (St. Helena, 1975, Part One: 9). Here the contrasting views of just two islanders can be quoted:

Also the road is not completed. When it rains its mud and water. Its [possible] to walk in only one small bay near the finish end. Only small cars can turn. Large vehicles have to keep reversing reversing. For the want of an under land drain, the dirt settle in the road and make a lot of mud. This is my complaint in life.

Another islander was more concerned that he and his neighbors were unable to get to the main road easily:

Really plenty can be done to help my neighbors and myself like we haven't got any sensible road, how if we got sick, we would have a hard time to get them on to the main road where a car can get. We take half an hour in walk to get there, and carrying only one its a hard job.

Lastly, a group of respondents had various complaints about the meagerness of the social benefits paid to them. One woman wrote:

I have seen the form that you wrote to someone, so now I am writing to you. My walk of life is this. I am 68 years of age. I have no father no mother no husband and no children. I am living with my sister who is in the same circumstances as I am. I applied to the social welfare twice for help. All they can afford to give me is £1.8 per week. It is not enough to give me the food that I require. A person of my age should have an income and to retire from worries.

The islanders' responses to the development plan seem, in short, to have little to do with the expectations and intentions of the planners. Most of those surveyed knew little about the plan; those who did were often hostile to, or critical of, the proposals in the plan. Even the small number of islanders who approved of the plan did not show a close identification with the planners' priorities. The islanders wanted different, more modest, more piecemeal improvements, which had little to do with the assumed needs that the planners gave priority to. Under these circumstances, it is perhaps not surprising that the islanders' representatives in the Legco found little enthusiasm for the development aims of the government and, with one exception, showed little inclination to activate their constituents in helping to implement the stated objectives of the government.

CONCLUSION

It is perhaps not too grand a generalization to suggest that colonial governments tend to encourage inertia and the preservation of the status quo and, by their very nature, are incapable of galvanizing the social changes necessary to transform a society. This generalization is lent particular force in St. Helena for three reasons. First, the administration comprises virtually the last cohort of British colonial officers. Unlike a minority of their predecessors who, in a remote district, might have experimented with a more populist style of administration, the officers in St. Helena are anxious not to blot their copybooks and are clearly conscious of Whitehall looking over their shoulders. Second, the civil servants in Whitehall are, for their part, primarily concerned with shedding Britain's remaining colonial responsibilities with the minimum of diplomatic and political fuss. Third, the social situation on the island itself encourages stasis. This stems partly from the conservatism of the small settler element, but also from the difficulties islanders have experienced in forming themselves into effective political lobbies. This stems in turn not from some inherent passivity or apathy, but partly from the all-too-recent experience of exercising a democratic choice and the small number of islanders who are self-employed and therefore immune from their felt obligations as government employees. The educational system and the narrow basis of consultation, representation, and participation permitted by the government also allows little room for the expression of opinions and grievances.

The St. Helenian government is, on the whole, successful in maintaining the traditional goals of colonial state—just government, the maintenance of law and order, the preservation of legal and constitutional formalities, and the more paternal goal of trusteeship and protection for the inhabitants of the island. But these characteristics of colonial rule proved wholly inadequate to the challenges confronting St. Helena in the 1970s. The colonial government was unable to harness private entrepreneurship to its stated task of reducing St. Helena's dependence on the United Kingdom and, in the face of a challenge from this quarter, retreated to its prior position of trusteeship. It was also unable, despite formally adopting the modern goals of community development and self-reliance, to build in or activate the structures of consultation and participation that would have made the realization of these goals possible. Instead "development" remained an abstraction, far removed from the needs and wishes of the people in whose name it was propagated.

REFERENCES

COHEN, R. (forthcoming) "Education for dependence: aspirations, expectations and identity on the island of St. Helena." Manchester Papers in Development (November).

The Guardian (1974) April.

HUGHES, C. (1958) "Report of an enquiry into conditions on the island of St. Helena." St. Helena Government Printer.

JACKSON, E. L. (1903) St. Helena: The Historic Island. London: Ward, Lock & Co.

KAY, G. (1975) Development and Underdevelopment: A Marxist Analysis. London: Macmillan.

MELLISS, J. C. (1875) St. Helena: A Physical, Historical and Topographical Description of the Island. Kent: L. Reeve & Co.

St. Helena (1972) The St. Helena Government Gazette Registers of Electors X, 12. St. Helena Government Printer.

——— (1975) Development Plan 1974 to 1979. Parts One and Two. St. Helena Government Printer.

St. Helena Labour Party (1975) The St. Helena Manifesto. Jamestown: St. Helena Labour Party.

United Kingdom Government (1973) Information transmitted to the Secretary-General of the United Nations by Her Majesty's Government in the United Kingdom in accordance with the provisions of Article 73(c) of the United Nations Charter concerning the territory of St. Helena and the dependency of Ascension for the period 1st April 1972 to 31st March 1973. Transcript copy.

6

CAPE VERDE:
SURVIVAL WITHOUT
SELF-SUFFICIENCY

DEIRDRE MEINTEL
McGill University

PORTUGUESE COLONIALISM IN CAPE VERDE

Cape Verde (*Cabo Verde*), a Portuguese colony until 1975, is an example of a small nation, possessing limited resources, whose very survival for the foreseeable future depends on external aid. The following section outlines some aspects of its colonial history that have shaped its present social and economic context, along with the factors of climate and geography that will partially determine the lines of possible development in the future. Despite its extreme poverty, and despite a disastrous drought that has marked most of the period since independence, Cape Verde has managed so far to utilize foreign assistance in a way that appears not to have compromised its political autonomy, but rather to have fostered local economic initiative and to have engaged its popular classes in the process of national development. This, I suggest, is due to capable administration by the government and to the emphasis given to the ideological formation of a mostly illiterate, rural populace. Pressure to develop the forces of production has not taken precedence over the gradual, slow but consistent, effort to transform the quasi-feudal relations of production that prevailed under colonial rule. Cape Verde's relative success in defining its own path of development makes it a particularly interesting case for study for students of development in the Third World and for those concerned for practical and political reasons with the survival of nations whose material circumstances preclude total food self-sufficiency as a realistic goal—

145

nations for whom a self-sustaining economy can only be conceived of in a context of interdependence.

Early Settlement and the Slave Trade

When the ten islands, nine of which are presently inhabited, that make up the archipelago of Cape Verde were claimed by Portugal in 1455, they were uninhabited. Located some 500 km west of what is now Senegal, they were probably known to some West African groups but appear not to have hosted a permanent population until a few years later, when European colonists and their African slaves arrived in Santiago, the largest of the islands (991 km^2). (Total surface area of Cape Verde: 4033 km^2). At first Portugal hoped to exploit the archipelago for sugar cane export production, as it had done successfully in the Azores and Madeira a few decades earlier, using African slave labor. This ambition was not to be realized, owing to the archipelago's dry and unreliable climate. (Average yearly rainfall is only 250 to 300 mm, and even that figure encompasses great annual variations).[1] Today sugar cane, maize, manioc, beans, and a variety of other food crops are grown in the five mountainous islands, with their many microclimates resulting from variations of relief and altitude, while the other low-lying islands have traditionally been used for raising goats and cattle. Yet these activities, while occupying about 90 percent of the population in recent times, never provided more than a marginal, undependable subsistence base.

Rather, slaving was the nexus of the Cape Verdean economy for over four centuries. Other economic activities—including the trade in textiles woven by slaves using West African techniques,[2] the exportation of animal skins and hides, and the victualing and repair of passing vessels—tended to revolve around the slave traffic, for which the archipelago became an important center during certain periods.[3] From a relatively small cohort of Europeans, including many Portuguese criminals and political exiles, and a much larger proportion of slaves there developed a racially mixed, creole (*Crioulo*)-speaking population that numbers approximately 330,000 today.

Initially, settlers were lured to the new colony by the prospect of extensive trading privileges granted by the Portuguese monarch Alfonso V in 1466. These were rescinded a few years later when the Crown established a system of contracts awarded to individuals based in Lisbon who obliged to pay heavy taxes on the even more lucrative slave commerce. Later rights over slaving and other forms of trade were ceded to monopoly companies, such as the Company of Grão-Pará and Maranhão (1755-1778), which, during the rule of the Marquês de Pombal, was allowed almost complete control of Cape Verde's economic and political life to the point of being empowered to nominate its governors (Carreira, 1969). Stringent trade regulations, often astonishing in their detail and rigour, covered such matters as the type of goods to be bought and sold, engagement of interpreters, destinations, and ports (Carreira, 1972). In fact, these measures simply turned many white and mulatto Cape Verdeans, now supposedly excluded from most commerce, into smugglers. Corruption flourished on a prodigious scale, to the point that governors, bishops, and even the Crown's own contractors engaged in contraband trade (Carreira, 1972; Duncan, 1972). Illegal commerce in all manner of goods remained prevalent until the very end of colonial rule.[4]

Most troublesome for the Crown's efforts to control the profits of the slave trade were the *lançados* (*lançar:* "to send out"), the agents of Santiago-based merchants sent to establish trading relationships among the riverine peoples of coastal Guinea. Often these emissaries were the mulatto sons of their white employers. The *lançados* usually adopted the garb, customs, and languages of the African groups they traded with, sometimes marrying into chiefly lineages (Rodney, 1970; Carreira, 1972). Condemnations and threats of both death and excommunication by Lisbon merely resulted in the *lançados* severing ties with Santiago and enlarging their commerce with other Europeans. Nonetheless, they constituted the most effective Portuguese presence on the mainland until the late nineteenth century, making the Cape Verdean creole language, *Crioulo,* something of a lingua franca among various ethnic groups of present-day Guinea-Bissau. The *lançados* were in a sense historical archetypes in that their activities prefigured the roles taken by Cape Verdeans in the late nineteenth and twentieth centuries as colonial intermediaries for the Portuguese on the African mainland, as discussed below.

Two Migrations

In the decades after slavery ended in Cape Verde, in 1858, a new traffic in human beings engaged the colony. Now its own drought-stricken peasants, mostly former slaves and their descendants, were recruited, sometimes under pressure, as labor for the islands of São Tomé and Principe, which together comprised a Portuguese colony in the Gulf of Guinea. The atrocious conditions of the cacao plantations there constituted what one observer called "*A Modern Slavery*" (Nevinson, 1968) and did not substantially change until Portugal's colonies became the focus of international attention in the late 1960s. Carreira's account of this migration cites accounts of whippings and torture noting that such violence continued "into our own times" (1977: 158). Between 1941 and 1970, according to his figures, there were 56,504 Cape Verdean laborers in São Tomé and Principe (1977: Annexo I, Table 11).[5]

A more elite migration of Cape Verdeans also began in the late nineteenth century as Portugal began to require missionaries and administrators on the African continent in order effectively to occupy and maintain its claim to the mainland colonies against pressure from Germany and Great Britain. Cape Verdeans came to fill the lower and middle echelons of the colonial apparatus in Guinea (now Guinea-Bissau) and to a lesser extent, in Angola and Mozambique, as missionaries, teachers, government administrators, and small businessmen.[6] The utility of Cape Verdeans to Portugal as buffers in the colonial process owed as much to their mixed racial background and their creole culture, with its strong Portuguese influence, as it did to their alleged capacity to adapt to the climatic conditions of the other colonies. The importance of the Cape Verdeans as "proxy colonizers" for the Portuguese is attested to by the founding of a seminary-*liceu* (i.e., secondary school) in 1866, followed after its demise by the *liceu* established in the city of Mindelo on the island of São Vicente in 1917.

Cape Verdeans as Colonizers and Colonized

The two very different migrations of Cape Verdeans to the other African colonies just mentioned illustrate very well the ambiguous position of Cape Verde in the Portuguese empire. On one hand, Cape Verdeans were always regarded as Portuguese citizens and were never subjected to the invidious distinctions made in the other colonies between so-called indigenous (i.e., "uncivilized") and assimilated persons under Salazar's rule. The latter category never numbered more than a miniscule proportion of the total population of a colony.

Officially, Cape Verde's status was that of an overseas province, or colony, depending on the prevailing terminology of any given period,[8] like Angola, Guinea, and the other African territories. But when the Colonial Act of 1930 brought the facism of Salazar's New State to the colonies and with it the *indigenato* policy, Cape Verdeans were given the status of "assimilated" (*assimilados*) and, unlike most other Africans under Portuguese rule, were thus considered citizens. In Caetano's words (1951: 8-9), "The whole population is civilized and the legal statute for *aborigines* (natives leading a tribal life . . .) is not applied to the black people." (At the time the latter category comprised 57,400 of the total population of 180,000, of whom 5,600 were counted as "white" and the rest as "mixed"). Under the 1946 Organic Law, a blueprint for colonial policy, it was expressly prohibited to treat Cape Verdeans as natives (*indigenos*).

Nonetheless, just as the repeal of *indigenato* by no means signaled an end to colonial racism, as Bender demonstrates for the case of Angola, so the fact that it was never applied in Cape Verde should not be taken to mean that this territory was somehow exempt from the racism inherent in Portuguese colonial policy, a fact suggested by the unconscious racism of Caetano's phrase, cited above. (Evidently it was only Blacks whose civilized status was in question). It was the darker, and poorer, inhabitants of Santiago and Fogo who constituted the bulk of Cape Verdean laborers in São Tomé, recruited on a commission basis by white merchant-landlords. The same sector of the population has predominated in the labor migrations of the 1970s to Portugal, where incidents of racial discrimination have been common. It was traditionally Black Cape Verdean peasants who suffered disproportionate fatalities in the many famines that have occurred. I have argued elsewhere that race, in terms of both phenotype and ancestry, constituted an important factor in determining an individual's "life chances" in colonial Cape Verde (Machado 1981). The roles of Cape Verdeans as proxy colonizers on the African mainland contributed to Cape Verde's ideological significance as a showcase for Portuguese colonialism and created the context for an ambivalent relationship with Guinea-Bissau that would affect both the revolutionary struggle and political relations between the two nations after independence. At the same time it was this possibility of formal education (considerably greater than in Guinea-Bissau, and for a certain time, greater even than in the metropole itself) that would provide qualified Cape Verdeans to lead the revolutionary movement in Cape Verde and Guinea-Bissau (the PAIGC, *Partido da Independência de Cabo Verde e Guiné*). The unusual number of well-educated Cape Verdeans, many of them exiles under the former regime, has also been an important factor in the country's postcolonial development.

Yet most Cape Verdeans were likely candidates for labor on the infamous cacao plantations or for labor migrations elsewhere. (These will be discussed briefly at a later point). This was not, of course, the simple result of an unfortunate climate but rather a consequence of Portugal's callous "underdevelopment" of the colony, to use Walter Rodney's term (1972). It is to this problem to which I now turn.

Portuguese "Underdevelopment" of Cape Verde

Many Portuguese were surprised when, little more than a year after the coup d'état that ended the Salazar-Caetano dictatorship in 1974, over 90 percent of the Cape Verdean electorate chose independence rather than continued affiliation with Portugal. Certainly some of this response resulted from the antagonisms created by the heavy Portuguese military and police presence during the wars waged on the African mainland. But probably of greater importance were the five centuries of administrative ineptitude, neglect, and flagrant exploitation on the part of Portugal that, once independence achieved, left Cape Verde's new leaders faced with a truly catastrophic situation.

In 1975 certain parts of the archipelago were facing their tenth consecutive year of drought. Exports accounted for under 7 percent of imports, the balance of payments being largely dependent on emigrant remittances from the United States and Europe. During colonial rule, famine accompanying periodic drought had routinely taken tens of thousands of lives; those of 1941-1943 and 1947-48, for example, had killed by conservative estimates about 38,000 (Carreira, 1977: 238). Only the international interest in Portugal's colonies prevented similar death-tolls in the early 1970s, and even then relief programs were only stopgap measures. Medical services were minimal; barely a dozen overworked physicians serviced the entire archipelago, and three of the islands were without a resident doctor. Malnutrition and intestinal parasites afflicted much, if not most, of the population, and infant mortality was high, at 120 per 1000 live births (Decraene, 1977). During my research,[9] which lasted for eleven months in 1972, I observed many cases of elephantiasis, pelagra, and leprosy, malaria having been brought under control only a few years earlier. At that time interisland transport was seriously deficient, and a small island such as Brava,[10] where I spent the greater part of my stay, could go for as long as six weeks without maritime contact with the outside world.

Though formal schooling enjoyed great prestige in Cape Verde, in part because it represented practically the only route to upward mobility (through colonial service), educational facilities had declined over Salazar's rule, and this, it could be argued, was perhaps the result of deliberate policy.[11] As a result, some 80 or so percent of the population was illiterate at the end of the colonial era. For most, in fact, the only hope of improving their circumstances was emigration. An estimated 200,000 Cape

Verdeans and their descendants live in the United States, to which they have been emigrating since the mid-nineteenth century. Counting the 40,000 resident in Portugal, most of them laborers, and those in France, Holland, and elsewhere, there are now over 300,000 Cape Verdeans living abroad, or roughly the equivalent of the population of the archipelago itself.

When I asked about this high outmigration as a solution to Cape Verde's economic problems, a high-ranking colonial official replied, "Better than the Malthusian one." In fact, Portugal's stunning neglect of the archipelago's fragile resources had done much to make "every Cape Verdean a potential migrant," as one writer put it (Araujo, 1966: 20). Deforestation by goats left to forage freely and by famished human beings had caused serious erosion; this was aggravated by occasional torrential rains that instead of being caught in anticipation of future droughts, were allowed to wash into the sea, along with precious topsoil. Only 1500 hectares of cultivated land were under irrigation, most of these being owned by a few banana exporters. The land had been mostly fragmented into tiny parcels, with fewer than 3 percent of the holders owning more than five hectares, and most having less than one (Davidson and Pelissier, 1980: 251). Cultivation was done by primitive methods using technology no more sophisticated than a digging stick.

Industry was minimal, consisting of a few archaic fish canneries, a small furniture factory, a flour mill, and the dredging of salt. Fishing was done in tiny 3-man rowboats unable to go far from shore, so that fish was actually scarce in most of the archipelago. Credit for technical improvements in fishing or agriculture was unavailable to all but the wealthy: to get credit from the state, a guarantee equivalent to the size of the loan was required, making state-supplied credit available only to a few already well-off landowners.

The underdeveloped state of Portugal itself (see Bender, 1978) gave little stimulus for promoting capitalist development in a colonial backwater such as Cape Verde. Instead, the mercantile, protectionist policies of the eighteenth and nineteenth centuries continued into the twentieth, administered with much the same inefficiency as before. Along with restrictive trade policies that forced Cape Verdeans to pay high prices for substandard Portuguese imports, rights to fish Cape Verdean waters and to export Cape Verdean salt were leased to foreign concerns. The few attempts to form cooperatives were stifled, while share-cropping and its equivalent in the fishing sector (whereby two-thirds of the catch went to the boat's owner, this usually being an individual possessing a number of vessels) remained prevalent.

Not surprisingly, seigneurial patterns of social relations continued, with prosperous landlords and merchants (often the same individuals played both roles) expecting and receiving deference, if not servility, from large clienteles of dependent tenants, sharecroppers, debtors, and the like. (Loans, particularly important for emigration, were usually made at 100 percent interest). Most of the colonial regime's administration in the twentieth century was composed of individuals closely related to the few notable families, and so were seen and deferred to as petty patrons.

Such patterns were reinforced by colonial racism, since positions of wealth and power tended to be held by those of lighter complexion. Portuguese propaganda focused more on "culture" than on race; nonetheless, the impact was the same, since cultural elements deemed "European" were considered modern and civilized, whereas those ascribed African origin (not always correctly) were defined as primitive and "backward." The significance of this racial ideology in Cape Verde's colonial heritage is not to be underestimated; five centuries of *effective* Portuguese occupation (in contrast to the mainland colonies where this took place only beginning around the turn of the century) along with the absence of an indigenous cultural base from precolonial times made for a much more thorough penetration of colonialist ideology into popular culture, though not without contradictions or counterinfluences.

Adding to the ideological tasks faced by the new regime was the fact that although the leadership of the PAIGC was mostly Cape Verdean, no guerilla warfare had been waged in Cape Verde, owing to its physical characteristics and to massive Portuguese troop deployment there. Thus, until 1974, Cape Verdeans in the islands had no concrete experience of the PAIGC's social and political program, put into practice earlier in the liberated areas of Guinea-Bissau, as was the case with FRELIMO in Mozambique and the MPLA in Angola.

For the brief period that General Antonio da Spinola governed Portugal, attempts were made to separate the future of Cape Verde from that of Guinea-Bissau, and to keep the former as part of Portugal. Though unsuccessful, this underscores the paradox that marked the whole colonial era. That is, Cape Verde's natural resources made it more an unprofitable albatross than a prize acquisition for the metropole, except for the fact of its geographical position. It was its location that conferred on Cape Verde whatever economic value it had for the colonizers during the slaving period and that later gave it tremendous strategic value during the African wars. Its governors of today are faced with the task of maximizing whatever international concern for its welfare can be gained from the archipelago's position as a "springboard to Africa," while attempting to develop human and natural resources to the greatest benefit of its population.

ECONOMIC DEVELOPMENT SINCE INDEPENDENCE

In some respects the economic situation of Cape Verde has worsened over the postcolonial period. Per capita income has risen from $65[12] as of 1967 to $130 in 1980 (Beaudet, 1981: 12, 23),[13] but not nearly as much as prices for some basics (see Davidson and Pelissier, 1980: 255), reflecting in part the world economic crisis of recent years. Exports have fallen to a mere 5 percent of imports (Legum, 1981: 486) a result of the severe drought that has continued almost without respite until the present, and of the abrupt departure of the Portuguese and other Europeans. Fortunately, emigrant remittances have increased substantially, from $7.95 million in 1974 to about $20 million in 1979, and large sums of foreign aid, totaling over $60 million in 1979 (Beaudet, 1981: 19) have been received from a variety of sources, to be discussed shortly.

Highest in Cape Verde's priorities for survival and future development is the assurance of adequate fresh water, first for the population's needs, and second, for agriculture and animal husbandry. Thousands of small dikes and embankments have been constructed, and over 2 million trees (acacia, pine, and eucalyptus) planted, all of which will improve water retention in the soil. Irrigation has been improved and extended; it is hoped that by the year 2006 over 8000 hectares will be under irrigation (Dumont and Mottin, 1980: 231). At present most of this land goes into sugar cane production (for locally consumed *aguardente*) and bananas (for export), though with time more irrigated land should be given over to subsistence production. For now, state policy has been to limit the extension of cash crop cultivation rather than to abolish it.

Nevertheless, even with these measures and the construction of a second desalinization plant (the first having been constructed during Portuguese rule), Cape Verde can meet only 30 percent of its food needs, and this only under optimal climatic conditions, according to an FAO report (Legum, 1981: 486). It is thus imperative to develop other sources of food and revenue. The most promising appears to be fishing. Since 1974

a new large refrigeration facility has been built (one was already functioning in Mindelo), and hundreds of small craft motorized. A state company
runs the industrial fishing sector and another such company is reestablishing crawfish exports, formerly controlled by a Portuguese firm. Small
fishermen have been aided through construction of small refrigeration
plants and improvements in port facilities and distribution services. The
goal is to make fish cover 15 percent of the local diet (Beaudet, 1981: 30).
The fishing sector has, in fact, shown considerable increases in production
and in quantities exported since independence.[14]

Industry offers but limited prospects in Cape Verde given the small
local market, transportation costs, and the fact that Cape Verdean labor is
relatively expensive ($2.75/hour) for Africa. At the same time, though, it
is also somewhat more qualified and reliable, so that certain types of
manufacture on the small scale but requiring some technical training might
eventually prove feasible as a source of state export revenue (Beaudet,
1981: 31).

Other sources of income include the international airport on the island
of Sal, now solvent for the first time. The harbor at Mindelo is now being
improved, a fact that will be important for Cape Verde's fishing exports. A
cement-making plant has been set up in Santo Antao, rich in deposits of
possolana (a type of rock high in silicone content and useful for insulation).
Though not currently being exploited, basalt and mineral waters both
offer export possibilities. Finally, wind and sun resources, both of them
considerable, are being studied as potential sources of energy. Tourism has
been prudently left aside for the present, given the country's fragile
infrastructure.

Besides the improvements at the level of production that I have summarized here, important progress has been made in education and public
health. Despite a shortage of teachers, facilities, and materials appropriate
to the present economic and political context, illiteracy has been reduced
(to 70 percent) and primary education extended from four to six years
and is now available to all children. (About 90 percent are in fact enrolled.)[15] Public health has improved because of carefully distributed food
aid from abroad (discussed later) and the emphasis put on preventive
education. While physicians are still lacking, some 75 nurses have been
trained and health centers oriented to women and children established
(Beaudet, 1981: 32). This has helped to alleviate in great measure the
bronchial ailments and intestinal parasites that chronically afflicted much
of the population before.

International Aid

Three aspects of Cape Verde's international policies can be delineated as having a direct bearing on the development aid it receives: first, any offer of aid with political conditions attached to it is refused. Second, Cape Verde avoids alignment with major power blocs on international issues. Third, it has cultivated a wide and multifaceted range of ties with other nations, including, of course, bilateral relations with contributing nation states, but putting emphasis on multilateral affiliations with other African states that allow access to other international sources of aid.

A propos of the first two points, the minister of economic coordination (Oswaldo Lopes da Silva) describes the Cape Verdean international stance as an "anti-bloc" policy, neither pro-East nor pro-West, but "for Cape Verde" (Beaudet, 1981: 37). The prime minister, Pedro Pires, asserts that "no aid that might have political constraints attached to it will be accepted" (Eisenloeffel, 1978: 17). In fact, the largest share of aid comes from Western countries, with the United States an important contributor but less so than the Netherlands and Sweden, sources of support for the PAIGC before independence and whose assistance comes mostly through nongovernmental organizations. Soviet contributions are of moderate importance, while the role of the Chinese is minimal. Both the possibility of a Soviet naval base and a NATO base have been categorically refused. However, the strategic potential of the archipelago remains an important consideration for potential donors such as the United States, as per a 1980 AID report (Beaudet, 1981: 38), and no doubt for the Soviet bloc countries as well. In a sense, Cape Verde maximizes the value of its strategic potential by refusing to actualize it. At the same time, as a small and extremely poor nation, it has been able to avoid involvement in issues not directly related to it interests (e.g., Afghanistan), while voicing support for revolutionary movements such as that of East Timor and the Polisario.

Besides the donor nations mentioned already, Portugal has given multiform assistance of great practical, if not monetary, significance. France, Belgium, and West Germany have given food, loans, and technical help. Various sorts of exchange have been set up with Senegal, Mozambique, and Angola. Relations with Guinea-Bissau did not hold crucial economic importance even before the rupture of late 1980; one French observer, Diannoux, dismisses their project of union, now apparently abandoned, as "the addition of one penury to another" (1980: 16). Cape Verde's membership in such organizations as the Lomé Convention, the Committee of Sahelian Countries (CILSS), and the Organization of African States has opened the way for assistance from bodies such as the European Economic Community and OPEC. United Nations assistance has been considerable, including a special program that consigns $95 million over a five-year period to a series of development projects in areas such as transport, reforestation, and irrigation (Beaudet, 1981: 38).

This adroit conjugation of various sources of aid constitutes more than the pragmatism of a small nation seeking to maximize its advantages. It is, rather, the manifestation of, and a necessary condition for, a broadly based program of national development whose most essential component is ideological; that is, the cornerstone of Cape Verdean policy regarding development at both the international and national levels is the political goal of creating an egalitarian, economically viable society, one in which the process of national development engages the broadest possible popular base. This process of development includes not only economic transformation through the development of the productive forces, but also political and ideological initiatives. Not only a healthy economy but one characterized by new social relations (i.e., relations of production) must be created.

That Cape Verde's priorities are social, political, and ideological is manifest in the fact that while the extraordinary budget for development provided by foreign aid is larger than the ordinary one, funds from the former are not used to balance the latter. To accomplish this, a policy of extreme austerity has been adhered to beginning with the $7000 per year salary of the prime minister (Beaudet, 1981: 15). Diplomatic expenses are minimized by maintaining only four embassies (at Conakry, Dakar, Lisbon, and Washington). Other evidence of the strength of the ideological commitments guiding the use of aid lies in the fact that food aid from abroad (some 70,000 tons in 1979) is sold, rather than distributed (except for that given to children, the aged, and infirm), at state-controlled prices. This is done as an incentive for work and as a precaution against cultivating a welfare mentality, with the secondary effect that a possible source of administrative corruption is thus avoided. Fair access to food and other essentials is facilitated by state employment policies, to be taken up shortly.

Of key importance for the integration of international assistance with national priorities is the Cape Verdean Solidarity Institute, a nongovernmental organization directly responsible to the ruling political party, the PAICV[16] (formerly the PAIGC). The Institute has two main functions, one being to initiate a certain number of its own projects, as it has done in the areas of education and local transport. The other is to oversee the activities of some forty nongovernmental organizations from ten or so different countries that are currently sponsoring development projects in Cape Verde. The Institute coordinates their contacts with the various government ministries and channels their efforts in directions considered positive for political as well as economic development.

Funds are encouraged more than are volunteers; unlike most Third World countries, Cape Verde, largely because of its special role under colonialism, does not lack human resources in the form of qualified personnel. Moreover, the local infrastructure is unable to support many foreign residents, given the shortages of food, lodging and energy resources and the problems of local transport. This is not to say that Cape Verde has entirely escaped the contradictions and ironies so abundant in Third World development programs elsewhere. Dumont and Mottin (1980: 230) point out that the equipment and techniques contributed by foreign agencies are often ill-conceived for the Cape Verdean context: petrol-hungry trucks pass long lines of girls and women walking with enormous water containers on their heads, yet there is not a single animal-drawn cart in sight. Costly tractors are sent to the state experimental farms, whose terrain is often too irregular for their efficient use, yet no one seems to have thought of a plow using animal power.

Despite the dangers of rapid population growth in a situation in which there are 340 inhabitants per arable square kilometer (Davidson and Pelissier, 1980: 250) and the rate of natural increase at 3.5 percent, there has been no organized campaign for population control. Information on family planning is promulgated through the National Commission for the Organisation of Women in Cape Verde but this organization is relatively new and poorly funded, with only one full-time staff member (Beaudet, 1981: 35). The reluctance to give more prominence to this issue probably represents a choice not to provoke a confrontation with the Catholic clergy, some of whom have given open support to the new regime. At present about 90 percent of Cape Verdeans are at least nominally Catholic, the rest being Nazarenes or Adventists.

National Development in Cape Verde

Unlike other African states, Cape Verde does not face the problem of integrating diverse ethnic groups into a new nation-state, but it does face the problem of insularity and, even within each island, of geographical isolation of villages from each other. The integration of its popular classes (mostly peasants, agricultural laborers, and fishermen) into the development of a new society implies giving priority to improving transportation both within and between islands, an area that has seen considerable progress. It also requires the decentralization of the development process and the encouragement of projects on the small scale. This has been done, to a large degree, in the domain of water conservation by emphasizing the multiplication of many small public works (e.g., dams, dikes, wells, and so on) that also have the advantage of safeguarding local ecology. In both the agricultural and fishing sectors, a similar decentralization is evident. Apart from several experimental farms run by the state, most development efforts are oriented toward the small cultivator, in the form of technical assistance, help in information of cooperatives (about which more in a moment), and extension of state credit. Similarly, development of fishing has focused not only on the state-run export sector but also on small fishermen, providing for local subsistence needs, again using the means of credit, cooperatives (for both production and distribution), and technical aid.

Cooperatives extend the development process to the village level while, as structured in Cape Verde, allowing for a large measure of local autonomy. The National Institute of Cooperatives works to encourage and facilitate, rather than to sponsor or itself found, cooperatives. These have already been formed: seamstresses, woodworkers, stonemasons, as well as agriculturalists and other associations now in formation may eventually result in cooperatives. Agriculturalists' cooperatives have had to confront inequalities of access to both land and water remaining from the old regime, and do so without receiving specific directives from the Institute (Beaudet, 1981: 35). Over the long run cooperatives should prove important vehicles for confrontation with the merchants and larger landlords. At present over 70 percent of cultivators are either renting or share-cropping (Davidson and Pelissier, 1980: 251), though both forms of tenure are now regulated by laws giving the tenants more rights than before, and a few large properties were nationalized immediately after independence, with indemnities paid to the former owners. Land tenure is in fact a complex issue, with many local variations, and it is enmeshed in traditional patterns of social relations, which explains the government's reluctance to institute a drastic program of land reform.[17] According to the prime minister, a more serious problem lies in the need to utilize land now lying idle, including plots belonging to emigrants or to landlords now living abroad and to peasants who already hold more than they can farm themselves (Chonchiglia, 1979: 21).

For the moment, given the extreme poverty of the population and the un- or underemployment of most agriculturalists during the long drought, an important element in the policy of equalizing the fruits of development is the state regulation of employment in rural development projects, which include about 30,000 jobs in water conservation-related projects alone (Beaudet, 1981: 26). An effort has been made to distribute jobs equitably among different geographical areas and by household, in accordance with the degree of economic need (Dumont and Mottin, 1980: 230). This helps equalize purchasing power among the rural population, about 40 percent of which is supported by development projects. Indirectly, then, access to food donated by foreign sources is equalized, and in a way likely to foster economic responsibility. The fall in real per capita income, noted earlier, may not be reflected in a lower standard of living for the popular classes, whom all reports suggest are materially somewhat better off than they were before.

Creation of employment is seen as important for eventually reducing the rate of emigration. While admitting that Cape Verde could not possibly absorb a massive return of emigrants from abroad, Pires and others in his administration see emigration as posing problems for the economic and political direction of the nation. Though remittances are necessary for the balance of payments, these funds go almost exclusively for family consumption and, as in the past, not necessarily in forms appropriate to the local context. By way of example, refrigerators from the United States have been used as storage cabinets in areas where electricity had not yet been introduced. Conspicuous and wasteful spending patterns (e.g., for cars, imported clothing and luxury foods, and elaborate houses made of largely imported materials) pose, as the prime minister has remarked, a threat to local society by "creating illusory needs that are impossible to satisfy within the country's means" (Beaudet, 1981: 20), needs which of course tend to stimulate further emigration (see Bougnicourt, 1974). The demographic effects of the absorption by emigration of a large proportion of the country's active labor force, especially males, are of course another serious consideration for the long term. Present efforts are geared at creating jobs in fishing and construction in order to reduce the necessity of emigration. One might ask whether it is not possible to build closer ties with emigrant communities and to somehow involve them more closely in the economic and political process now underway.

CONCLUSIONS

In the decade preceding independence, Portuguese aid occasioned by the drought in Cape Verde took the form of make-work projects paying workers less than a dollar a day. Though some of these projects were no doubt useful, they were nonetheless devoid of long-term planning, much less of any conception of structural change in Cape Verde's economic system. Essentially, the changes in Portuguese assistance since the mid-nineteenth century were quantitative ones, except for the somewhat improved conditions allowed the Cape Verdean workers. Most Cape Verdeans perforce had no recourse but passive dependency on government "support" (*apoio*), as Portuguese famine relief was termed in colonialist parlance, or similarly passive reliance on remittances from abroad. Enterprising individuals' only hope for improving their living conditions and for eliminating the danger of starvation was the individualistic or at best familistic solution of migration. Neither Portuguese aid nor the role of emigration as the "solution" to Cape Verdeans' problem of survival did anything to foster collective responsibility in the populace, which indeed would have been inimical to the colonial regime.

The strategies adopted by Cape Verde since independence for utilizing large sums of aid from abroad have been largely successful in avoiding the dangers not only of narrow economic and political dependency on one or another world power bloc but also of fostering the dependent mentality, and this despite facets of the colonial experience alluded to above.

Though little mention has been made of the political structure of the PAICV in this essay, it should be evident that the process of development in Cape Verde outlined above represents in its pragmatism and flexibility and above all, in its emphasis on popular participation based on ideological awareness, an attempt to put into practice the principles promoted by Amilcar Cabral. In particular, these include the respect for popular culture, the necessity of gradual construction of a new "national culture," and the profound understanding of the fact that the achievement of political independence is but a moment in the process of national liberation, comprehending "the complete liberation of the productive forces and the construction of economic, social and cultural progress of the people" (1973: 52). The cautious attitude taken by Cape Verde's present governor toward landlords and merchants is wholly consistent with Cabral's program;[18] it was his understanding that the petite bourgeoisie would undergo a gradual suicide, rather than a drastic annihilation, in its incorporation into the postcolonial process of development and liberation.[19]

Also important is the fact that quite in keeping with the approach of Cabral, today's leaders in Cape Verde have adopted a form of political discourse striking in its simplicity and in the avoidance of jargon, whose effects would be to foster external alignments and dependencies, as well as to limit the participation of the popular classes in Cape Verde. In the words of Pedro Pirès, "We are blessed with a progressive, nationalist, democratic and revolutionary regime but we are neither communist socialist nor bourgeois" (Decraene, 1977).

Finally, it is worth pointing out the remarkable similarities between the process of national development in Cape Verde and the general outlines of the Sandanista program in Nicaragua. Both nations face similar temptations to increase production rapidly at the expense of creating new relations and a new "national culture"; both nations experience pressures for dependent alignments with foreign powers, and both have struggled to maintain the participation and support of as wide as possible a popular base, without outright exclusion of the more privileged classes. Both nations are struggling to utilize economic development not as an end in itself, but in the pursuit of an essentially political objective, the construction of a more egalitarian and democratic society oriented to the needs and aspirations of their popular masses. Whatever the long-term outcomes, both these nations have despite certain economic and political differences, adopted broadly similar strategies for constructing a new society in today's international context, and have done so with some considerable success to date; this offers grounds, perhaps, for some guarded and constructive optimism to those concerned with the future of nations and territories such as those discussed in this volume.

NOTES

1. These range from 37 mm, in only seven days of rain, to 1050 mm in 47 days (Ribeiro, 1960: 66).

2. Duncan (1972: 210) estimates that some 28,000 slaves were transshipped through Cape Verde to the New World over the sixteenth century.

3. These were cotton cloths about a yard wide and five to six feet long featuring indigo designs on a white background. Such textiles were a prerequisite for trade on the Guinea coast during the sixteenth and seventeenth centuries, and those produced in Cape Verde were considered especially desirable. During certain periods they served as a measure of value and a form of currency in the archipelago (Carreira, 1968; Duncan, 1972: 219).

4. Several Portuguese army officers report cases of smuggling that involved collusion between Portuguese military officials and Cape Verdean merchants during

the late 1960s and early 1970s. Contraband in electrical appliances, pharmaceuticals, and various luxury goods appeared to be a common occurrence from what I was able to observe in 1972.

5. This figure includes 796 children born of Cape Verdean parents in São Tomé and Principe.

6. Also, between 1962 and 1968, 524 Cape Verdean peasants and fishermen were brought to planned agricultural colonies (*colonatos*) in Angola, in the hope that they would serve as racial and cultural intermediaries between Portuguese and Africans in these settlements (Bender, 1978: 110).

7. For example, in Angola in 1950, only 7 percent of the African population was classified as "assimilated" (Bender, 1978: 151). Duffy (1962: 166) notes that during the thirty years in which the *indigenato* existed, only 5 percent of the African population moved from "native" (indigenous) to "assimilated" status.

8. Bender (1978: XXn) has discussed the vicissitudes of official usage of the terms "colony" and "overseas province." During most of Salazar's dictatorship the former term was in favor, until 1951, when international criticism resulted in a return to the "overseas province" designation, a term whose first official use dates from 1822. The euphemistic nature of the term under Salazar and Caetano is belied by the fact that after the 1974 coup d'état in Portugal, the word "colony" was once again used to designate Cape Verde and the other territories claimed by Portugal outside its borders.

9. This was sponsored by traineeship grant and travel subsidy from the National Institute of Mental Health (Washington, DC).

10. This small island (64 km^2) was the one of greatest historical importance in the emigration to the United States that began sometime in the first half of the nineteenth century and became increasingly heavier until the restrictive immigration laws of the 1920s.

11. In the 1930s, the "virtues" of illiteracy were defended in Portugal's National Assembly and the public fora by partisans of Salazar's dictatorship (Mónica, 1979). The normal schools were closed by the ruler, resulting in a decline in availability of education both in the metropole and in the colonies.

12. Cash figures are given in U.S. dollars throughout the text.

13. I am particularly indebted to the Service Universitaire Canadien Outremer (SUCO), Montreal, Quebec, for providing a copy of Pierre Beaudet's (1981) comprehensive and well-documented report on aid and development in Cape Verde.

14. According to FAO statistics published in Davidson and Pelissier (1980: 253-255).

15. According to the prime minister (Chonchiglia, 1979: 20; see also Beaudet, 1981: 33-34).

16. *Partido Africano da Independencia de Cabo Verde.* The change in the title came after the 1980 rupture with Guinea-Bissau and the subsequent separation by the Cape Verdean branch of the PAIGC.

17. According to Dumont and Mottin (1980: 229), the popular tribunals created after independence tended to favor tenants in disputes with landlords. However, the protests of the latter eventually led to the suppression of these "people's courts" in the interest of "national unity."

18. One aspect of the postcolonial economic program envisaged by Cabral (1969: 171) was the following:

Four types of property: Co-operative exploitation on the basis of free consent will cover the land and agricultural production, the production of consumer goods and artisan articles. Private exploitation will be allowed to develop according to the needs of progress, on the condition that it is useful in the rapid development of the economy of Guinea and the Cape Verde Islands. Personal property—in particular individual consumption goods, family houses and savings resulting from work done—will be inviolable.

19. For complex reasons, one of which is the great scarcity of well-educated revolutionaries in Guinea-Bissau compared with Cape Verde, the PAIGC in Guinea-Bissau has not been as successful as in Cape Verde its political incorporation of various classes into national development. This issue, along with that of the significance of and reasons for the 1980 rupture between Guinea-Bissau and Cape Verde, warrant separate treatment elsewhere.

REFERENCES

ARAUJO, N. (1966) A Study of Cape Verdean Literature. Boston: Boston College.

BEAUDET, P. (1981) Le Cap Vert. Montréal: Rapport de Recherce, Service Universitaire Canadien Outre-Mer.

BENDER, G. (1978) Angola Under the Portuguese. Berkeley: University of California Press.

BOUGNICOURT, J. (1974) "La migration contribuera-t-elle au développement des zones retardées?" pp. 191-214 in Samir Amin (ed.) Modern Migration in Western Africa. London: Oxford University Press.

CABRAL, A. (1969) Revolution in Guinea. New York: Monthly Review Press.

——— (1973) "Identity and dignity in the context of the national liberation struggle," pp. 57-74 in Return to the Source. New York: Monthly Review Press.

CAETANO, M. (1951) Colonizing Traditions, Principles and Methods of the Portuguese. Lisbon: Agência Geral do Ultramar.

CARREIRA, A. (1968) Panaria Cabo-Verdeano-Guineense. Lisbon.

——— (1969) As Companhias Pombalinas de Navegação, Comércio e Tráfico de Escravos do Occidente Africano para o Nordeste Brasileiro. Porto: Imprensa Portuguesa.

——— (1972) Cabo Verde: Formação e Extincão de Uma Sociedade Escravocrata (1460-1878). Lisbon.

——— (1977) Migrações nas Ilhas de Cabo Verde. Lisbon: Universidade Nova, Ciéncias Humanas e Sociais

CHONCHIGLIA, A. (1979) "Quatre ans d'indépendance." Afrique-Asie 188 (May 28): 20-21.

DAVIDSON, B. and R. PELISSIER (1980) "The republic of Cape Verde," pp. 250-259 in Africa South of the Sahara 1980-1981. London: Europa.

DECRAENE, P. (1977) "Facing up to drought—and independence." The Guardian (Sept. 18): 12.

DIANNOUX, H. (1980) "La Guinée Bissau et les iles du Cap-Vert." Afrique Contemporaine 19, 107: 1-16.

DUFFY, J. (1962) Portugal in Africa. Baltimore: Penguin.

DUMONT, R. and M-F. MOTTIN (1980) L'Afrique Etranglée. Paris: Seuil.

DUNCAN, T. (1972) Atlantic Islands: Madeira, the Azores and the Cape Verdes in Seventeenth-century Commerce and Navigation. Chicago: University of Chicago Press.

EISENLOEFFEL, F. (1978) "Nous ne voulons pas être un peuple de mendiants." Afrique-Asie 161 (May 15): 16-17.

LEGUM, C. (1981) "Cape Verde Islands: another year of drought," 484-487 in Africa Contemporary Record: Annual Survey and Documents. New York: Africana.

MACHADO, D. (1981) "Idéologie et terminologie raciale aux iles du Cap-Vert." Culture 1, 1: 115-124.

MÓNICA, M. (1979) "Moulding the minds of the people: views on education in 20th century Portugal." Presented to the International Conference on Modern Portugal, June 21-24, Durham, New Hampshire.

NEVINSON, H. (1968) [1906] A Modern Slavery. New York: Schocken.

RIBEIRO, O. (1960) A Ilha do Fogo e as Suas Erupções. Lisboa: Junta de Investigações do Ultramar.

RODNEY, W. (1970) A History of the Upper Guinea Coast 1545-1800. London: Oxford University Press.

——— (1972) How Europe Underdeveloped Africa. London: Bogle-L'ourerture Publications.

7

DIEGO GARCIA:
THE MILITARIZATION OF AN
INDIAN OCEAN ISLAND

JOONEED KHAN

Montreal

The struggle for control of strategically situated islands was an essential part of European colonial expansion. Falling into the rimland category of geopolitical history, islands served, in times of conventional weaponry, either as strategic bases in themselves (defense-cum-resting posts along vital trade routes) or as springboards for the penetration of neighboring heartlands (Mahan, 1890). In these days of remote-control, push-button, planetary weaponry, however, one would expect islands to have lost the dubious relevance they once enjoyed, when sailing ships overran the oceans of the world.

Far from it. The intensive militarization, by the United States, of the Indian ocean island of Diego Garcia, a tiny, horseshoe-shaped atoll 13 miles long and 6 miles at its widest, to the tune of hundreds of millions of dollars proves that the strategic importance of islands has not changed in spite of the advent of ultra-sophisticated weaponry. And no one else knows that better, and more bitterly, than do the 1500 or so islanders who were deported to make way for this new advanced post "for the defense of the Free world" (Carlucci, 1981), situated at the very heart of the Indian Ocean.

The Diego Garcia story is all at once a simple and a complex one. Simple because it illustrates, once again, that might is right and that, in the name of high-sounding moral principles, small societies can be trampled on and exterminated with impunity when superpower interests are at stake. And complex not only because it pits a small nonaligned country, Mauritius, against historically tested Anglo-American guile, but also because it exposes the forty or so countries surrounding the Indian Ocean to the terrible dangers of renewed superpower rivalry at a time of accelerated reversal to the Cold War (Langelier, 1981). Above all, the Diego Garcia story is only partially known, for various reasons, not least of which being the highly secretive conditions that continue to surround it (McDowell, 1981) and the ambiguous stance of the Mauritian government of Sir Seewoosagur Ramgoolam over the whole issue (Jeune Afrique, 1980).

BACKGROUND

The story begins, from recorded sources, with the arrival of Portuguese navigators in the Indian Ocean around the turn of the 15th century. But the "unique" character of the coralian island system undoubtedly developed without waiting for the Portuguese, who named this "totally insular" world the Chagos Archipelago. It is in fact an ecological system of three groups of "pure oceanic islands," atolls of characteristic coral origin, dispersed along the rim of the Chagos Grand Bank, an irregular oval 95 miles long and 54 miles wide lying between the fourth and seventh parallels and between the seventieth and seventy-second meridians (Toussaint, 1972).

To the west of the Grand Bank lie Trois-Frères, l'île d'Aigle, l'île aux Vaches, and l'île Danger, nothing more than uninhabited outcroppings; to the north of it and away is the Peros Banhos and Solomon group, with île Boddam, most fertile of the Chagos islands with dense vegetation including coconut and rare tropical essences; and to the south lie the Six-Iles group (or Egmont Islands) and Diego Garcia, an almost closed atoll with an internal lagoon that nearly dries up at low tide any that turn-of-the-century geographer S. Gardiner called the "contour of an island" (Toussaint, 1972: 18).

The emergence of French and English names in the once Portuguese Chagos toponymy reflects colonial rivalries that, by the beginning of the nineteenth century, resulted in placing the Chagos as well as the Mascarenhas (minus Bourbon, or Réunion Island) and the Agalega and Cargados groups firmly under British rule. Over time, all of these British possessions came to be administered from Mauritius (Scott, 1961).

In 1903, however, the 92 or so islands of the Seychelles archipelago were separated from Mauritius. By the end of the 1950s, British Indian

Ocean possessions seemed destined to crystallize into two independent island-states, Mauritius and Seychelles, the first with a predominantly Indian population and the second with a predominantly African one: British fairplay would be seen to triumph again.

In 1965, however, while Anthony Greenwood, minister in charge of the Colonial Office in the then Labor government of Sir Harold Wilson, was stating publicly that Mauritius was "ripe for independence," his ministry was secretly detaching the Chagos archipelago from Mauritius and the islands of Aldabra, Farquhar, and Desroches from Seychelles to form the British Indian Ocean Territory (BIOT), destined to serve as military bases in time of war (Toussaint, 1972: 305). Those were the days of passionate and nostalgic public debate in Britain about "strategy East of Suez" (Toussaint, 1961).

Conveniently for the West, however, the then government of Seychelles did not appear too keen on independence (Cadoux, 1974: 65), and, of the Chagos archipelago, only Diego Garcia was integrated to the BIOT, the rest of the island-group being placed under Seychellian administration. Mauritius was given sovereignty over Rodrigues, Agalega, and the Cargados Carajos groups.

While Britain was quite ostentatious about the democratic path it was following toward decolonization after the winds of change of the 1960s, it was, on the other hand, secretive and unilateral about the formation of the BIOT and, needless to say, the inhabitants of the Chagos, Aldabras, Farquhar, and Desroches islands were never consulted about the project. Indeed, even the peoples of Mauritius and Seychelles were kept in the dark, in the first place by their own leaders, one of whom, Ramgoolam of Mauritius, is said to have been described by Harold Wilson as "my favourite Prime minister."

Those were also the days of growing U.S. military involvement in Indochina. Anticommunist crusading then had a heroic John Wayne type of ring to it. There would not be another Cuba anywhere else in the world. The shriveling up of the ever-sunny British Empire was leaving a dangerous vacuum, notably in the Indian Ocean, a strategic lake shared in common by three continents, which the United States, natural heir to the decadent European imperial powers since the Spanish-American War of 1898, could not leave unfilled.

Ramgoolam may have been Wilson's favorite prime minister, but he was playing in the little leagues. Besides, could one trust him, his successors, or anybody else in those parts with the protection of vital oil lines, strategic mineral deposits, and captive, dependent markets? Gaullist France was actively cultivating its bases in Réunion, the Comoros, and the Malagasy Republic including the disputed islands of Europa, Bassas da India, Juan de Nova, les Glorieuses, and Tromelin, which control access to the Mozambique Channel. The Soviet navy was rearing its head everywhere, threatening "freedom of navigation" (Toussaint, 1961).

A quick reminder of the geopolitical dynamics of the time in the region may be in order. In the first place, the status of the Indian Ocean as an extension of the Middle East cannot be sufficiently emphasized: True since the opening of the Suez Canal in 1869, this role had only increased with the emergence of petroleum as the West's basic source of energy from the 1900s onward. And the oilfields were on the Indian Ocean side of the Middle East, not on the Mediterranean side. This was also the region in which the USSR had been trying to realize the old Russian dream of a warm water port: The Soviets had settled firmly in Nasser's Egypt, which controlled the Suez Canal (nationalized in 1956) and influenced Arab policy against the West (Prats, 1974: 122-124).

China was cultivating ties with Pakistan, conveniently located on the Indian Ocean, and had just fought a successful border war with India. Somalia, Kenya, and Tanzania had achieved independence in 1960, 1961, and 1963, respectively. Madagascar had achieved independence in 1960. In 1964, the Zanzibari Revolution had taken place and, with Chinese support, the new United Republic of Tanzania was embarking on a nonaligned and socialistic path. The Tanzania-based Molinaco party had spelled out the demand for the independence of the Comoros in 1963.

The Maldives, where the future of the British military base of Gan was uncertain, and Singapore, where British military installations were in a similar quandary, were both heading toward independence by 1965. War was raging throughout both Yemens, with Egyptian and Saudi interference, while Oman, where oil was discovered in 1964, was faced with a strong guerilla movement in the Dhofar: This turbulence posed an immediate threat to the security of both Bab-al-Mandab, the opening of the Red Sea into the Indian Ocean, and of the Strait of Hormuz, linking the Persian Gulf to the Indian Ocean (Cadoux, 1974).

These then were the considerations that led to the creation of the BIOT in 1965. The immemorial, close-knit, and original Ilois community inhabiting the Chagos archipelago where, alongside their traditional fishing activities, colonial economic imperatives had forced them to undertake coconut oil extraction, had little weight in the balance. As it turned out, they had none. The Ramgoolam government was paid U.S. $8 million (Houbert, 1981).

The most amazing part of the whole story, as it has surfaced in bits and pieces over the years, is that, in the very words of Radha Ramphul, the Mauritian representative at the United Nations, "no document was ever signed" between Mauritius, then a crown colony enjoying internal self-government, and Britain, over Diego Garcia. It was a "gentlemen's agreement." In the months that followed, it was widely but misleadingly reported in Mauritius and in the world press that "Mauritius had sold Diego Garcia to Britain for $8 million."

Wasting no time, Britain leased Diego Garcia to the United States for 50 years. The terms of the lease have been kept secret, and as late as 1981, Ambassador Ramphul would not say what income Britain was deriving from the lease. The *London Sunday Times* wrote, in 1976, that the U.S. administration of Johnson, Rusk, and McNamara had agreed to a secret cut-price deal on Polaris missiles to be purchased by Britain, provided the British took care of the islanders (Ellsworth-Jones, 1976). The "rebate" is said to have amounted to U.S. $14 million (Houbert, 1981).

In late February 1982, the *Sunday Times* reported that "the United States will offer the most generous terms of any Anglo-American nuclear weapons deal if Britain agrees to buy the U.S. Trident II missile system [with up to 14 warheads and a range of 6,000 miles] before it ever deploys Trident I [eight warheads and 4,000 miles] as the replacement for its Polaris [three warheads] fleet" (UPI, Feb. 21, 1982). The new agreement would replace the one made between Prime Minister Margaret Thatcher and President Carter in June 1980 for the purchase of Trident I at an estimated cost of $5 billion, the report added.

After independence, in 1968, as questions were increasingly raised in Mauritius about the affair, Ramgoolam's confidants floated the following explanation: "It was blackmail. Britain told us we had to give up Diego Garcia or we would not get independence. We were in no position to refuse" (Cadoux, 1974: 57). It took two to three years before Mauritians discovered that it was in fact the whole of the Chagos archipelago that Mauritius had ceded for $8 million. And by 1971, while the opposition Mauritian Militant Movement (MMM) was raising embarrassing questions about what the government had done with the money, the Ilois population of Diego Garcia began to land in Mauritius in waves of hundreds of destitute men, women, and children (Ellsworth-Jones, 1976).

Britain, after having maintained that the BIOT islands were uninhabited, had begun deporting the population of the one island that the United States had chosen for their major naval base of the 1980s in the Indian Ocean. The shameful deportation continued into 1976, when the

London Sunday Times reported from Mauritius that the deportees were coming not only from Diego Garcia, but from Peros Banhos and the Solomon islands as well (Ellsworth-Jones, 1976). A Mauritian representative in Britain admitted in 1975 that the deportation had been taking place "with a minimum of publicity." When the British press unveiled the scandal, the government announced that it had paid a further $1.5 million to Mauritius for the resettlement of the deportees. But the *Guardian* reported in September 1975 that 422 families of deportees had written to the British and U.S. governments complaining that they had never received any compensation (Cadoux, 1974: 57).

UNITED STATES STRATEGY IN THE INDIAN OCEAN

In retrospect, it does seem that the United States had contingency plans for military bases in the Indian Ocean since the Kennedy-Johnson era (Houbert, 1981: 83-84). The creation of the BIOT by Britain in 1965 was only the first step. By leasing Diego Garcia for 50 years the following year, the United States had opted for a strategic articulation point located midway between the Strait of Malacca and the Cape of Good Hope, between northwest Australia and the Horn of Africa. The subsequent militarization of Diego Garcia was thus ominously inherent in its very geographical location.

There were other contributing factors. The geological structure of the atoll, "with no adequate ports" and where "accosting could be dangerous," made it an impregnable platform from which aeronaval operations could be confidently carried out (Toussaint, 1972: 16-20). Its political status was in transition—Diego Garcia was only one of some 30 atolls that were "dependencies" of a small island nation, Mauritius, situated some 1200 miles to the south and itself a colony hesitatingly on the way to a precarious independence, with Britain holding the upper hand (Houbert, 1981: 84).

As it turned out, Britain had no difficulty in detaching it to suit American military purposes, with a little help from its favorite prime minister. The fact that there is practically no winter in the Chagos, with an almost constant 30-degree (celsius) temperature throughout the year hardly varying between night and day, with cyclones being almost unknown and rainstorms rare, was another advantage for the United States (Toussaint, 1972: 20). Moreover, Diego Garcia was tiny. It may have been independent in splendid isolation before the Europeans came, but recorded history had always categorized it as a dependency, and it could not seriously pretend to any form of viable independence in the modern world. Besides, it had only a handful of inhabitants who could be easily waylaid without any powerful friends raising hell and venting embarrassing denunciations in the outside world (McDowell, 1981). Their only support could have come from Mauritius but the Mauritian government chose to remain silent, deciding to speak out only when it was too late, and that too, in a revealingly half-hearted manner (Jeune Afrique, 1980). In any case, it was up to Britain to do the dirty job of detaching and emptying Diego Garcia—and Britain did it with gusto, even emptying in the process most of the Chagos archipelago (Ellsworth-Jones, 1976). The United States only moved in as an innocent tenant and heroic defender of the free world.

The choice of a tiny, population-free island enjoying the status of an absolute and exclusive property of the West, with no political claims against it, as the possible future lynchpin of Western military strategy in the Indian Ocean on the other hand reflects deep concerns in the minds of U.S. contingency planners of the 1960s about the future stability of friendship ties as existed then with imperial Iran and Ethiopia as well as with racist South Africa and fascist and colonialist Portugal in Mozambique (Larus, 1982: 44-45). These, and Pakistan as a member of CENTO, were then the real allies of the United States in the Indian Ocean area. The winds of change were blowing, and even in "friendly" new states like Kenya and the Malagasy Republic nationalist sentiments were too intense to accommodate installation of American military bases. Since these winds of change were blowing against Western colonialism and domination, areas of opportunity were opening up for the USSR and China, not for the United States (Cadoux, 1974). The Stars and Stripes would therefore have to be planted in a territory free of potential political embarrassments, where the United States would not have to be answerable to anybody—the "errors" of the Canal Zone in Panama and of the Guantanamo naval base in Cuba would be avoided—and Diego Garcia offered itself fatally to anyone who could read a map at the Pentagon.

The United States, though it obtained Diego Garcia in 1965, announced only in 1974 that it had decided to "extend" its "military facilities" on the island (The Nation, 1974). Developments on two fronts during the intervening 8-year hiatus had silently sealed the fate of the islanders: Britain had effectively asphyxiated the coconut oil and copra economy of Diego Garcia, as a pretext for the "evacuation" of the islanders—thereby "honoring" the latter part of its deal with the United States; but more important, while the Nixon-Kissinger team had taken over from Johnson, world political changes had confirmed the choice of the Diego Garcia plan, in the minds of Washington strategists, as the best location for the United States in the Indian Ocean and had forced it from the back burner into the forefront of U.S. political decision making. Besides, a second Anglo-

American Agreement concluded on October 24, 1972 "specifically dedicated Diego Garcia to their joint military use" (Larus, 1982: 46).

The islanders began arriving in Mauritius in 1971 but, as *The Nation*
wrote in an editorial entitled "Island of Shame" in October 1975, "the
fate of the Diego Garcians was largely hidden" until September 1975,
when the *Washington Post* and the *Manchester Guardian* broke the story,
relying both on the tough reporting by David B. Ottaway from Mauritius.
The Nation added that as early as 1972, "Robert B. Semple, Jr., reported
in the *New York Times*" that Diego Garcia's population "consisted almost
entirely of American naval personnel," but apparently nobody then asked
to know if the island had been inhabited and, if yes, what had happened to
this population. Ottaway wrote that the islanders "were forcibly removed
before 1972 to make way for a controversial American naval base there"
and that he found them "living in abject poverty" in Mauritius (*The
Nation*, 1975).

When it leased out Diego Garcia to the United States, Britain took over
direct control of the economy of the Chagos group, while the Seychellian
outlying dependencies of the Aldabras, the Desroches islands (in the
Amirantes group) and the Farquhar islands, also forming part of the BIOT
since the previous year, continued to be administered by the British
governor of the Seychelles, and their fishing, coconut, and guano resources
continued to be exploited by private companies (Cadoux, 1974: 26). Until
then, the lucrative coconut oil and copra economy of the Chagos had been
controlled by Chagos Agalega Limited, a private company that had
bought out Diego Limited in 1962, which itself had replaced in 1941 the
Société huilière de Diego et Peros, the private firm that had been running
the economy of these "oil islands" since 1883 (Toussaint, 1972: 272-273).
What the Chagos revenues of Chagos Agalega Limited were in 1966, when
direct British control of the economy came into effect, is a secret shared
only by Britain and the owners of the Seychellian company. Another such
secret is the compensation paid by Britain to the company itself. The data
probably lie on the dusty shelves of the archives of the Government of
Mauritius in Port-Louis, but Mauritian public opinion was superficially
content in the knowledge that the Chagos (together with Agalega, Saint-
Brandon, the Cargados, and Rodrigues) were "dependencies as the
speaker of the Mauritius Broadcasting Corporation unfailingly reminded
listeners on its special Sunday radio broadcasts. This seems to have been
sufficient in lulling Mauritians into showing little or no interest in the
actual social and economic realities of the oil islands.

An October 1975 editorial of *The Nation* noted, however, that in 1968,
"evidently on London's orders, copra production was allowed to deteri-
orate" on Diego Garcia, adding that

by 1971, work had ceased, the island's economic infrastructure [was] ruined, the Diego Garcians [were] moved to Mauritius, 1,174 miles away. . . . Following up Ottaway's work, Bernard D. Nossiter wrote in the *Washington Post,* from London, that the British government admitted that its closing down of Diego Garcia's copra production facilities led to the evacuation, though, he said, the government preferred not to describe its measures as forced.

Will Ellsworth-Jones of the *London Sunday Times,* who had reported from Mauritius in 1975 on the plight of the deported Diego Garcians, returned in June 1976 and wrote that "a year later, the poverty, squalor and neglect go on." His most dramatic discovery, however, was that deportees continued to come not only from Diego Garcia but from the adjoining islands of Peros Banhos and Solomon as well. Quoting a fisherman who said he had visited Peros Banhos illegally in 1975, he wrote that "while American servicemen had moved on to Diego Garcia, with loud pop music and all, there still stood on the adjoining islands the emptied homes, furniture and cooking oils still in place, a pitiful reminder of what the islanders lost when Britain ordered them out."

The U.S. government, after maintaining officially that the islands were uninhabited, later said that the plight of the islanders was strictly a matter between Britain and Mauritius. But as public outrage mounted against Britain, the United States became implicated. As Simon Winchester of the *Guardian* wrote from Washington, quoting naval sources, the United States gave Britain a $10-million discount on missiles and missile parts in return for emptying Diego Garcia of its residents. Quoting Capitol Hill sources, he added that the arrangement was "probably not completed at Cabinet level but at senior levels in the two Defense Departments."

According to *The Nation,* Democratic senator Gary Hart said he had details on the transaction but could not release them because of their confidential classification. He asked for an investigation, and Democratic senators John Culver and Edward Kennedy cosponsored a resolution demanding a history of American involvement in the deportation. Yet nothing has come of this initiative. *The Nation* (1975) editorial concluded that

the removal of the Diego Garcians from their homeland smacks of an international arrogance that raises profound questions about the nature of Anglo-American foreign policy. The secrecy and deception surrounding the evacuation once again provokes concern about other acts now unknown. The people of Diego Garcia deserve full compensation and, if they wish, return to their homes. The age of colonialism is supposed to be over.

The evacuation of the Diego Garcians, on the other hand, took on an increasing urgency for U.S. strategy as world events unfolded rapidly over these years. Ironically enough, the single most decisive development was taking place outside the Indian Ocean area, in Indochina. Ever since Eugene McCarthy had defeated Lyndon Johnson in that fateful New Hampshire primary of February 1968, Americans were haunted by the suicidal dangers of engaging their fighting men in massive numbers on any land mass anywhere around the globe (SRB, 1981-1982). Strategists for the Nixon-Kissinger team, knowing that the Vietnam War could not be won, were concentrating their efforts on peace with honor, which meant how best to disengage from Indochina and save Uncle Sam's face at the same time.

But they were also putting in place U.S. strategy "after Indochina," and, as far as the Indian Ocean was concerned, the Diego Garcia contingency plan appeared to be the best possible one: From a secure base in the middle of the Indian Ocean, the United States could control events in the Middle East, in the Gulf area, on the South Asian subcontinent, on the Eastern flank of Africa, in the Cape of Good Hope area, and in the Malaysia-Indonesia-Australia sector, where the waters of the Indian and Pacific oceans mingle (Prats, 1974: 127).

The next most important event of these intervening years was undoubtedly the Indo-Pakistani War of 1970-1971, which led to the independence of Bangladesh. India had intervened in Bangladesh after signing a long-term Friendship and Cooperation Treaty with the Soviet Union, and the U.S. navy took seven days to reach the Bay of Bengal—too late to be of any help to Pakistan (Prats, 1974: 126). Besides, one wonders whether the Americans ever seriously contemplated engaging their troops on the South Asian mainland at a time when their one major preoccupation was to extricate themselves from Vietnam.

The lesson American strategists drew from this experience was twofold: the Diego Garcia option had to be exercised full steam and some kind of Rapid Deployment Force (RDF) had to be set up on the atoll (SRB, 1981-1982: 48-51). Such a force could not only be deployed rapidly from a short distance, as its name implies, but it could also be withdrawn rapidly to its oceanic fortress, thereby avoiding for the United States the wasteful embarrassment of getting bogged down in a Vietnam-like quagmire.

The Somali Revolution of 1969, the emergence of the People's Democratic Republic of Yemen and the rise of the MMM in Mauritius that same year, the return of the Bandaranaike government to power in Sri Lanka in 1970, followed by the Jathika Vimukthi Peramuna (JVP-National Liberation Front) uprising of 1971, the Malagasy Revolution of 1972, the Arab-Israeli War of 1973, and the Ethiopian Revolution of 1974 were further events perceived as setbacks from Washington, where the newly acquired Soviet naval facilities of Berbara and Kismanya, in Somalia; of Hodeida and Socotra, in South Yemen; of Chittagong and Vizhakapatnam, in the Bay of Bengal; and of Tamatave, in Madagascar, loomed as so many threats that were actively exaggerated by Pentagon and Navy lobbyists in order to get congressional approval for the reinforcement and extension of the Diego Garcia facilities (Prats, 1974: 123-124).

In subsequent years, the fall of the Portuguese African empire, the entry of India into the nuclear club, the independence of the truncated Comoros and the Seychelles followed respectively by the left-leaning coups d'état of Ali Soilih and France-Albert Rene, the British military withdrawal from Singapore, the independence of Djibouti, the Soweto uprising in South Africa, the fall of the Pahlevi dynasty in Iran, and the Soviet invasion of Afghanistan not only brought about the groundswell of American conservatism that landed the Reagan-Haig-Weinberger team into the White House in 1980, but also pushed the Diego Garcia plan, conceived in relative obscurity in the 1960s, into the forefront of U.S. anti-Soviet strategy in the Persian Gulf (McDowell, 1981).

The Diego Garcia plan has indeed come a long way from the uphill struggle it faced in Congress in the early 1970s. After persistent lobbying, the Pentagon obtained in August 1974 the approval of the Senate Armed Forces Committee for the extension of the naval facilities at the base. In July 1975, with Gerald Ford filling in for Richard Nixon at the White House, Congress authorized credits to the tune of $29 million for this purpose (Prats, 1974: 127). By then, the Chagos had been emptied of their population "abject islanders uprooted in a game of strategic chess," as the *National Geographic* put it in an October 1981 issue with the cover story entitled "Crosscurrents Sweep the Indian Ocean." The story, researched by Bart McDowell and Steve Raymer, makes the point that "for reports on Diego Garcia, one must rely on congressional hearings, photographs, old maps and hearsay" and that "British landlords have allowed no journalists ashore since 1977."

Jimmy Carter, whose administration squarely addressed the Rapid Deployment Force (RDF) issue as the main component of U.S. strategy after Indochina, determined the fate of Diego Garcia when he spelled out the so-called Carter Doctrine, after the Soviet invasion of Afghanistan: "Any external threat on the Persian Gulf region would be considered a threat to the national security of the United States and would be met as such" (SRB, 1981-1982: 49). Ronald Reagan has further reinforced it by stating, in November 1981, that the United States "would never allow Saudi Arabia to become another Iran," meaning that American forces would intervene there even if the threat came, not from without, but from within (AFP and AP, November 1981). Since the US embargo against Iran, following the hostage taking at the U.S. Embassy in Tehran, Diego Garcia has become the pivot of U.S. naval operations in the region, and the pressure has been kept up as the Soviet military presence in Afghanistan prolongs itself.

Thus it was that in March 1981, Deputy Defense Secretary Frank C. Carlucci could announce without provoking much criticism, in testimony before a Senate panel, that the Reagan administration had nearly doubled to $4 billion the funding request for the Rapid Deployment Joint Task Force (RDJTF), "tailored for continued U.S. access to the Persian Gulf area," which provides 40 percent of the free world's oil, without which "the interrelated economies of the West cannot survive." He went on to outline the following "tracks" along which U.S. defense planning for the region was proceeding:

- a U.S. military presence, largely naval, consisting of one or two carrier battle groups and an afloat marine presence part of the time, coupled with frequent army and air force exercises;

- creation and deployment of the RDJTF, a headquarters, and planning organization;

- diplomatic efforts to gain access to facilities on the Indian Ocean littoral and a program to improve these facilities, including a systematic buildup of facilities on Diego Garcia;

- a program of prepositioning of equipment, together with sea and airlift capabilities, to shorten deployment time of U.S. forces.

It is clear we must have a presence in the region, and capability to reinforce in the region, if we are not to be presented with the fait accompli of Soviet military domination over the Strait of Hormuz and the shipment of oil. If we fail to deter such an occurence, the political-military shape of the world would change totally.

Thus said Deputy Secretary Carlucci, who continued:

> We should have substantial advanced warning of any large-scale Soviet agression in the Gulf region. The elements of time and distance are crucial to both sides. It is over 2,500 kilometres from the Trans-Caucasus to the Strait of Hormuz—over mountainous terrain with few roads and many bridges. Our air power could be used for interdiction and our RDF land forces could confront such a Soviet attack. This kind of invasion would not be a blitzkrieg, but rather a land war fought laboriously through narrow defiles, mountain pass after mountain pass.

After explaining how the RDF, while deterring the Soviets from "executing a lightning-like thrust in the Gulf region," would give time to "mass and employ our naval forces, with their inherent flexibility, at places of our choosing," he explained that the RDF would be integrated "into broader military options" and that the RDJTF "must be viewed as an evolving organization." He recalled that the RDJTF was created in October 1979 "as a separate subordinate element under the US Readiness Command (Redcom) at MacDill Air Force Base," with a mission "to conduct predeployment planning and training for non-NATO contingencies." It was to be under the National Command Authority (NCA) through the Joint Chiefs of Staff, but "with the increasing threat in South-West Asia, the mission of the RDJTF was narrowed to focus on planning and operations in that area alone."

Carlucci then went on to discuss the relative merits of various command structure alternatives for the RDJTF, including the creation of a totally new unified command, independent of U.S. command for Europe, the Atlantic, and the Pacific, with "the commander located in the Persian Gulf area, probably on a command ship." And he concluded by reminding the senators that "our secure, continued access to Gulf oil is absolutely vital" and that the RDF, "a credible instrument of force for that objective . . . merits our full support," adding: "Our security demands it" (Carlucci, 1981).

What was happening in fact was the emergence of a new U.S. inspired strategic alliance, pivoted on Diego Garcia, for the whole Indian Ocean area, where U.S. investments in 1975 were estimated at $10 billion (Prats, 1974: 127), where most of the world's oil supplies originated, and where lucrative markets for major arms deals and Western technology were waiting to be tapped (SRB, 1981-1982).

While he was supreme allied commander of NATO, General Alexander Haig had often complained publicly about the legal fetters that prevented the Atlantic Alliance from intervening in peripheral theaters where the Soviet Union was extending its influence, namely Africa, the Middle East, Asia, Latin and Central America, and the Caribbean. Since NATO would not overtly and officially become the policeman of the world, the United States came up with the expanded version of the Diego Garcia option, cheered on by British Prime Minister Margaret Thatcher who, on a visit to Washington in February 1981, announced that Britain was prepared to join "a rapid-deployment, multinational force to protect the Gulf." She was immediately accused of "bellicose demagogy" by the British Opposition (Reuter, AFP, March 2, 1981).

Three days after Deputy Secretary Carlucci's testimony, William H. Durham, U.S. International Communications Agency (USICA) security affairs correspondent, quoting U.S. defense officials, wrote that "the United States had begun a five-year project to improve military facilities in Egypt, Oman, Kenya, Somalia, and on the Indian Ocean island of Diego Garcia." Defense Secretary Caspar Weinberger, he said, reviewed the plan shortly after taking charge of the Pentagon, and then enlarged it as part of the Reagan defense plan for the coming five years. Among the projects listed by Durham are the improvement of port and military facilities at Ras Banas, on the Egyptian side of the Red Sea, opposite a key oil terminal in Saudi Arabia ($106.4 million); reconstruction of an old British airfield on the island of Masirah, off Oman's coast ($75 million); enlargement of the Omani airfield at Seeb and Thumrait, as well as improvement of the Omani ports of Mutrah and Salalah; repair of oil facilities at the Somali port of Berbera ($24 million), improved in the early 1970s by the Soviets who were then forced out in 1977; improvement of the Berbera airfield, on the Gulf of Aden, and use by U.S. air and naval forces of the port and airfield of the Somali capital of Mogadishu; improvement of the Kenyan port of Mombasa ($26 million) and use of Kenyan airfields at Embakasi and Nanyuki; and finally, "the Indian Ocean island of Diego Garcia is scheduled for $237.7 million in improvements . . . a large part of it going into improving runways on the airfield so that it can handle large transport and cargo aircraft such as C-141s and C-5s."

All of these improvement projects are geared to one single purpose: providing oil storage tanks and shelters for U.S. naval supplies and accommodating surveillance planes, jet fighters, and military transport aircraft as well as staging areas for ground troops that might be deployed elsewhere in the Persian Gulf area. U.S. defense officials did say, however, that "under the agreements, all improvements made to the various military facilities at U.S. expense will become the property of the host countries"—no doubt a new Reaganomical approach to development aid to the Third World (Durham, 1981).

To top it all off, Richard Burt, director of the Bureau of Politico-Military Affairs of the State Department, told Marie Koenig, USICA diplomatic correspondant, on March 23, 1981, that while the Reagan administration, in increasing U.S. military construction and presence in the Persian Gulf area, aimed at demonstrating that "it pays to be America's friend," he also stressed that "in moving further to strengthen our capabilities in the region . . . we will be sensitive to the political problems that a permanent presence would entail." He went on to underline State Secretary Haig's call for a strategic consensus to counter the Soviet Union from Pakistan to Egypt, and including Saudi Arabia, Israel, and Turkey, but emphasized: "We are not seeking a formal NATO role," although "the Western Allies' stake in the region is at least as great as our own." He concluded by "calling on Western Allies to increase their economic support to friendly countries in Southwest Asia and the Eastern Mediterranean" (Koenig, 1981).

Since then, the U.S.-Pakistani and U.S.-Israeli "strategic" alliances have been formalized, to the tune of billions of dollars worth of military aid. The assassination of Anwar Sadat has precipitated the sale of AWACS to Saudi Arabia and the joint U.S.-British Bright Star military maneuvers in the Egyptian desert and from Bab-al-Mandab to the Strait of Hormuz. In early February 1982, Defense Secretary Caspar Weinberger undertook a nine-day tour of the Persian Gulf and Jordan during which he announced the establishment of a Joint Saudi-U.S. Military Commission "to promote military cooperation," an objective the United States had been trying to achieve since 1974 (UPI, AFP, Reuter, February 9, 1982).

The militarization of Diego Garcia appears absolutely irreversible against such a backdrop. The dispossessed Ilois community seems condemned to oblivion.

THE POLITICS OF THE DIEGO GARCIA ISSUE

This is only a superficial impression, however, because the issue had been kept alive from three quarters, in spite of the Mauritian government's thunderous silence: the MMM opposition within Mauritius itself, neighboring governments from Africa to Asia who are interested in seeing the Indian Ocean become a nuclear-free zone, and the growing antinuclear movement within the British Labor Party.

The issue was officially raised for the first time at the United Nations in October 1980 when Prime Minister Seewoosagur Ramgoolam, addressing the 35th General Assembly, deplored the rapid and intensifying militarization of the Indian Ocean, which "has gradually expanded beyond its own waters" and "is now linked to the States of South-East Asia . . . and to the most vital features of the Middle East." Since it is the only mention of the Diego Garcia issue by Mauritius on record at the United Nations—15 years after cession of the Chagos, 12 years after Mauritian independence and 10 years after the deportation of the Ilois community—the single paragraph in Ramgoolam's speech deserves to be quoted *in extenso:*

> It is necessary for me to emphasize that Mauritius, being in the middle of the Indian Ocean, has already at the last meeting of the Organization of African Unity reaffirmed its claim on Diego Garcia and the Prime Minister of Great Britain in a parliamentary statement has made it known that it will revert to Mauritius when it is no more required for global defence of the West. Our sovereignty having been accepted, we should go farther than that and disband the British Indian Ocean Territory and allow Mauritius to come into its natural heritage as before its independence. The United States should make arrangements directly with Mauritius for its continued use for defence purposes. And then there are the inhabitants of Diego Garcia who are domiciled in Mauritius and for whom better arrangements should be made. It must be the duty of both the United States and Great Britain to discuss with the Mauritius Government how best to give satisfaction to all concerned and at the same time provide better prospects to the islanders [Ramgoolam, 1980].

The following day, however, Sir Anthony Parsons, Britain's ambassador to the United Nations, contradicted Ramgoolam in the following terms: "I wish to make it clear that the United Kingdom has sovereignty over Diego Garcia and has not accepted that the island is under the sovereignty of Mauritius," adding that the government of Mrs. Thatcher had made no firm promises to return the atoll but had only announced that it would be willing to consider ceding sovereignty to Mauritius in the event that Diego Garcia was no longer needed for Anglo-American defense purposes (Larus, 1982: 49).

The 17th OAU summit, meeting in Freetown in July 1980, had indeed adopted a resolution demanding that "Diego Garcia be unconditionally returned to Mauritius and that its peaceful character be maintained," since it "was not ceded to Britain for military purposes" and since its "militarization is a threat to Africa, and to the Indian Ocean as a zone of peace" (UN General Assembly, 1980). It seems, however, that this resolution was adopted not so much at the urging of Mauritius but rather under the impetus of some other African governments deeply concerned with the militarization issue. At the 35th Council of Ministers of the OAU immediately preceding the 17th summit, two similar resolutions were adopted, one reaffirming "the sovereignty of the Federal Islamic Republic of the Comoros over the island of Mayotte" and the other, with "reservations expressed" by Mauritius and the Comoros, among others, reaffirming that "the Glorious, Juan de Nova, Europa and Bassas da India constitute an integral part of the Democratic Republic of Madagascar" (UN General Assembly, 1980).

Since the UN General Assembly adopted, on December 16, 1971, a declaration making the Indian Ocean a "zone of peace," the OAU, the Non-Aligned Movement, and various other forums have pushed further by demanding that the Indian Ocean be made a nuclear-free zone. One resolution adopted at the 35th Council of Ministers of the OAU recalled that the 6th Non-Aligned Summit in Havana in September 1979 had adopted such a resolution and that the UN General Assembly (1980) had decided in 1980 to convene a meeting on the Indian Ocean in 1981. The Special UN Committee on the Indian Ocean, totaling no less than 46 member states, was into its 162nd meeting on August 25, 1981, and still striving toward a "harmonization of views" over the timing of a UN Conference on the Indian Ocean (UN General Assembly, 1981b).

Sri Lanka, one of the first to protest extension of the Diego Garcia military facilities when the decision was announced by Britain on December 15, 1970, was the country that submitted the Zone of Peace resolution to the UN General Assembly the following year (Prats, 1974: 131). Forty-nine countries chose to abstain. Among them were the two superpowers, who said they preferred bilateral negotiations (Langelier, 1981). A ministerial meeting of the Organization of Solidarity of Afro-Asian Peoples scheduled for 1981 in Colombo never materialized (Afrique-Asie, 1981: 8).

India, which sees itself as the main actor in the region, also protested the 1970 decision on Diego Garcia and has been most active on this issue, but with a difference. Accusing the United States of having triggered the arms race in the Indian Ocean by commissioning the North West Cape Very Low Frequency Communications station, in Australia, in the mid-1960s, India argues that the Soviet naval presence is "reactive" and "defensive" (Seth, 1975: 646-649). Rejecting the "power vacuum theory" as "colonialism in another garb," India, member of the nuclear club since 1975, in the name of a new "assertive nationalism," has proposed that the coastal states themselves police the Indian Ocean, within the eventual framework of a "common market"—a modified version of the Brezhnev Plan calling for military protection of the Asian coastline through an alliance centered on India (Prats, 1974: 132).

America's Indian Ocean strategy follows a nineteenth-century gunboat policy that ignores India, External Affairs Secretary Eric Goncalves told American reporters in Delhi on the eve of a visit to Washington in April 1981. "We are prepared to be as pro-Western as you will permit us to be, but every time we try to make an opening, you kick us in the teeth. It's a bit difficult," he said, describing India as "the only stable, basically strong country in the region" (AP, April 12, 1981). In February 1982, the Indian Ministry of Foreign Affairs made public a report of its own experts saying that the USSR had strengthened its naval presence in the Indian Ocean (34 to 36 vessels with major bases at Dakhla, in Ethiopia, and Aden, and facilities at Da Nang and Cam Ranh, in Vietnam), although the U.S. war fleet in the region was still the most important one (AFP, February 6, 1982).

Australia, New Zealand, Malaysia, and Indonesia protested when the 1974 Anglo-American Agreement on Diego Garcia was announced. At the 21st Commonwealth Parliamentary Conference, held in Delhi in 1975, a resolution was adopted, after heated debate and in spite of British objections, calling for the dismantling of the military installations on Diego Garcia (Prats, 1974: 131).

Moves are afoot to make the South Pacific a nuclear-free zone as well, with the Opposition Labour Parties of Australia and New Zealand in the forefront. Australian Labour leader Bill Hayden has said that if he became prime minister after the 1983 elections, he would ban U.S. nuclear-armed ships from Australian ports. "That would make the maintenance of the ANZUS Treaty as we know it of the greatest difficulty and it is difficult to see how we could survive," Australian Foreign Minister Tony Street commented at the June 1982 council meeting of the ANZUS—Australia, New Zealand, United States—Pact in Canberra (Reuter, June 21, 1982).

The pro-Western Ramgoolam government in Mauritius had decided, back in 1965, not to rock the boat of Western global defense planning in the Indian Ocean. In return, Britain has signed an Agreement on Mutual

Defense and Assistance committing itself to look after the island's "internal and external security" after independence (Houbert, 1981: 86). In congratulating U.S. President-elect Ronald Reagan in November 1980, Ramgoolam offered his government's "close cooperation" in the global strategy for "the defense of the Western world" and for "the reestablishment of a healthier situation in the Indian Ocean" (AFP, November 7, 1980), a pledge that he verbally renewed in the White House rose garden while visiting President Reagan in October 1981.

As far as the deportation of the Diego Garcians was concerned, the largely Indian-based Ramgoolam government no doubt counted on anti-African feeling among the majority Indian (Hindu and Muslim) community of Mauritus to keep the issue dormant since the Ilois community of deportees would be assimilated to the "creoles," a term that, in Mauritian parlance, denotes the descendents of mainly African slaves who to this day remain at the very bottom of the island's racial power pyramid (Favoreu, 1970: 18).

The Ilois deportees, were, however, taken under the protection of the Organisation Fraternelle (OF), a church-based movement led by a handful of Catholic priests of African origin (Afrique-Asie, 1981: 18). This movement is dedicated to uplifting the minority creole community, packed in fishing villages and urban slums and generally left in the lurch with the advent of universal adult suffrage after having been politically manipulated by the French plantocracy before 1959 (Durand and Durand, 1975: 121-131). Though anti-marxist, the OF is quite close to the opposition Mauritian Militant Movement (MMM) because of the latter's class-based assault against racial politics in Mauritius (Durand and Durand, 1975: 147-195).

Throughout the 1970s, the OF and the MMM thus organized public campaigns against the inhuman treatment of the Ilois deportees, the MMM using the occasion to attack Ramgoolam's betrayal of Mauritian sovereignty and the general subservience of his foreign policy to imperialist interests. After the 1976 general elections, when it became the most widely supported political party on the island (though it was effectively kept out of power through yet another coalition between Ramgoolam's Labour party and ex-Foreign Minister Gaëtan Duval's right-wing PMSD), the MMM opposition has been actively pursuing the demilitarization of Diego Garcia and the denuclearization of the Indian Ocean with the left-wing governments of Mozambique, the Malagasy Republic, and the Seychelles (AP, June 15, 1980).

The OF campaign was largely responsible for the belated doubling of compensation ($3 million) decided by Britain in 1979 for the deported Diego Garcians. The MMM campaign for the return of Diego Garcia to

Mauritius, on the other hand, gained the natural support of the various forums already constituted on the demilitarization and denuclearization issues since the early 1970s. The participants, from Africa, Asia, Australia, and New Zealand, not wanting to see the Indian Ocean become yet another theater for superpower rivalry, indeed seem to have been thwarted in their campaign by the very "default" of the Ramgoolam government and the refusal of Mauritius, the one legal claimant to sovereignty over Diego Garcia, to join in the struggle.

As for the Soviet bloc, it has been pushing, in spite of the Vietnamese occupation of Kampuchea and the Soviet occupation of Afghanistan, and in spite of expressed Soviet preference for bilateral negotiations, for international debate on the Indian Ocean demilitarization issue within the Non-Aligned Movement. The USSR favors strengthening peace in the Indian Ocean because it wants to avoid a new strategic threat to its security from the south and to secure the maritime routes linking Soviet Europe to the Soviet Far East, said Lev Mendelevitch, chief Soviet delegate to the UN Special Committee on the Indian Ocean in March 1981 (AFP, March 10, 1981).

Theodore Wilkinson, chief U.S. delegate, told a special meeting of the Committee in 1979 that "America cannot support banning nuclear weapons from war ships," at least not "until our common objective of eliminating all nuclear arms from the face of the earth has been achieved" (AP, March 7, 1979). As far as the Soviet-U.S. bilateral talks are concerned, Paul Warnke, then director of the U.S. Arms and Disarmament Agency, said in Moscow in June 1980: "When mutual interests are at stake, chances are good that concrete results can be attained."

Experts interpreted these cryptic words to mean that the bilateral talks were primarily aimed at maintaining in the Indian Ocean the same conditions of global balance that form the basis of détente elsewhere. President Carter was quoted as saying that the objective of the talks was "to preserve the status quo and to avoid any reinforcement of military potential in the region" (AFP, July 10, 1980). Since then, the Reagan administration has considerably reduced all bilateral contacts with the Soviet Union and substantially reinforced U.S. military potential there.

But Washington's uneasiness over the future of Diego Garcia has been further heightened by the increasing radicalization of the British Labour party. Following the failed U.S. rescue mission for the Tehran hostages, in April 1980, Labour MPs pressed Prime Minister Thatcher in the Commons to confirm or deny Diego Garcia's use as a staging site in light of a 1976 Anglo-American Agreement requiring the United States to consult with Britain whenever the facilities are to be used in circumstances other than "normal." "I cannot get myself into a position where I have to confirm or deny movements through allied bases," Mrs. Thatcher answered in what is described as "a blocking reply."

Amid increasing concern over the danger of Britain being drawn by U.S. strategic interests into "an intervention at the wrong time, in the wrong place and on the wrong side," as Labour leader Michael Foot put it in March 1981 (Reuter, March 2, 1981), and indeed into a world war or even into a nuclear war, the Labour party adopted at its 1980 Blackpool meeting a resolution calling on the party to include in its Manifesto a "firm commitment opposing participation in any defense policy based on use or threatened use of nuclear weapons" and "a pledge to close all nuclear bases, British or American, in Britain or in British waters." This last phrase has raised concern in Washington, which considers Britain as the landlord of Diego Garcia and which would see the eventual election of Labour to power in London as a potential danger to its strategic plans in the Indian Ocean (Larus, 1982: 50-53).

The net result has been a dramatic internationalization of the Diego Garcia issue, "Dodge City," as U.S. pilots have nicknamed the atoll in a burst of Far West nostalgia, not having lived up to its original billing, as the October 1981 *National Geographic* survey put it, that "no population meant no problem." The Ramgoolam government itself, faced with growing opposition at home over the handling of the issue and threatened with defeat at the forthcoming general elections, was forced by circumstances to become more pressing on the subject in spite of the fact that Port-Louis was being viewed as the new focus of moderation in the southern Indian Ocean after the fall of Philibert Tsiranana in Madagascar (Cadoux, 1974: 57).

The Ramgoolam government also joined the fray, albeit in its own moderate manner, in the light of other more recent developments as well. Britain, in granting independence to the unwilling James Mancham government in 1976, not only restored the territorial integrity of the Seychelles by returning the islands of Aldabra, Desroches, and Farquhar it had detached in 1965 to form the BIOT; it also placed under Seychelles jurisdiction responsibility for the fate of a major U.S. Air Force satellite tracking station perched on a hilltop above Victoria, and the remaining islands of the Chagos Archipelago, minus Diego Garcia, detached originally from Mauritius, thereby driving a territorial wedge between Victoria and Port-Louis.

In demanding the return of Diego Garcia to Mauritian sovereignty in his 1981 speech before the UN General Assembly, the foreign minister of the "progressive" Seychelles government significantly omitted any mention of the rest of the Chagos archipelago (UN General Assembly, 1981c). Moreover, the emergence of the Law of the Sea debate in the 1970s brought home to the Mauritian government, struggling to free the overpopulated island from the fetters of its one-crop sugar cane economy (Durban, 1981), the unsuspected importance of underwater mineral resources, including the possibility of oil deposits, in the vast oceanic area occupied by the Chagos archipelago.

The present position of the Ramgoolam government on the Diego Garcia question was explained by UN Ambassador Radha Ramphul in an interview in New York in October 1981. Mauritius, he said, as a non-aligned nation, cannot tolerate military bases by any of the superpower blocs on any part of its territory, and Diego Garcia is very much part of Mauritian territory. But as a small nation, Mauritius cannot, on the other hand, declare war on the United States to obtain evacuation of the atoll.

So the Ramgoolam government has decided, since the 50-year U.S. lease of Diego Garcia has already run 16 years, to concentrate its efforts over the remaining 34 years, "with our friends in the OAU and the Non-Aligned Movement," on obtaining payment of U.S. rent money directly to Mauritius and ultimate recognition by both the United States and the United Kingdom of Mauritian sovereignty over Diego Garcia. It goes without saying, added Ambassador Ramphul emphatically, that the lease will not be renewed on expiration in the year 2015.

The previous month, an Anglo-American consortium, Raymond Brown and Root Mowlem, and the Mauritius Builders' Association, had signed a million-dollar contract providing for military and residential construction on Diego Garcia. The signing ceremony took place in the Port-Louis offices of Harold Walter, minister of Foreign Affairs, Tourism and Emigration, in the presence of U.S. Ambassador Robert Gordon (Advance, 1981). The deal calls for the employment of some 270 Mauritian construction workers on the Diego Garcia construction project and the purchase of some construction material from Mauritius, a practice very much in line with the new Reaganomical approach to development aid.

According to Ambassador Ramphul, this was a "clever ploy" by Mauritius "to establish its nationals for the first time on Diego soil"—as if the Ilois community, often claimed by Britain and the United States to have been "migrant workers," who had been living there for generations before their deportation, had never been Mauritian nationals. He added with a hint of self-satisfaction that on expiration of the lease all installations on Diego Garcia would revert to Mauritian ownership.

This being, in a nutshell, the current Mauritian policy on Diego Garcia, pieced together in response to growing pressure from within (the MMM opposition) and from without (progressive neighbors, the Non-Aligned Movement, and the OAU), one can assume that the Mauritian government still wishes to dampen the issue. Such a policy contains no element whatsoever that might create fears in Washington or in NATO circles. Such would indeed be the case if Mauritius were a one-party dictatorship, but this is far from being the case (Favoreu, 1970: 30-35). The fact that it is a vigorous, pluralistic society with electoral politics being very much alive throughout the island is giving nightmares to the planners at the Pentagon.

The situation is simple enough: Ramgoolam's Labour party, which lost to the MMM in the 1976 general elections but managed to hold on to power thanks to a new coalition with Gaëtan Duval's third-place PMSD, faced an uphill struggle on the road to the general elections of June 11, 1982. Its slim hopes of rebirth and rejuvenation were dashed when a group of "Young Turks," tired of playing dissident backbenchers, left the Labour party to form the Mauritian Socialist party (MSP). Its chances of re-election dwindled further when the mainly Hindu MSP formed an alliance with the leftist MMM, thereby threatening Labour with a massive defeat at the polls. The irony is that this exercise in democracy in a remote corner of the globe also threatens the U.S. strategy of defending free world interests in the Indian Ocean because the election of an MMM-MSP alliance to power in Port-Louis will definitely upset the Diego Garcia applecart, apart from possibly creating opportunities for Soviet influence in Maritius.

This is how the Diego Garcia tide, launched in secrecy 17 years earlier, could engulf Mauritius itself. Feverish movements are already afoot. One plot came to light after Senator Barry Goldwater, chairman of the House Select Committee on Intelligence, sent President Reagan a letter in early August 1981 protesting assassination attempts planned by the CIA against Libyan strongman Muammar Qaddafi. The State Department admitted CIA assassination plans existed but denied they were directed against Libya, saying instead that the target was Mauritania.

The confusion between Mauritania and Mauritius being a familiar one, the MMM immediately launched enquiries and soon enough learned that the assassination plot was indeed targeted at Paul Berenger, secretary-general of the MMM (South, 1981). By mid-August, the *Wall Street Journal*, the *Washington Post*, the *Observer*, and the *Guardian* confirmed that the plans concerned Mauritius, adding however that the CIA did not plan any assassinations but was simply engaged in "a quiet attempt to funnel money to the Mauritian government in order to counter Libyan aid to the opposition" (Afrique-Asie, 1981: 14-15).

The Libyan connection, which the Ramgoolam government has itself lucratively exploited in return for the teaching of Arabic as an optional third language in Mauritian schools, has suddenly become embarrassing for the octogenarian prime minister, since the Reagan administration in Washington has decided that Libya is the ringleader of international terrorism, a codeword for all anti-U.S. liberation movements around the world. In keeping with this, Ramgoolam decided in January 1982 to limit the activities of the Libyan diplomatic mission in Port-Louis, prohibiting Libyan aid to any public or private organization in Mauritius, and directing Tripoli to deal with the Mauritian government when it wishes to invite Mauritian citizens to Libya (Reuter, January 31, 1982).

In the meantime, after the failure of the South African-backed mercenaries squad of "Mad Mike" Hoare to topple the government of the Seychelles in November 1981, information minister Suresh Moorba accused the Albert René government of "interfering in Mauritian domestic affairs by financing the MMM" (Gupte, 1981).

More ominous still are the desperate efforts of the Labour party to mobilize Hindu communal feelings as a last-ditch attempt to retain power, since Hindus constitute the majority of the population (Gunesh, 1981a). Such an attempt is uphill work in a highly literate society that has been trained through nearly 15 years of class politics since independence. Ramgoolam further suffers from his sagging popularity in Delhi, where Indira Gandhi seems to find the youthful Berenger more exciting because of his clear stand on Diego Garcia (Gunesh, 1981b).

But the old-guard leadership of Labour is not a bunch that gives up easily. Stories circulating in Mauritius at the time of writing (April 1982), more than three months before election day, indicate clearly the Labour propaganda line, which goes as follows: "If the MMM takes power, the Arabs will take over Mauritius, and we, Hindus, proud descendants of the coolies—indentured labourers who replaced the African slaves on the sugar plantations—will lose control over the rich oil and other mineral resources of the Indian Ocean."

As the first secretary of the Mauritian Embassy to the United Nations put it to me last October: "Mauritians know that the old man [Ramgoolam] is doomed. But they know him only too well and they expect he'll pull some last-minute trick to try and win the elections. They are also fed up with the Labour government and it doesn't seem they will fall for any more tricks, but they are still curious to see what he will do." One horrible political rumour even suggests that Ramgoolam might be so desperate as to foment bloody communal riots between Muslims and Hindus, which could serve either to split the MMM-MSP alliance or to give the government the pretext it wants to postpone the June elections.

The fact that the Diego Garcia story is a constantly evolving one only adds to its complexity as we now find ourselves a long way from the secret routine colonial operation of 1965 affecting a forgotten atoll in the middle of the Indian Ocean and faced with the prospect of direct or covert Western intervention in the internal affairs of a free, sovereign, and democratic country, Mauritius. This dangerous situation not only illustrates the short-sightedness of the Ramgoolam government, but it also dramatizes, in the world as it is presently constituted, the destabilizing propensities of superpower interests when small countries stand in their way, especially when such small countries play the double game of running with the hares and hunting with the hounds for the sake of survival.

The world as seen from the Pentagon, with the United States on the defensive, with "a new kind of imperialism stalking the world, namely Soviet communism," as President Reagan put it in unveiling his Caribbean Basin Initiative before the Organization of American States in February 1982, offers no substitute to the Diego Garcia strategy of a fixed aeronaval base for new anti-Soviet military alliances in the Indian Ocean. If the present U.S. policy on El Salvador and Central America is any indication—indeed U.S. defense policy as a whole—the Reagan administration is just not prepared to reexamine its Indian Ocean strategy—and any demilitarization of Diego Garcia is therefore out of the question as far as it is concerned.

The British government, too, remains intransigent. As late as March 27, 1982, with the Mauritian Parliament recessed since the preceding June and with the whole island engulfed in election fever, the Ramgoolam caretaker government, after protracted negotiations, signed a new agreement with Great Britain giving some $8 million in compensation to the deported Ilois. However, the agreement was signed by Mauritius only after Britain "accepted not to insist on the inclusion of a clause whereby Mauritius would have recognized British sovereignty over the Chagos archipelago" (AFP and Reuter). Mauritius, in return, failed to obtain recognition of its sovereignty over the islands and, as part of the bargain, it accepted to provide land to the deported Ilois population. This eleventh-hour patchwork has somewhat defused the Ilois question as a campaign issue in Mauritius, but it leaves untouched the problem of Mauritian sovereignty and the even larger concern about the militarization of Diego Garcia.

In early March, Pentagon officials disclosed that the U.S. Defense Department was "exploring the possibility of gaining access for U.S. military planes at bases in several countries of the Western Caribbean" along the pattern set "in other parts of the world" where "this type of arrangement, formal and bilateral, would be provided to Congress but not ratified." The AP news report quoted here went on to underline that "the reference to other parts of the world means especially the Indian Ocean-Middle East area" (AP, March 3, 1982).

In this light, the Anglo-American alliance against Argentina over the Malvinas and their South Georgia and South Sandwich dependencies takes on a special significance. Beyond the internal problems of the Argentine junta and the rumours of oil in the region, could it be that the Argentine occupation was an attempt to thwart an extension of the Diego Garcia model to the South Atlantic? The Anglo-American resolve to wrest the islands back through an absurdly disporportionate use of force, not to mention "honest mediator" Alexander Haig's early proposal for the United States to have a say in the future of the islands, can hardly find adequate explanation without reference to the Diego Garcia model.

The joint Anglo-American use of Ascension Island in the Malvinas campaign is in itself quite instructive. Between April 16 and June 19, 1982, according to Captain Bob McQueen, commander of the support forces on the Mid-Atlantic ocean base, the 34-square-mile island had allowed helicopters to make 5352 sorties delivering 125 tonnes of materiel to the Royal Navy Task Force off the Falklands and served as point of transit for 20 million liters of fuel, its civilian population doubling to 2000 between March and April, not to mention the fighting men (AFP, June 19, 1982).

But an equally significant, though contradictory, object lesson was offered on the same June 19 by about 1000 Marshall Islanders who organized a "sail-in" leading to the "functional closure" of the U.S. missile range on Kwajalein Island, the main feature of Kwajalein Atoll, a ring of about 90 Micronesian islands 2400 miles southwest of Honolulu, in the south Pacific. They were protesting their government's signing of a "compact of free association" with the United States and objecting specifically to the terms regarding use of Kwajalein lands for the missile range (UPI, June 28, 1982).

A cynical twist was provided by Prime Minister Margaret Thatcher's speech before the British House of Commons on April 14, 1982, declaring that "the freedom of choice and the rights of self-determination of the Falklanders themselves must be primordial in any settlement of the crisis." The same day, Sir Anthony Parsons, British ambassador to the United Nations, delivered a letter to the Security Council that declared that "the inhabitants of the Falkland Islands, like other peoples, are entitled to their right of self-determination" (AFP, April 14, 1982).

The British government, which only two weeks before had bought for $8 million the right to self-determination of the 2000 and more Ilois deportees as well as their right to their homes and their islands, was now embarking on a costly crusade to defend the self-determination rights of an equal number of Falklanders. Two weeks later, former Labour Prime Minister Harold Wilson, who presided over the creation of the BIOT, added his own bit of racist irony by declaring, in a speech before students on the campus of Youngstown State University, in Ohio, that only the 1800 residents of the Falklands should decide who governs the South Atlantic islands. "Whatever they want, they should have it," proclaimed Sir Harold, adding he would personally support self-government for the islands (AP, April 28, 1982). His favorite Prime Minister is thankful, no doubt, that Sir Harold did not propose self-government for the Chagos, but he must certainly regret that Great Britain has consistently ignored these same noble considerations of sovereignty and self-determination vis-à-vis Mauritius in its handling of the Chagos issue.

U.S. Admiral Alfred Thayer Mahan is reported to have predicted, at the turn of the nineteenth century that "Asia will belong to the power which will achieve control over the Indian Ocean, and the future of the world will be decided in its waters" (Cadoux, 1974: 73). On his retirement in 1974, U.S. Admiral Elmo Zumwalt, chief of operational planning for the U.S. Navy, announced that the Indian Ocean would be the keystone of the great strategic readjustment of the 1980s (Prats, 1974: 133). The militarization of Diego Garcia, seen against such a background, means that, beyond the dignity and livelihood of 2000 Ilois and beyond the sovereignty of Mauritius, the fate of billions may be threatened.

REFERENCES

Advance [Mauritian Daily] (1981) September 1.

Afrique-Asie (1981) No. 250 (October 12): 8-18.

CADOUX, C. (1974) "Esquisse d'un panorama politique des pays de l'Océan indien," pp. 47-77 in Annuaire des pays de l'Océan indien. Aix-en-Provence.

CARLUCCI, F. (1981) "Excerpts from testimony to Senate panel." USICA Press Release (March 9). Washington, DC: USICA.

DUPON, J-F. (1974) "L'Océan indien et sa bordure: présentation géographique," pp. 19-46 in Annuaire des pays de l'Océan indien. Aix-en-Provence.

DURAND, J. et J-P. DURAND (1975) L'île Maurice, Quelle independance? Paris: Anthropos.

DURBAN, D. (1981) "Un avenir economique incertain." L'Economiste du Tiers monde 56 (Otober).

DURHAM, W. H. (1981) U.S. Improving Middle East, Indian Ocean Military Facilities." USICA Press Release (March 12). Washington, DC: USICA.

ELLSWORTH-JONES, W. (1976) "The islanders that Britain sold." London Sunday Times (June 20).

FAVOREU, L. (1970) L'île Maurice. Paris: Berger-Levrault.

GUNESH, T. (1981a) "Mauritius: castely considerations." India Today (October 31).

––– (1981b) "Mauritius: time to choose sides." India Today (December 31).

GUPTE, P. B. (1981) "Mauritius sees Seychelles meddling." New York Times (December 6).

HOUBERT, J. (1981) "Mauritius: independence and dependence." Journal of Modern African Studies 19, 1: 75-105.

Jeune Afrique (1980) Diego Garcia: un réveil tardif." No. 1019 (July 16).

KAUFMAN, M. T. (1981) "Supremacy at sea: the race in the Indian Ocean." New York Times (April 19).

KOENIG, M. (1981) "U.S. reviewing options for increased Mideast presence." USICA Press Release (March 23). Washington, DC: USICA.

LANGELIER, J-P. (1981) "L'Ocean indien, nouveau coeur du monde." Le Monde (February).

LARUS, J. (1982) "Diego Garcia: political clouds over a vital U.S. base." Strategic Review (Winter).

MAHAN, A. T. (1890) The Influence of Sea Power upon History. Boston: Little, Brown.

McDOWELL, B. (1981) "Cross-currents sweep the Indian Ocean." National Geographic (October): 422-457.

The Nation (1974) "A speck on the map." (March 16).

––– (1975) "Island of shame." (October 18).

PINCHER, C. (1981) "Soviet, West battle for naval supremacy." Sunday Telegraphy (June 21).

PRATS, Y. (1974) "L'Océan indien, zone strategique," pp. 121-133 in Annuaire des pays de l'Océan indien. Aix-en-Provence.

RAMGOOLAM, S. (1980) "Adress to the 35th United Nations General Assembly" Permanent Mission of Mauritius to the UN. October 9.

RIVIERE, L. (1982) Maurice 82. Port-Louis: Maurice Almanach.

SCOTT, R. (1961) Limuria: The Lesser Dependencies of Mauritius. London.

Seth, S. P. (1975) "The Indian Ocean and Indo-American relations." Asian Survey 15 (August): 75-105.

South (1981) "Getting it wrong." No. 11 (October).

State Research Bulletin [SRB] (1981-1982) Vol. 5, No. 4 (December-January): 41-52.

Time (1980) "Digging in at Diego Garcia." (July 14).

TOUSSAINT, A. (1961) Histoire de l'Océan indien. Paris: PUF.

––– (1972) Histoire des îles Mascareignes. Paris: Berger-Levrault.

United Nations General Assembly (1980) A/35/463 (September 29).

––– (1981a) A/AC.159/L.35 (March 5).

––– (1981b) A/AC.159/L.38/Rev.1 (August 27).

––– (1981c) A/36/PV.6 (September 22).

8

PROSPERING AT THE PERIPHERY:
A SPECIAL CASE—THE SEYCHELLES

RAPHAEL KAPLINSKY
University of Sussex

Capitalism—the dominant mode of accumulation in the world economy— shows a persistent tendency toward the concentration of production. Despite characteristic unevenness in this expansion of the forces of production, there has been a long-run tendency for the center of the system to be in North America and Western Europe. It is only relatively recently that the Far East has begun to emerge as another central node of accumulation.

In the context of this tendency toward concentration, the expansion of the forces of production in a small peripheral economy are heavily circumscribed, for a number of reasons. These include scale economies, which militate against production for small markets; dynamic external economies, which reinforce the benefits of producing at the center of the global system; high transport costs and infrequent communications to larger markets; and distance from the pressures molding final consumers' taste patterns.

Despite these seemingly overwhelming difficulties associated with accumulation at the periphery of the world economy, there are a number of discrete factors that suggest that particular paths of accumulation in

Author's Note: I am grateful to Robin Cohen and Bernard Schaffer for helpful comments on an earlier draft.

particular sectors may be viable, at least in the short to medium run. These include the perishability of some products (e.g., bread), commodities with high transport-to-value ratios (e.g., bricks), commodities that display significant weight/volume loss in processing (e.g., minerals), commodities that are unique to certain areas (e.g., handicrafts), and goods and services that are specific to particular regions (e.g., tropical fruit, beaches, and sunshine).

The Seychelles is one of a series of western Indian Ocean islands (the others being the Comoros, Reunion, the Maldives, and Mauritius,[1] which are characterized by extreme smallness, of both size and population, and by distance from major areas of accumulation and trade. Even within this group of island-states, the Seychelles is relatively small and unpopulated—its population, for example, is less than half that of its next smallest neighbor, the Maldives. I have argued that a priori this isolation and smallness will probably militate against substantial accumulation in the Seychelles. Yet, as we shall see below, there are particular advantages that stem from remoteness, a small population, and geographical dispersion that have worked to further development in the Seychelles. But before we consider these, it is helpful to detail some demographic and geographical factors and to present some details of the development of the Seychelles economy.

The Seychelles is made up of over 100 islands, covering a total of 171.4 square miles. While, due to the lack of a definition of "an island," it would be improper to quote an exact number, it is generally recognized that the group consists of around 100 named islands" (Republic of Seychelles, 1978). Forty of these islands are granitic and the remainder are coralline; the former group is much more hospitable to habitation and accounts for over 99 percent of the population. Some of the coralline islands are in fact submerged mountains and are almost entirely covered by water at high tides. The scattering of these 100 or so islands over 400,000 square miles of ocean may hinder intra-Seychelles communications, but it does provide a lien over an enormous area of the Indian Ocean, which has identifiably large fishing resources and may well also harbor extensive oil deposits. Oil rigs are currently drilling at the edge of the plateaux, some ninety miles from the main island, Mahe.

Historically, before technical change in communications reduced the cost of international travel and exchange, the combination of rugged granitic islands and swampy coralline islands placed a constraining limit on population and agriculture. Fully 50 percent of the land mass is unsuitable for any form of agriculture, and 90 percent of the remainder is suitable only for tree crops and shrubs, giving a total of only around 100,000 acres to meet the subsistence, residential, and other needs of over 60,000 people (IMF, 1979). In neighboring Kenya, for example, it is estimated that even on soil with high potential, a ratio of one acre per person is required to meet minimum subsistence requirements aside from land required for residential, industrial, and administrative needs. Moreover, contrary to the first expectations of the visitor (who is confronted on arrival with lush vegetation), the fertility of the soil on even these 100,000 acres is low by comparison with many other tropical countries.

The population of the Seychelles (around 61,900 in 1977, and growing at 2.1 per annum) is concentrated on three major granitic islands that are within 70 miles of each other. Mahe alone accounts for 35 percent of total land mass and had 88 percent of total population, with a further 7 percent on Praslin and 3 percent on La Digue. By comparison with other less developed countries (LDCs), a significant proportion (37 percent) are urbanized, and (as we shall see later) and even greater proportion are in paid employment.

THE SEYCHELLES IN THE WORLD ECONOMY

Three factors have dominated the historical development of the Seychelles. The first of these is *location,* where the isolation of the islands has had two divergent implications. On the one hand, it has cut the Seychelles off from migration and trade, thereby contributing to political and social isolation. And on the other, its commanding position in the Indian Ocean has been a strategic attraction to military powers, thereby forcing particular forms of contact with the external world. Second, its *small size* has inhibited expansion through extensification; expansion through intensification of technology required indigenous technological capabilities that have not been available in the islands, characterized as they are by limited population and resources. Moreover, the *small population* has limited the market for domestic production. Third, the absence of *natural resources*—including fertile soil—has reinforced the contribution of location and size to political, economic, and social isolation.

Over the past thirty years a number of factors both within and (especially) without the Seychelles have wrenched the islands out of their political, cultural, and social isolation. Some of these have sprung from developments internal to the islands. Of primary importance here has been the contact with the external world resulting from steady emigration (sometimes only temporary). This exodus had occurred for a number of reasons. The growing social horizons of the *grand blancs* (that is the large landholders, predominantly of French origin) have led them to venture abroad. Moreover, to some extent, and particularly in recent years, the momentum of political opposition has forced remnants of this class to seek security in other countries. At the same time a narrow stratum of *skilled workers* has emigrated in search of higher incomes and wider horizons, and a significant proportion of *younger women* have left, either by marrying Americans manning the satellite station, or by working as domestic servants in the Gulf. Between 1945 and 1972, therefore, about 7000 Seychellois had left the islands, and their contacts with remaining family and friends have contributed to the breakdown of the islands' isolation.

Changes in the external world have, however, had a more significant impact on opening the Seychelles to the world economy. Five of these stand out in importance.

(1) The pressures toward decolonization in other Third World countries had an inevitable spillover effect on the Seychelles. This occurred not merely as a general phenomenon of growing political consciousness, but also took specific forms. The most important of these was the financial and political support given in the early 1970s by the OAU to the Seychelles Peoples United party (SPUP), led by Albert Rene. The SPUP opposed the Seychelles Democratic party (SDP) which, in the pre-independence period, renounced the goal of independence. However, when the SPUP's policies grew in popularity, they were coopted by the SDP, which formed a coalition with the SPUP and led the Seychelles to independence in 1976.

(2) With the closure of the Suez Canal in 1967, the Indian Ocean began to assume great importance to the Western powers, who anxious to maintain control over oil supplies. The Seychelles, while not directly on this oil route, was strategically placed to exert such control—moreover, even if the Western powers did not directly exercise its facilities, there was the ever-present concern that the socialist bloc might fill the vacuum.

(3) Other strategic concerns—notably the use of the Indian Ocean as a launching pad for submarine missiles aimed at Russia, and the intention to use Diego Garcia, one of the islands discussed in this book, as a stepping stone for a Western military presence in Asia—combined to reinforce the growing geopolitical importance of the Seychelles and other western Indian Ocean islands.

(4) The development of cheaper air travel led to the rapid growth of a long-haul tourist industry, placing the Seychelles on the map as a major attraction for European and North American tourists. From the year in which the airport was opened (1972) the number of tourist arrivals increased rapidly from 15,197 to 78,852 in 1979, a growth rate of 26.5 percent per annum over the period.

(5) The Seychelles holds the property rights over a segment of the Indian Ocean that is rich in fishing resources and is a breeding ground for tuna and whales. Consequently, foreign firms (from Japan, Taiwan, and Korea) have approached and reached agreement with the Seychelles to "farm" this resource on payment of an annual royalty of about Rs 12m (Rs 13.8 = £1 in 1980). More significantly, the rich potential of tuna fishing has led the Seychelles into an agreement with the French government (anxious to maintain employment in a declining shipbuilding industry) for the "aided" purchase and manning of technically sophisticated longline tuna fishing. And finally, growing international concern with the depletion of global whale resources has thrust the Seychelles (with a delegation of 17 members, funded, advised, and partly staffed by developed country ecologists) into a leading role in international negotiations to limit whaling.

These factors, external and internal, have had a major impact in opening up the Seychelles to the world economy and in changing the horizons of its population. But despite this growing internationalization, the future of the Seychelles will continue to be constrained by the three factors that have influenced its historical development, namely its small size, its distance from the centers of the world economy, and its resources. I return to these themes below, but we will first concern ourselves with the dimensions of development in the Seychellas economy.

THE DEVELOPMENT OF THE SEYCHELLES ECONOMY

A Brief Historical Overview

Although the Seychelles had been visited since the eighth century, and used as a watering base by pirates in the fifteenth and sixteenth centuries, the first known residents (emigres from Mauritius) arrived in 1771. In these early years trade in timber and tortoises was the major economic activity, but after official intervention the settlers turned to subsistence crops. (It is a common belief that the felling of these valuable indigenous timber resources removed a protective cover from the soil, so that the thin, fertile covering of soil over the granitic islands was washed into the sea. This is supposed to be a major reason for the poor fertility of the islands). The growing political ferment of the French Revolution filtered through to these settlers, and in the early 1790s an attempt was made to declare UDI from Mauritius. The upshot was direct rule from France by the legendary de Quinssey, who is reputed to have had both English and French uniforms, regalia, and flags. When English ships entered the Seychelles to assert their supremacy, they were met by Mr. Quincey running up the Union Jack and wearing English regalia; when the French arrived, they were met by de Quinssey in French uniform, running up the Tricolour. Even in this early period, therefore, the strategic importance of the islands had an impact on domestic policies.

Ceded to England in 1814, the island remained under the domination of the original French settlers (the grand blancs), with their coterie of slaves. But the liberation of the slaves in the 1830-1840 period, led to mass migration and a halving of the population from 8500 in 1830 to 4360 in 1840. This was a turning point in the economic history of the Seychelles, which until then had been largely self-sufficient in food, a position that has never been attained since. It was not until 1871 that the population again exceeded 8000, the immigrants being made up of freed slaves. But the shortage of land and the established position of the original grand blancs set the pattern of class hegemony that endured until the early 1970s, namely, the large landholders (the grand blancs) and an employed proletariat made up of ex-slaves and their descendants. This proletariat was a rural rather than an industrial one. The Seychelles is particularly unusual compared to other Third World economies in relation to the size of proletariat compared to that of the peasantry. Some 88 percent of the working population is employed, with two-thirds of the total labor force in capitalist production, and the balance being unemployed, self-employed, or domestic servants (Le Brun and Murray, 1980).

The origins of political opposition to this hegemony are to be found in the process of political democratization. At the outset of this process in 1948, the legislative council was made up of four elected and two nominated members. But until 1967 the electorate was confined to literate taxpayers and, not surprisingly, the dominant political grouping in these years was the Seychelles' Farmers and Taxpayers Association, representing the interests of the landowning and merchant classes. In 1964, the SDP and the SPUP were both formed. The SDP, under the flamboyant personal leadership of Mancham, came to represent the alliance between merchant capital, foreign capital, and the grand blancs. Mancham was characterized by himself and others as being an international playboy. The SPUP newspaper parodied this rather neatly—"The Chief Minister is still on holiday in Seychelles—He has not yet resumed his duties abroad" (cited in Ostheimer, 1975: 166). Its position was anachronistically conservative, rejecting independence until 1975, championing links with South Africa and lampooning the "socialism" of Tanzania. But by that time the SPUP's policies of "independence now" and a reduction in inequalities were becoming increasingly popular. However, this was not always represented in the legislative council. Despite achieving 47.6 percent of the votes in the 1974 election, the SPUP gained only 13 percent of the seats. However, Mancham eventually capitulated to popular pressure and coopted the SPUP's policies and formed an alliance with them in 1975. Independence arrived in June 1976 and a coup, led by the former SPUP leader Albert Rene, deposed Mancham in 1977.

This coup is commonly characterized as a move against the personal style of Mancham. However, it was much more than this; it represented an overthrow of the alliance between merchant capital and landowners by an uneasy alliance between the petty bourgeoisie and the working class.[2] Foreign capital had no difficulty in adjusting to this change in hegemony. As we shall see, this uneasy alliance had produced its own tensions but it can be safely concluded that the coup set the seal on the demise of the grand blanc landowners.

The Changing Economic Structure

Little empirical evidence exists for the Seychelles economy in the period prior to the mid-1960s. As we have seen, a brief period of international trade in timber and tortoises and self-sufficiency in food production was followed by almost two centuries of subsubsistence agriculture. Deficits in food production were largely covered by exports of guana fertilizer to Mauritius (from the turn of the century) and the gradual expansion of copra (made from coconuts) and cinnamon exports from the grand blanc estates. No figures exist for living standards or for growth in the economy in this period.

However, the introduction of the first air service in 1971 and the opening of the international airport in 1972 (partly built as a staging post for the proposed Concorde route to Australia) signified momentous changes in the Seychelles economy. Although the inflow of tourism was not the only changing parameter—for example, as can be seen from Table

TABLE 8.1   Terms of Trade: Index of Copra and World Import Prices,
             1960-1978

Year	Copra Export Prices (1)	Developed Country Import Prices for All Commodities (2)	Terms of Trade £ (1 ÷ 2)
1960	100	100	1
1961	79	99	80
1962	77	98	79
1963	89	100	89
1964	92	102	90
1965	117	103	114
1966	87	104	84
1967	88	104	85
1968	117	103	114
1969	96	106	91
1970	NA	112	NA
1971	99	118	84
1972	65	127	52
1973	135	155	87
1974	315	221	143
1975	247	240	103
1976	310	216	144
1977	481	235	205
1978	530	259	205

SOURCES: Developed Country Import Prices from various editions of the IMF
         Financial Statistics: The period 1960-1963 refers to world import prices,
         not just to those of developed countries. Copra prices from Barclays
         Bank DCO reports on Seychelles and from 1978 Annual Trade Report.

8.1, the terms of trade of the major export commodity fell significantly between 1960 and 1973—it has played the major role in the significant structural changes that have occurred.

The basic fact is that in terms of international competitiveness, the Seychelles is a high-cost agricultural producer with poor soil fertility, overaged plantations, and high labor costs. By comparison, in the tourist sector the Seychelles creams the international market with exceptionally high all season occupancy rates[3] at high prices. Consequently wages and profits[4] in tourism are much higher than are those in agriculture—for example in 1977 wages in the tourist sector were on average 32 percent higher than were those in agriculture. Similarly, the fishery industry provides higher returns than agriculture does. While manufacturing is also internationally uncompetitive, protection allows for higher returns in industry than in agriculture (e.g., wages in industry were 233 percent of those in agriculture).

As a consequence of initially adverse terms of trade and then growing uncompetitiveness with other domestic sectors there has been a consistent decline in production of traditional export crops, which has been matched by a growth in frozen fish exports and in earnings from tourism. The details can be seen in Table 8.2, which shows an absolute decline since 1972 in earnings from cinnamon and negligible earnings from vanilla and guano. Even copra exports, which benefited from a substantial increase in prices in the mid-1970s (see Table 8.1) fell in volume terms by 16 percent between 1971 and 1979. Interestingly, the dependence of the Seychelles on copra as a source of visible export earnings has actually risen over the past 15 years. This has been a consequence of a lucrative export market to Pakistan (which is particularly vulnerable given that country's balance of payments deficits) and the almost complete extinction of other traditional export crops.

To some extent the decline in commodity exports has been compensated by a growth in production of vegetables, fruit, and poultry, some of which has found its way into the tourist sector. Although only fragmentary evidence exists there is some sign that the tourist sector had bid food resources away from the indigenous population (with January 1974 = 100), the index of food prices (other than fish) rose to 221.5 in December 1978, while that of nonfood items rose only to 199.6. And, although the share of food stuffs in total imports has fallen slightly,[5] the absolute value of food imports almost doubled from Rs 39.5 million in 1974 to Rs 77.2 million in 1978.

Even these figures on domestic production of foodstuffs overestimate the implicit relative profitability of agriculture since a proportion of marketed output arises from part-time farming, where labor is uncosted. Thus whereas in 1978 there were estimated to be 73 large farms (over 50 percent of which farmed coconut, poultry, and livestock, a large proportion of which were being held for speculative purposes), and 634 small-scale commercial farmers (again, many of whom were not farming their plots commercially), there were over 4500 "backyard" farmers depending on no-cost family labor. (Unfortunately, no information exists on the concentration of landholdings.)

TABLE 8.2 Major Export Items (Rs 000)

| Year | Total Visible Exports | Traditional Exports—Agriculture | | | | | Nontraditional Exports | | |
| | | Cinnamon | Guano | Vanilla | Copra | (Copra as % of Total Visible) | Fish | Tourism | |
								Gross /	Net[a]
1960	NI	1458	NI	539	4768	NI	0	Negl	Negl
1961	NI	1473	NI	146	4383	NI	0	Negl	Negl
1962	NI	1853	NI	281	4534	NI	0	Negl	Negl
1963	6867	1354	NI	86	5179	75.4	0	Negl	Negl
1964	8661	1601	NI	51	6567	75.8	0	Negl	Negl
1965	10098	2815	NI	48	6049	59.9	0	Negl	Negl
1966	9021	2296	NI	175	5021	55.7	0	Negl	Negl
1967	10518	3427	NI	53	5557	52.8	0	Negl	Negl
1968	16308	8031	NI	30	7179	44	0	Negl	Negl
1969	NI	6635	NI	7	5843	NI	0	Negl	Negl
1970	NI	NI	NI	Negl	NI	NI	0	Negl	Negl
1971	7916	3332	332	Negl	3574	45.1	0	Negl	Negl
1972	9528	5938	546	Negl	2346	24.6	0	NI	NI
1973	12969	7208	447	Negl	4657	35.9	0	NI	NI
1974	18721	7047	270	Negl	9932	53.1	466	48000	19200
1975	12903	3629	471	Negl	7299	56.6	513	80000	32000
1976	17940	3664	1110	Negl	8817	49.2	3354	135000	54000
1977	24385	3311	1319	Negl	14503	59.5	3161	170000	68000
1978	24705	1895	1738	0	16157	65.4	3550	208000	83200

SOURCE: Tourism from IMF (1979); others from Annual Trade Report and Barclays DCO Reports on Seychelles.

NI = No information.

Negl = Negligible.

a. Estimated at 40% of gross figure. See IMF (1979: 13).

The major growth sector of the past decade has therefore been the tourist industry, which despite low retention ratios (i.e., total foreign exchange receipts minus foreign exchange costs), has contributed significantly to the growth of the economy (see later). In recent years the fishing industry has also begun to expand. The Seychelles is particularly blessed with high fishing yields—per capita fish consumption is already around 80 kilograms per annum (the highest in the world), largely accounting for the relative absence of malnutrition among children. Frozen fish is a growing export item, and it is anticipated that the tuna fishing venture will provide substantial net benefits in the future.

All these structural changes have a certain economic rationale, but the growth of the manufacturing sector in recent years can only be explained as a political phenomenon, reflecting in part the uneasiness of the alliance between the petty bourgeoisie and the proletariat. A number of these petty bourgeois families have begun to exploit their new links with the state to set up "industries" behind tariff barriers (e.g., dairy and animal feed production). At the same time, the state sector, under the illusion that industry necessarily leads to wealth, has attracted foreign capital to the islands. The result has been that a number of inappropriate industries have been established that sell high-cost commodities to the islands' consumers, with little hope that these costs will be reduced as the industries move down the learning curve. A few examples illustrate this:

- The dairy industry (which has particularly strong personal links with the state) sells cream at Rs 47 per liter, while imported cream, CIF and duty paid, could be sold at Rs 35 per liter.

- The two plastic plants sell inferior, unprinted containers for Rs 0.25 and Rs 0.36, whereas imported printed containers, duty paid, cost Rs 0.19.

- Imported refined cooking oil costs Rs 15 per liter, whereas unrefined local oil sells at Rs 24 per liter.

- It is planned to assemble 300 motor cars a year at Rs 40,000 each, with an import content of over Rs 27,000.[6] Fully built cars, of better quality, can be imported for Rs 19,000 to Rs 22,000, CIF.

This tendency toward "inefficient" industrialization is by no means unique to the Seychelles. Moreover, as in other countries it has similar explanations in the realm of political economy in that it reflects the power that the accumulating class has in persuading the state to erect tariff barriers and quotas to protect local industries. Nevertheless, the Seychelles

TABLE 8.3   Sectoral Shares of GDP, 1977

Sector	Percentage Share
Agriculture and forestry	8
Fishing	2.9
Manufacturing and handicrafts	3.4
Construction	9.2
Hotels and restaurants	10.9
Government services	18.8
Transport, communications and distribution	27.3
Other services	17.7
All other	1.7
GDP per capita	$1,500

economy has seen significant growth over the past decade in which the economy grew at a real rate of over 5 percent per annum over the 1972-1978 period (IMF, 1979). By 1978 the sectoral contribution of tourism almost equaled the combined shares of agriculture and industry (see Table 8.3). All this occurred within a context of a healthy balance of payments in which a growing visible trade deficit (from Rs 121.4 million in 1974 to Rs 306 million in 1978) was covered by earnings on tourism and grants from abroad. Foreign debt, though rising substantially from Rs 8.6 million in 1977 to Rs 27 million in 1978, is still only a small proportion of total imports (Rs 402 million in 1978). The real contribution of the tourist sector to economic growth can be seen from Table 8.3, from which it is evident that estimated net earnings from tourism in 1978 were 3.4 times those of total visible exports and 5.2 times greater than those from copra, the next largest foreign exchange earning activity.

The Distributional Impact of Growth

However it is measured, the distribution of income in the Seychelles is relatively equal in comparison with that in other countries, particularly those on the African mainland. The Gini coefficient of .46 (as estimated by the 1978 Household Expenditure Survey) is substantially lower than that of neighboring Kenya (.59). Partly as a consequence of this and partly because the level of per capita income (around U.S. $1500) is relatively high, real standards of living of the mass of the population are better than in many other LDCs. This shows up in a relatively high average industrial salary of around U.S. $200 per month and an average agricultural salary of

TABLE 8.4   Comparison of Fiscal Revenues, Kenya and Seychelles (1977)

	Percentage of Fiscal Income Arising from Various Sources	
	Seychelles	Kenya
Income tax	16.1 ⎫	⎫
	⎬ 28.4	⎬ 39.7
Corporation tax	8.3 ⎭	⎭
Import duties	33.9	19.9
All indirect taxes (including import duties)	71.6	60.3

SOURCE: Kenya, Statistical Abstract (1977); Seychelles, IMF (1979).

around $100 (all 1980 prices). Other indicators of noncash income make this point even stronger:

- Life expectancy at birth is 62.5 years for males and 69.9 years for females.

- About 47 percent of homes have fresh water inside the house, with only 29 percent dependent upon a well, a river, or a stream.

- Some 97 percent of children finish six years education, and 72 percent finish eight years. (Despite this, standards of education are low. Some estimates are that 25 percent of the population is functionally illiterate).

- Only 4 percent of homes are not made from wood, cement, or stone.

- Some 86 percent of households possess a radio.

Nevertheless, much remains to be done. The fiscal system, which taxes corporations at 35 percent and provides for a maximum marginal rate of taxation (after numerous generous personal allowances, including education overseas) of only 35 percent, is regressive. Not surprisingly, the proportion of taxes raised through indirect, regressive measures is high, even by comparison with its unequal neighbor, Kenya (see Table 8.4). Overall, 25 percent of the population live in households that qualify them for low-cost, self-help housing (i.e., less than Rs 700 per month). It is in fact possible to identify the relatively poor (i.e., those in households earning less than Rs 200 per month) as those living in households of one to two persons. Most of these 3500 people are old and living on inadequate pensions and welfare benefits.

The relatively high absolute standard of living of even the poorest segment of the population is explained by two main phenomena. The first of these is the ready availability of fish, which is cheap and highly nutritious. By a quirk of good fortune the fish favored by the export markets has little local demand and is caught at the same time as the preferred local varieties. Consequently, even if future economic growth is partly led by the expansion of fish exports, the cross-subsidization possible between these two types of fishing activities is unlikely to remove a major item of food from local diets. And second, unemployment is scarcely a problem on the islands, and most families have regular incomes. Although 10 percent of the population has registered themselves as unemployed, the institution of a full employment scheme by the state in early 1980 (which provided benefits in excess of minimum wages) had a poor rate of take up by the "unemployed." This suggests that real unemployment is substantially lower than 10 percent and that most of those who registered did so in the expectation of obtaining better jobs.

Reflecting the changing composition of the state, a number of measures have been taken in recent years to reduce inequalities further. These include:

- a concerted attempt to reduce salary differentials within the state, which fell from 21:1 in 1976 to 11.9:1 in 1978;[7] at the same time, separate civil service pensions rights and automatic annual increments in salary have been abolished;

- the Land Acquisition Act has been passed, giving the state the right to purchase, *at use value,* land not used productively;

- the institution of a full employment scheme; and

- expansion of secondary education to widen educational opportunities and an attempt to introduce an egalitarian National Youth Service to build a "pre-figurative form of Socialist Society" (Le Brun and Murray, 1980).

The Role of Foreign Investment

It is noticeable that the post-coup state, while undertaking a number of measures to reduce inequalities, has left foreign capital untouched. This is partly evident in relation to the absence of exchange control, to the low corporation tax (35 percent), and to the absence of withholding payments on dividends or interest, the latter two of which are common practice in other LDCs. More surprisingly, it is also evident in relation to the decision not to disturb foreign shareholdings, which are dominant in both tourism and industry. For example:

- all 5 large hotels, 8 out of 45 small hotels, and 4 out of 46 guest houses are foreign owned;[8]

- most "large-scale" manufacturing establishments are foreign owned, including the dairy, the brewery (Seybreweries), and the major furniture (Bodco), plastics (Seychelle), paints (Tropicolour), and cigarette (Silhouette) factories. Those large-scale enterprises that are not foreign owned—e.g., the bakery (Seybakery), metal working (Seysteel), Mahe Construction,—are owned by foreign nationals resident in the Seychelles, who in 1977 constituted 4 percent of the population.

It is possible here to distinguish between the attitude of the post-coup state to the capitalist powers—where the Seychelles has played a more even role of providing balanced access to the Soviet and Western fleets—and to foreign capital, which has remained undisturbed. Hitherto, foreign capital seems to have been happy with the policies of the post-coup state. But if it should become more radical—for example, by mobilizing the trade unions—or if it should act more consistently in the interests of the bourgeoisie by pressuring for sale of shareholdings to Seychellois, the attitude of foreign capital could easily change. Moreover, foreign capital has a ready constituency of foreign capitalist powers and internal groups that have been squeezed since the coup.

PROSPERING AT THE PERIPHERY: THE PROSPECTS

As we have seen, the Seychelles is in an unusual position compared to many other peripheral economies. In most of these economies there has been, and continues to be, a tradeoff between distributional policies (including full employment) and economic growth. By contrast, when most of the world's economies were stagnating in the 1973-1979 period, the Seychelles experienced unprecedented rates of economic growth, combined with full employment and significant movement toward greater equality. (Although, we have seen that there is some evidence that the tourist sector has raised the relative price of food excluding fish, thereby affecting those on low incomes disproportionately.) Ironically, the very factors that led to the Seychelles' isolation and low incomes in the previous two and a half centuries—namely its isolation, its small size, and the absence of valuable resources—have been the source of the "success" of the tourist sector over the past decade since tourists have flocked to the unspoilt beaches and isolation. Our attention obviously turns, therefore, to the question of whether this happy confluence between distribution and growth will endure over the coming decades. A number of factors urge a cautionary judgment—while in discussing these I distinguish for the purposes of convenience between external and internal factors, they cannot be so divided analytically since there is a dialectical interplay between the external and internal world at the economic, political, and social levels.

External Factors

Strategic implications of location. We have already considered the vital strategic role held by the Seychelles. Events in the neighboring Comoros (where some islands were invaded by French mercenaries and a right-wing regime was installed), and the Gambia (discussed elsewhere in this volume), illustrate the very real dangers faced by the post-coup state. This is reflected both by the presence of up to 2000 Tanzanian soldiers resident on the islands (for whom there is little affection among the Seychellois) and the rising expenditure on the military between 1972 and 1978, from 12.2 percent to 15.8 percent of total government expenditure, compared to 11.2 percent on health and 8.2 percent on social security in 1978. There is no doubt, therefore, that the possibility of external military intervention is a very real one. The higher the strategic stakes in the Indian Ocean become and the more substantial the move to the left within the Seychelles (especially in regard to external policies), the greater is the possibility that external military involvement will disrupt the momentum of the 1970s, perhaps through the "democratic" restoration of Mancham, who is currently resident in the United Kingdom and who is actively lobbying for such intervention.

Vulnerability to dependence upon tourism. We have seen how over the past decade the Seychelles had become increasingly dependent on tourism as a major source of economic growth and foreign exchange. The tourist industry is, however, notoriously vulnerable to external economic factors (notably economic conditions in developed countries) and too great a dependence on this sector can lead to instability of the sort experienced by many primary commodity exporters. Moreover, tourism is also sensitive to the political climate within the Seychelles, and internal political tensions (perhaps actively fomented by external forces) may conceivably affect the health of the industry. Hitherto, with the possible exception of raising the price of many food items, tourism in the Seychellas has not had the negative social impacts visible in the Caribbean, the Gambia, or neighboring Kenya. But if this were to occur, the inevitably hostile and violent reaction of the locals would detract from the "specialness" of the Seychelles as a holiday destination for people from developed countries.

So far, the Seychelles has not suffered adversity from its high cost structure in tourism. Indeed, the doubling of the tourist industry turnover tax in 1980 from 5 percent to 10 percent (which provided no revenue in 1975, 4.3 percent of total government revenue in 1975, 4.3 percent of total government revenue in 1979, and about 7 percent in 1980) and which was immediately passed on to the customers, had little visible impact on demand. But as the industry expands from its present capacity (of 2430 beds) to the projected 4000 beds in 1985 and 5500 beds in 1990, it may become less and less of a marginal market that is able to cream off the higher-cost segment of the industry and become more susceptible to cost pressures.

Finally, it may well turn out that the fishery industry will grow substantially over the coming decade. If so, this may reduce the dependence of the islands on a single sector, that is, tourism. All of these factors, however, are uncertain—no one knows how price elastic the Seychelles tourist industry is or will be, how vulnerable it will be to economic recession in developed countries, or how negative will be the social impact of tourism. It does, nevertheless, suggest a question mark over continued tourist-sector-based growth in the 1980s.

Internal Factors

Political opposition. Although there is no firm "evidence" (e.g., referenda, elections) for the popularity of the post-coup state, the indications are that it has a strong measure of public support. This support has, however, declined over the years, and the positioning of Tanzanian troops and the fiasco of the National Youth Service have in particular eroded some of this popular sympathy. The decision to introduce compulsory National Youth Service led to major demonstrations in October 1979. It was initially based on residence in one of the outer islands, but political opposition forced a move to a voluntary scheme based on the most beautiful beach on Mahe, the major island in the Seychellas. More recently, however, a compulsory scheme was reintroduced to take the place of the last two years of school education. Seen as a "prefigurative socialist society," it aims to combine the two essential elements of education, that is, the "head" and the "hand": At the time of writing it is too early to gauge its success or future evaluation. Moreover, important pockets of opposition remain among the grand blancs, merchant capital, and the technical classes (which have suffered from the squeeze on the incomes of senior civil service and parastatal employees). It is doubtful whether this opposition will by itself be able to threaten the durability of the post-coup state, but any outside-sourced intervention is bound to have the support of these disaffected elements.

"Economic rationality." We have already pointed to the relatively special growth path of the Seychelles in the past decade in which there was little tradeoff between growth and employment or distributional policies. As argued, this arose from the comparative advantage Seychelles holds in tourism and fishing. But such competitiveness does not hold in other sectors—in agriculture, labor costs, on poorer productivity soil, are double those of the Philippines, a competitor in the copra trade; in manufacturing, unit labor costs are 3.5 times those of neighboring Kenya.

Despite these "facts," there are three major reasons for the continuance of local production. The first is the natural protection offered to domestic production by high transport costs, infrequent delivery, and the perishability of certain commodities. This has provided space for local production of a few specialized products such as fresh vegetables, bread, and beer. Second, there may be strategic reasons based on the concept of self-reliance that are particularly strong in relation to the production of basic foodstuffs. And third, there are powerful political pressures emanating from the local bourgeoisie for import substitution behind high tariff barriers; examples of both existing (e.g, plastics, paints, cream) and planned ventures (automobile assembly) have already been mentioned.

This latter pressure to import substitution raises a very real threat to the continuation of the Seychelles economic success. When there are alternative uses for labor and land (in tourism, fishing, and public services), the expansion of internationally uncompetitive industries must necessarily occur at the expense of economic growth. Moreover, insofar as such industries produce commodities for lower-income consumers, it will also make the distribution of income more unequal (in favor of industrial capital and possibly its labor force). Finally, by reducing imports (and therefore import duties) it will also have a negative impact on the finances of the state.

CONCLUSIONS

For most Third World economies at the periphery of the world economy, independence has been a predominantly "political" phenomenon,
reflecting the internal momentum of accumulation and class formation.
Economic "independence" and betterment of living standards have been
mirages, and in many parts of the Third World there has been a consistent
decline in the real incomes of the masses, particularly in the 1970s. The
Seychelles is an exception to this phenomenon, its success stemming in
part from its isolation, its strategic importance, its smallness of size, its
lack of resources, and the historical isolation that it faced given these
parameters. While some elements of this story (particularly the geopolitical
factor) can be seen in other peripheral economies, the Seychelles remains a
very special case, with only limited applicability to other Third World
economies.

It is a fascinating question whether the future holds as much promise as
the past does. In "theory" it is conceivable to design a set of policies that
maximize the Seychelles' strength in tourism and fishing and minimize the
weaknesses in agriculture and industry. But it is not possible to do so in
abstraction from concrete political-economic phenomenon. Most notably,
here are two possible configurations that might spoil the dream. The first
is the confluence between geopolitical strategic considerations and internal
political opposition, which might lead to violent conflict, threatening the
viability of the tourist sector. Should the tourist industry begin to have the
adverse social impact evidenced in the Carribean, this too will pose a threat
to future growth. The second concerns the grandiose expansionism of the
former petite bourgeoisie, which now has strong links with the state and is
bent on accumulation via high-cost import substitution. Nevertheless, the
situation is particularly fluid, and it is difficult to anticipate what the final
balance of forces will be over the coming decade.

All this brings us back to the special position of the Seychelles and its
relationship to the general problem of small peripheral economies, of
which African island enclaves are an extreme example. What has occurred
in the Seychelles has been prosperity without accumulation. There has, for
example, been no viable accumulation in any of the various economic
sectors. In both manufacturing and agriculture, further accumulation
shows signs of reducing prosperity, while in fishing, despite the Seychelles'
rich potential, its distance from major markets will always make this a
marginal sector. The most accurate characterization of these islands, there-

fore, is of a rentier-type of prosperity, arising from its "untouched," remote, and beautiful environment. The problem for rentier economies of this type, however, is that the scarce resource is seldom an absolute monopoly, that it is very fragile (e.g., as a consequence of a too-fast or ill-judged expansion of the tourist industry, or due to political disruption) and that it is heavily dependent on external demand. All of these problems face the Seychelles—so do they confront other island and small economies of this type.

POSTSCRIPT

In the late afternoon of November 25, 1981, a squad of 43 "mercenaries," aided by six colleagues already in residence as "tourists," were surprised before they had time to launch a planned coup designed to reinstate former President Mancham. They were beaten off by the Seychelles army, escaping by commandeering an incoming Air India airplane and forcing it to return them to South Africa, their point of origin.

The fact that most of these "mercenaries" were South Africans should not be misinterpreted as indicating that Mancham alone was behind the coup attempt (buying in the assistance of sympathetic soldiers), for it turns out that many of these "mercaneries" in fact belonged to the elite Second Reconnaissance Unit of the South African Army. Furthermore, underlying the South African connection lay the active support and connivance of parts of the Kenyan government and CIA.

How does this attempted coup affect the argument of this chapter on the Seychelles? Well, it clearly reinforces the conclusions reached in the earlier discussion. The only point of detail that could be added is that changing military technology increased the likelihood of this attempted coup. The Soviet Union's industrial base is vulnerable to submarine-launched missiles from either the North Pole route or the Arabian Sea. Until recently, the U.S. Polaris missiles had a range of about 2500 miles and required launching from the 15 degree north parallel. But the new Trident submarine missile has a range of 4000 miles and can reach the USSR's industrial heartland from the equator, making the Seychelles an important listening post for the Soviet Union. Clearly American interests lie in denying this vantage point to the Soviets and what better way to exercise this than through ensuring that a sympathetic regime controlled the archipelago, and who better to enforce this than the South African proxies?

NOTES

1. Neighboring Madagascar (area of 226,658 square miles), while large by comparison with the Seychelles, also fits into the standard definition of a small country (i.e., those with a population less than 10 million).

2. See Le Brun and Murray (1980), who include the "technical class" in this "revolutionary" alliance.

3. Which has been as follows: 1972 = 64 percent, 1973 = 53 percent, 1974 = 52 percent, 1975 = 62 percent, 1976 = 66 percent, 1977 = 68 percent, 1978 = 66 percent, and 1979 = 64 percent.

4. While no figures exist for profits in any of the sectors, casual empiricism confirms a higher rate of profit in manufacturing and tourism than in the plantation or small scale farming sectors.

5. From 24.6 percent in 1974, to 21.3 percent in 1975, 17.5 percent in 1976, 16 percent in 1977, and 19.2 percent in 1978.

6. These cost calculations are based upon a foreign investment that is free of corporate tax for ten years, free from tax on expatriates' salary for an unlimited period, has preferential sales to the state, and is free from all import duties and controls.

7. I am grateful to Chris Colclough for these calculations.

8. I am grateful to John Bryden for these data.

REFERENCES

Barclays Bank DCO (1965, 1967, 1970) The Seychelles: An Economic Survey. London: Barclays.

International monetary fund (1979) Seychelles—Recent Economic Developments. (mimeo)

KAPLINSKY, R. (1980) "Capitalist accumulation in the periphery: the Kenyan case reexamined." Review of African Political Economy, No. 17.

LE BRUN, O. and R. MURRAY (1980) The Seychelles National Youth Service: The Seed of a New Society. Brighton. (mimeo)

LEE, C. (1976) Seychelles: Political Castaways. London: Elm Tree Books.

Republic of Kenya (1978) Statistical Abstract 1977. Nairobi: Central Bureau of Statistics.

Republic of Seychelles (1978) 1977 Census Report. Mahe.

Republic of Seychelles (1979) Trade Report for the Year 1978. Mahe.

Republic of Seychelles (1979) Report on the 1978 Household Expenditure Survey. Mahe.

9

LES SURVIVANCES COLONIALES
AUX COMOROS

CLAUDE GASPART
University of Louvain

The process of decolonization in the Comoros, the author argues, has to be considered a failure, in both political and economic terms. The very fact of smallness has produced a situation of considerable political and economic dependence on the former metropolitan power, France. Political representatives of one of the four islands constituting the Comoro Archipelago, Mayotte, actually refused independence in favor of French protection. The author discusses the Mayotte crisis as well as other indicators of political instability from the colonial period, through to the "socialist experience" under Ali Soilah and the period of government under President Ahmed Abdallah. Claude Gaspart contends that the acute dependence on Paris propelled a prolonged crisis in leadership and a profound lack of confidence in the local capacity to solve political and administrative problems.

As in the other Indian Ocean territories surveyed in this book, the location of the Comoros—guarding the Mozambique Channel, which carries oil tankers from Indonesia and the Gulf—gives the islands an important strategic significance. Professor Gaspart sees the origin of the Mayotte crisis and the several coups d'état that followed independence as related to the intense political pressures that stem from outside interest in the area and the consequent attempts by local aspirants to political office to maximize their bargaining power. At the same time, it is doubtful whether any group has extracted a significant degree of leverage playing the strategic card.

—R.C.

L'archipel des Comores est situé à l'entrée nord du Canal de Mozambique dans l'océan Indien et est composé de quatre îles: Grande Comore, Anjouan, Mohéli et Mayotte, d'une superficie totale de 2034 km^2.[1] Les trois premières de ces îles ont accédé à l'indépendance, par décision unilatérale, le 6 juillet 1975 et forment à l'heure actuelle une République Fédérale Islamique tandis que la quatrième île, celle de Mayotte, est demeurée française, suite au voeu de ses habitants exprimé par référendum.

L'évolution politique et institutionnelle des Comores a été marquée, au cours des deux décennies écoulées, par une instabilité de caractère permanent: luttes des partis et tendances avant 1975; renversement par une coalition des partis d'opposition du premier président, M. Ahmed Abdallah, moins d'un mois après l'indépendance, le 3 août 1975. Son successeur, M. Ali Soilih gouverne dans un climat d'incertitude politique que la rupture de tous les liens avec la France contribue, au fil du temps, à approfondir; des mercenaires étrangers renversent Ali Soilih, le 13 mai 1978 etc. A l'heure actuelle, l'isolement diplomatique du pays consécutif au coup d'Etat, la sécession de Mayotte, l'election du socialiste François Mitterrand à la présidence française, le 10 mai 1981, une opposition active, tant à l'intérieur qu'à l'extérieur, sont autant d'eléménts qui concourent à donner à la situation politique comorienne un caractère instable.

A première vue, la décolonisation des Comores n'aurait pas dû poser de problèmes majeurs. Trois de ces îles sont françaises depuis moins d'un siècle; la population européenne se réduit à quelques centaines de personnes tandis que l'intérêt économique du territoire est presque nul. Reste, bien sûr, la position stratégique des Comores qui les habilite à contrôler le trafic pétrolier en provenance du Golfe arabo-persique et de l'Indonésie en direction de l'Europe et des Etats-Unis via le Cap.

En réalité, cette décolonisation s'est déroulée dans les pires conditions comme l'ont noté de nombreux analystes et est un processus raté à un point tel que c'en est presqu'un cas d'école. Cette décolonisation hâtive développe, aujourd'hui encore, ses effets sur la politique intérieure et extérieure de l'archipel. L'imbroglio politique et l'histoire récente du pays s'expliquent par le fait que les Comores sont devenues indépendantes sans posséder les structures tant politiques qu'économiques susceptibles de répondre aux besoins du moment. Mais aussi parce que le pays manquait d'hommes pour mener à bien l'accession à la souveraineté. Loin en effet de favoriser la mise en place d'authentiques élites locales, de former des administrateurs compétents, la France, puissance coloniale, s'est le plus souvent employée à préserver et même a renforcer les privilèges d'une petite caste d'affairistes prenant appui sur des structures féodales et un islam médiéval (Junqua, 1975: 15). Le passé récent de l'archipel (à l'exception de la période "soilihienne" 1976-1978) a consacré la primauté quasi absolue de la politique "politicienne" sur le fait économique. C'est pourtant celui-ci qui s'impose en dernière analyse et qui aurait dû mobiliser les énergies locales. Mais la colonisation française a été relativement peu entreprenante aux Comores et le pays doit faire face à un ensemble de défis qui dépassent ses possibilités actuelles.

Défi démographique d'abord: la plus récente projection de la population des quatre îles fait état, pour l'année 1982, de 438.310 habitants (World Bank, 1979: 127) (soit une densité moyenne de 215 habitants au km^2)^2 et d'un taux d'accroissement voisin de 2,7% . Ce problème démographique s'aggrave encore si l'on examine la densité par rapport à la surface agricole utile[3] notion importante dans ce pays où plus de 80% de la population vivent encore directement de l'agriculture: à la Grande Comore et à Anjouan, les deux îles les plus étendues de l'archipel, cette densité est de 407 et 568, respectivement.

Défi économique ensuite: la présence française a privilégié, à travers les sociétés coloniales, la production de cultures industrielles (essences à parfum, coprah, vanille, girofle) destinées à l'exportation et ce, au détriment des cultures vivrières. Ce type de développement agricole exerce, aujourd'hui encore, une influence prépondérante sur la structure de production agricole et la structure d'allocation des terres. Le déficit vivrier permanent qui en résulte et qui est une des caractéristiques essentielles de l'économie comorienne conduit le pays à être fortement dépendant de l'extérieur pour la couverture de ses besoins alimentaires.[4]

D'autres indicateurs enfin témoignent du sous-développement de l'archipel: le taux de scolarisation, à l'indépendance, d'à peine 33% dans le primaire et de 8% dans le secondaire; le système sanitaire quasi inexistant; le commerce encore largement basé sur le troc . . . Malgre l'urgence des problèmes économiques et sociaux à résoudre ceux-ci ne semblent pas avoir constitué une préoccupation majeure pour la classe politique comorienne au cours des deux dernières dècennies, exception faite de la présidence d'Ali Soilih. La politique "politicienne", on l'a déjà noté, a largement occupé le devant de la scène; c'est elle qui mobilisera ici l'attention, l'aspect socio-économique demeurant cependant en toile de fond.

La République Fédérale Islamique des Comores est un micro-Etat (ou un mini-Etat). Tous les critères lui conférant ce statut convergent (Taylor, 1971: 183-202). La petite dimension, jointe à l'isolement géographique relatif, a-t-elle pu, dans le cas des Comores, produire des conséquences sociales et politiques? Il semble, comme l'ont noté certains auteurs (Wood, 1967: 32) que la petite dimension entraîne une plus grande vulnérabilité aux crises et aux pressions de toutes sortes. Une conséquence importante de la petite dimension, dans le cas des Comores, est la dépendance politique. L'analyse de cette caractéristique structurelle constitue la première partie de la présente étude.

Il faut donc revenir sur le passé. C'est nécessaire pour un pays qui ne l'a pas quitté et dont on ne perçoit pas encore clairement l'avenir. Au fil de l'évolution politique des vingt dernières années, on montrera comment le mécanisme de dépendance politique s'est mis en place, comment il s'est développé, de quels appuis et forces il a pu bénéficier.

L'instabilité politique interne aux Comores que l'on a évoquée plus haut est un reflet de cette dépendance politique. Celle-ci s'est traduite principalement par le fait que la classe dirigeante comorienne a toujours voulu trouver à Paris une réponse aux problèmes politiques internes de l'archipel, même après l'indépendance, plutôt que de rechercher des solutions de manière autonome alors qu'institutionnellement elle en avait les moyens depuis 1961, date de la première loi d'autonomie interne. Mais l'on remarquera que la faiblesse du leadership politique n'est pas particulière aux Comores et qu'elle caractérise de nombreux micro-Etats du tiers monde (Selwyn, 1975: 18) Simultanément, on observe que la France n'a jamais eu de politique réellement cohérente à l'égard des Comores. On le montrera. Il est vrai que cette absence de cohérence a partiellement trouvé son origine dans un manque de continuité politique: entre 1958 et 1974, quinze ministres et secrétaires d'Etat se sont succédé au Ministère des Départements et Territoires d'Outre-Mer (DOM-TOM), à Paris.

Ces deux éléménts—recherche de solutions à Paris aux problèmes internes et absence de politique bien définie—expliquent dans une large mesure les péripéties de la vie politique comorienne: indépendance unilatérale, coups d'Etat, sécession de Mayotte etc.

L'anémie du pouvoir politique local apparaît clairement dans l'affaide Mayotte. L'analyse de cette crise constitue la deuxième partie de l'étude. La sécession mahoraise a eu, tant au plan national qu'international, de multiples implications et, aujourd'hui encore, domine le débat politique de l'archipel et les rapports avec la France. L'analyse de cette sécession permet de montrer comment l'Etat a été incapable de trouver en lui-même les ressources nécessaires pour surmonter une crise majeure du fait de l'affaiblissement de ses structures politiques internes.

Enfin, dans la troisième partie, on montrera comment la position strategique des Comores dans l'océan Indien n'est pas étrangère à la vie politique mouvementée de l'archipel.

L'ÉVOLUTION POLITIQUE ET INSTITUTIONNELLE DE 1960 À 1982 ET LA DÉPENDANCE POLITIQUE

La société comorienne est caractérisée par une structure féodale au sein de laquelle l'aristocratie, tirant de la possession des terres une influence politique, a longtemps joué un rôle essentiel. A l'heure actuelle, plutôt que d'aristocratie, il conviendrait de parler de *notables,* personnages influents qui détiennent l'essentiel de la puissance économique et politique. Ces notables sont très souvent, il est vrai, issus de la noblesse. Maise, de plus en plus, ils se recrutent dans la bourgeoisie marchande, tard venue dans la hiérarchie traditionnelle de la société comorienne (Martin, 1968: 62). En realite, depuis 1965, l'on assiste a une phase de transition de la societe comorienne qui se traduit par un recul de l'influence de la noblesse, recul lui-même lié à l'effritement de la notion de clan et du rôle croissant joué par les notables dans les divers aspects de la vie de l'archipel.

Dans le cadre d'une telle société, les divers partis politiques sont des partis sans idéologie bien définie: on appartient à tel ou tel parti parce que l'on est favorable au notable qui le dirige. Ainsi, le notable (cadi, cheikh, chef religieux . . .) influence considérablement le comportement politique des Comoriens (Saint-Alban, 1973: 83).

Le poids des structures féodales est tel que les paysans, lors des élections, votent de la facon indiquée par les chefs de village (Charpantier, 1976: 101). Le clientélisme est donc généralisé. Le maintien de structures politiques féodales a été favorisé par l'isolement géographique des Comores: l'administration française a eu peu de prises, durant la colonisation, sur les structures coutumières de cette société (Bourde, 1965: 91). En outre, le caractère traditionnel de ces structures est accentué par l'importance de l'islam dans la vie politique: la population, surtout dans les campagnes, est soumise aux chefs religieux, eux-mêmes soutenus matériellement par les chefs politiques en place.

Enfin, les rivalités interinsulaires sont une caractéristique genérale importante pour comprendre l'évolution politique de l'archipel (Ostheimer, 1975: 75). Ces rivalités ont non seulement facilité la conquête française au

19° siècle, mais elles exercent, de nos jours, une influence déterminante dans la vie politique notamment en ce qu'elles empêchent la formation d'un parti politique enraciné dans les quatre îles et la mise au point d'un programme économique commun. La jalousie interinsulaire est à la base du problème politique interne majeur auquel doit faire face l'archipel: unité ou séparatisme. Les rivalités sont évidentes dans le cas du conflit qui oppose Mayotte au reste de l'archipel. Mais elles sont également sensibles entre, par exemple, la Grande Comore et Anjouan. Dans certains pays du tiers monde, l'absence d'unité est parfois contrebalancée par la présence sur la scène politique d'une armée où se fondent les disparités. Ce n'est pas le cas aux Comores (Flobert, 1976a: 326).

La présence français aux Comores remonte au 19° siècle.[5] Par une pénétration échelonnée de 1841 à 1912, la France substitue progressivement sa souveraineté à celle des "sultans batailleurs" locaux. Par la loi d'annexion du 25 juillet 1912, les Comores deviennent une dépendance de Madagascar. "L'archipel cesse alors d'intéresser l'administration française, notent Chagnoux et Haribou (1980: 31), et va accumuler dans tous les domaines un retard dont les conséquences se font encore sentir aujourd'hui."

Plutôt que l'administration, ce sont les sociétés coloniales francaises, exploitant les plantes à parfum,[6] qui vont modeler l'évolution du pays. Ces sociétés coloniales ont en effet exercé une influence déterminante sur le devenir agricole de l'archipel du point de vue de la structure de la production et du régime des terres Mais cette influence s'étend également au domaine politique: comme c'est le cas ailleurs, les caractéristiques économiques des plantations insulaires de petite dimension engendrent une structure politique au sein de laquelle l'intérêt des planteurs et des sociétés d'import-export est prédominant (Crusol & Crusol, 1980: 1027).[7]

Malgré les réticences coloniales, l'archipel se détache de Madagascar en 1946. De 1946 à 1956, l'organisation administrative du territoire est définie par les décrets du 24 septembre et du 25 octobre 1946: le premier, conférant aux Comores l'autonomie financière et administrative (mais non politique) érige l'archipel en "territoire d'outre-mer" (TOM) et accroît les pouvoirs de l'administrateur supérieur (français); le second, innove en creánt une Assemblée territoriale élue[8] possédant un pouvoir délibératif sur les questions non politiques (La Vie Publique en France, 1975: 17).

La décentralisation administrative est renforcée par la loi-cadre de juin 1956, appelée "loi Defferre" et par le décret du 22 juillet 1957 qui crée un Conseil de gouvernement chargé d'exécuter les décisions de l'Assembléé territoriale. En outre, cette dernière peut désormais délibérer sur tous les problèmes touchant aux intérêts locaux et se voit conférer de larges pouvoirs réglementaires.

En 1958, les Comoriens approuvent à une très large majorité le projet de Constitution de la V° République française et se prononcent pour le maintien du territoire dans l'ensemble français. L'Assembleé territoriale opte, le 11 décembre de la même anneé, pour le maintien du statut de territoire d'outre-mer, mais doté d'un caractère "évolutif" (C'est-à-dire un statut autorisant plus d'autonomie) (Flobert, 1976a: 343). Les relations difficiles entre l'archipel et la métropole commencent à se préciser dès ce moment car hommes politiques comoriens et autorités françaises n'interprètent pas l'expression "statut évolutif" de la même manière. A partir de cette époque, et jusqu'à l'indépendance, les relations entre Paris et Moroni seront marquées du sceau de l'ambigüité car les autorités françaises n'ont jamais voulu répondre clairement à cette question essentielle: la France entend-elle garder les Comores? (Flobert, 1976a: 345).

Deux séries de réformes institutionnelles vont alors conférer au territoire une autonomie croissante: les lois d'autonomie interne de 1961 et 1968. Au plan formel, ce qui distingue ces deux lois, c'est la manière dont les compétences d'Etat et les compétences territoriales sont respectivement délimitées: dans la première loi, ces dernières sont limitativement énumérées, les autres domaines relevant des autorités métropolitaines. Dans la seconde loi, c'est la compétence de la République française qui est déterminée, celle de l'archipel devenant de droit commun (Chagnoux et Haribou, 1980: 34). La loi du 22 décembre 1961 organise l'autonomie de gestion et se caractérise principalement par une plus large décentralisation administrative et un pouvoir accru des autorités locales dans les matières d'intérêt territorial tandis que l'Administrateur supérieur est remplacé par un Haut-Commissaire, représentent le pouvoir central. La première loi d'autonomie interne se heurte, dans son application, à une série de difficultés et, en 1966-1967, de nouvelles discussions ont lieu pour modifier le statut de 1961 et conduire l'archipel à la pleine autonomie interne.

Le projet de loi proposé à Paris répond à trois préoccupations principales: donner aux organes institutionnels du territoire le pouvoir de régler eux-mêmes leur mode de formation, leur fonctionnement et leurs rapports; élargir et définir les compétences territoriales et les distinguer nettement de celles de l'Etat; enfin, préciser dans quelles conditions s'exprimera la personnalité des circonscriptions (Flobert, 1976a: 348). Le statut est adopté à la fin de l'année de 1967 et rentre en application le 3 janvier 1968: c'est la deuxième loi d'autonomie interne.

On assiste donc, au cours de la période 1946-1968, à un élargissement continuel de l'autonomie de l'archipel sans toutefois que la France définisse une politique cohérente ni qu'elle précise le terminus ad quem de ce processus. Comme l'écrivent justement Chagnoux et Haribou (1980: 33) "l'évolution institutionnelle vers l'indépendance (. . .) semble caractérisée plus par des mesures destinées à satisfaire le besoin de considération de la classe politique, que par des transformations profondes." Pour les hommes politiques, comoriens, l'évolution vers l'indépendance signifiait recevoir plus de considération et de subventions de la métropole. Ce n'était certes pas pour exercer davantage de responsabilités. Mais qui sont ces hommes politiques comoriens et que représentent-ils?

Les deux principaux partis politiques apparaissent vers 1946, au moment où les Comores deviennent un territoire d'outre-mer: les "Verts," parti fondé par Saïd Mohamed Cheikh et les "Blancs" du prince Saïd Ibrahim. Il conviendrait de parler de *tendances* plutôt que de partis politiques: en effet, il s'agit avant tout, on l'a déjà relevé, de rassemblements créés autour d'un homme, sans qu'il y ait une idéologie ou une doctrine politique bien définie (Saint-Alban, 1973: 77-78). Le clivage politique observé ne correspond pas à la classique distrinction gauche-droite. L'appartenance à l'une ou l'autre tendance est fonction de l'attachement de chacun pour l'un ou l'autre des leaders. De plus, les vieilles rivalités villageoises n'ont pas disparu et expliquent, dans une certaine mesure, l'absence de partis politiques réels jusqu'à une date encore récente. Ces deux partis—les Verts et les Blancs—n'ont ni structures, ni organisation, ni programme économique. Les deux seules différences que l'on puisse trouver entre eux se situent d'abord du point de vue de la composition de leur électorat (les "Blancs" recrutant leur clientèle plutôt parmi les gros commerçants et les "Verts" parmi les fonctionnaires); ensuite, quant à leur attitude par rapport à la France: les "Blancs" sont peut-être plus nationalistes que les "Verts" attachés plus durablement à une amitié avec la France (Flobert, 1976a: 329). Ces deux formations dominent entièrement la scène politique comorienne de 1946 à 1961, date à laquelle ils fusionnent, mettant ainsi un terme aux luttes qui n'étaient souvent que des conflits de personnes.

Au cours de la période 1961-1968, l'on assiste à la création de deux partis politiques d'opposition: l'un à l'intérieur, le Mouvement Populaire Mahorais (MPM) (parti dont il sera question quand la présente étude traitera de l'affaire mahoraise) et l'autre, à l'extérieur, le Molinaco (Mouvement de Libération Nationale des Comores).

Créé en 1963 à Dar Es Salam, soutenu et financé par l'OUA, l'Union Soviétique et certains pays progressistes africains, le Molinaco a essentiellement joué le rôle de catalyseur dans le mouvement d'indépendance des Comores, même si son influence, à l'intérieur même de l'archipel, est très réduite.[9] Son prolongement à l'intérieur des îles, le PEC (Parti pour l'Evolution des Comores) rencontre, lui aussi, peu d'audience.

En janvier 1968, des grèves et des manifestations de lycéens sont réprimées brutalement à Moroni. Ces événements déterminent la création d'un autre parti politique: le RDPC (Rassemblement Démocratique du Peuple Comorien). Fondé par le prince Saïd Mohamed Jaffar et Mouzaoir Abdallah, le RDPC, implanté essentiellement à la Grande Comore et composé d'éléments assez jeunes de la bourgeoisie, ne se caractérise pas par une idéologie particulière sinon que ses membres sont plus libéraux que les membres des partis traditionnels.

Au cours de cette même année 1968, le Pasoco (Parti Socialiste des Comores) voit le jour. Ce parti occupe, sur l'échiquier politique comorien, une place importante, sans commune mesure avec le nombre de ses adhérents (Saint-Alban, 1973: 86). C'est le premier parti politique comorien 'a parler, sur le plan interne, d'indépendance.[10] Actif surtout 'a la Grande Comore et à Mohéli, le Pasoco est principalement composé d'intellectuels formés en France, partisans d'un socialisme à la ligne assez indéfinie mais qui tendrait à se rapprocher du "modèle tanzanien."

A la mort de Saïd Mohamed Cheikh, en mars 1970, le prince Saïd Ibrahim—leader du parti "blanc"—devient président cu Conseil de gouvernement et fait dissoudre la Chambre des deputés qui, élue en 1967 sur la liste de Saïd Mohamed Cheikh, ne reflète plus la situation politique. Saïd Ibrahim cree des lors l'UDC (Union Democratique des Comores) qui se veut un parti "au-dessus des partic." Il se détache ainsi du parti "blanc."

Au début des années 1970, on se trouve ainsi en présence de deux partis dominants—l'UDC et le RDPC—qui rassemblent grosso modo les trois-quarts de l'électorat comorien traditionaliste et qui sont devenus les héritiers spirituels, en quelque sorte, des partis "vert" et "blanc," respectivement. Si l'on excepte le MPM dont la position sur la scène politique comorienne est particulière, les partis d'opposition sont au nombre de deux—Pasoco et Molinaco—auxquels il covient d'ajouter l'ASEC (Association des Stagiaires et Etudiants Comoriens), fondé en 1966 et qui a été la pépinière où se sont formés les dirigeants du Pasoco.

Le 12 juin 1972, le prince Saïd Ibrahim de l'UDC est renversé sous l'action du RDPC. Mais, paradoxe, ce dernier s'associe, le 10 septembre, au parti "vert" pour former l'OUDZIMA (unité) tandis que les partisans du prince créent l'UMMA (Parti du peuple, en arabe).

A partir de ce moment, l'indépendance est à l'ordre du jour de tous les partis politiques, qu'ils y soient favorables ou hostiles. L'objectif de l'UMMA, initialement, était de lutter contre l'idée d'indépendance: ce parti prônait un resserrement des liens avec la France (Vallier, 1977: 14). La position de l'UMMA évolue ensuite puisqu'il réclame lui aussi l'indépen-

dance. En realite, l'UMMA du prince Saïd Ibrahim est favorable à l'indépendance mais avec l'accord et dans l'amitié avec la France, tandis que la
coalition RDPC du prince Saïd Mohamed Jaffar se prononce en faveur
d'une "indépendance rapide." Ainsi que le remarque Saint-Alban: "La
rapidité avec laquelle l'UMMA a su se constituer une importante clientèle
électorale reflète bien la crainte d'une fraction non négligeable de l'opinion
devant une marche vers l'indépendance qui a été insuffisament préparée"
(Saint-Alban, 1973: 85).

Le vote de la deuxième loi d'autonomie interne de 1968 (cf. supra) n'a
cependant pas été d'une grande utilité au plan politique interne, et les
difficultés entre Paris et Moroni persistent. Saïd Ibrahim est favorable à
une "association étroite avec la France" tandis que d'autres hommes
politiques au pouvoir estiment que "la France accule petit à petit les
Comores à vouloir l'indépendance." Ainsi, à partir de 1972, la classe
politique, féodale et commerçante, reprend à son compte la revendication
d'indépendance des partis d'opposition.

A la suite du renversement du prince Saïd Ibrahim s'amorce une
nouvelle phase du processus d'accession à l'indépendance avec, le 23
décembre 1972, le vote par la Chambre des députés des Comores, d'une
résolution demandant "l'indépendance dans l'amitié et la coopération avec
la France." Les négociations menées entre une délégation comorienne
conduite par M. Ahmed Abdallah—porté à la présidence avec pour mandat
de négocier l'indépendance—et le ministère des DOM-TOM aboutissent, le
15 mai 1973, à la "declaration commune sur l'acces des Comores à
l'indépendance" (Documents de l'actualité internationale, 1973: 523-527);
qui prévoit l'organisation, dans un délai de cing ans, d'un référendum sur
cet accès à la souveraineté. Il s'agit d'un texte, important sur lequel on
reviendra dans l'analyse de l'affaire mahoraise. A la suite de cette "déclaration commune," ambigüe comme on le montrera, les événements vont se
précipiter. Au lieu de préparer une transition en douceur, les politiciens au
pouvoir vont accélérer le processus dans la hâte et l'improvisation.

Le référendum prévu a lieu le 22 décembre 1974: 95% des votants se
prononcent en faveur de l'indépendance tandis que 64% des électeurs de
Mayotte choisissent de demeurer français (Africa Research Bulletin, 1975:
3466).[11] Ces résultats vont précipiter l'indépendance. Invoquant à
l'origine la déclaration du 15 juin 1973, Ahmed Abdallah considère que la
réponse positive des populations au référendum confère *ipso facto* à la
Chambre un pouvoir constituant[12] et au président du Conseil de
gouvernement les compétences de chef de l'Etat. Il annonce donc son
intention de soumettre directement le projet de Constitution à référen-

dum. S'agissant du contenu des institutions, il ecarte toute solution de partition de l'archipel, même sous une forme fédérale et se borne à prôner une régionalisation dont il ne précise pas le contenu. Les partis d'opposition, regroupés, en 1974, dans un Front National Uni (au sein duquel l'UMMA est le plus influent) dénient toute valeur juridique aux accords de juin 1973. Ils souhaitent que les autorités françaises désignent un organe collégial chargé d'expédier les affaires courantes et organisent l'élection d'une Assemblée constituante, le projet ainsi élaboré étant ensuite soumis au référendum. Mais tout en réclamant le respect des particularismes insulaires, ils ne choisissent pas clairement entre un Etat authentiquement fédéral et un Etat unitaire décentralisé. Quant au MPM, s'appuyant sur le dernier alinéa de l'article 53 de la Constitution française selon lequel "nulle cession de territoire n'est valable sans le consentement des populations intéressés," il considère que l'île de Mayotte ne peut être dissociée de la France puisqu'elle a voté majoritairement contre l'indépendance (La Vie Publique en France, 1975: 20).

Le Parlement français vote finalement, le 30 juin 1975, une loi selon laquelle un Comité constitutionnel, largement représentatif, établira un projet de Constitution garantissant la personnalité politique et administrative des îles composant le futur Etat. Ce projet de Constitution sera soumis au référendum avant la proclamation de l'indépendance, à une date qui sera fixée par le Comité constitutionnel.

Cette "indépendance sous conditions" est jugée inacceptable par Ahmed Abdallah et le 6 juillet 1975, la Chambre des députés des Comores proclame l'indépendance unilatérale—par 33 voix sur 39, en l'absence des députés mahorais. Mayotte fait sécession, à partir de ce moment, et demeure française. Il s'agit pour Ahmed Abdallah plus d'une fuite en avant qu'autre chose: déclarer l'indépendance de façon unilatérale sans attendre la mise en place d'accords classiques de coopération, c'était donner un alibi à la France qui pouvait ainsi se désintéresser de l'archipel sans trop de scrupules.

Moins d'un mois après l'indépendance, le 3 août 1975, Ahmed Abdallah est renversé par le Front National Uni, coalition des partis d'opposition. Le principal instigateur de ce coup d'Etat est le prince Saïd Mohamed Jaffar, ancien président du Conseil de gouvernement de juin à octobre 1972, date à laquelle il avait démissionné pour entrer dans l'opposition[13] (Afrique Contemporaine, 1975: 16). Mais "l'homme fort" du nouveau régime, c'est Ali Soilih qui, dès la fin du mois d'août 1975, impose l'idée d'une "révolution" et constitue un gouvernement avec, au sommet, un Conseil National de la Révolution dont dépend un Conseil Exécutif National, ce dernier présidé par Said Mohamed Jaffar (Vallier, 1977: 17). Une délégation conduite par Mouzaoir Abdallah, ministre chargé de la Coordination, se rend à Paris, à l'automne 1975, pour tenter de négocier des accords transitoires avec le gouvernement français et pour proposer des garanties constitutionnelles facilitant la réintégration de Mayotte (Chagnoux et Haribou, 1980: 67). Les négociations échouent. Une des conséquences de cet échec est l'annonce, par le représentant francais à Moroni, du rapatriement des fonctionnaires métropolitains "car il n'y a pas d'accords de coopération d'Etat à Etat" "entre Paris et Moroni. Ce retrait marque pratiquement la fin de toutes les relations–économiques, politiques et diplomatiques–avec la France. Malgré la conclusion d'accords de coopération avec d'autres pays (cf. infra), le nouvel Etat indépendant va désormais devoir "compter sur ses propres forces."

Le 2 janvier 1976, les membres du Conseil Exécutif National et du Conseil National de la Révolution élisent Ali Soilih chef de l'Etat en remplacement du prince Jaffar. Dès le lendemain, le Conseil National de la Révolution est remplacé par un Conseil National des Institutions. Commence alors ce que l'on a coutume d'appeler la "révolution comorienne." La plupart des analystes distinguent quatre phases dans cette révolution qui va de janvier 1976 à la mi-mai 1978: a) une phase dite de "consolidation de l'Etat" (janvier 1976-aout 1976); b) une phase de "démocratie populaire" (août 1976-avril 1977); c) une "période transitoire" (avril–mai 1977); d) une "phase économique."

La première phase dite de "consolidation nationale" est une période au cours de laquelle il a fallu, après la rupture des relations avec la France, empêcher l'effondrement du pays et composer avec les structures existantes (commercants, notables, grands propriétaires . . .) (Maestre, 1979: 26). Cette période se caractérise par trois éléments principaux (Chagnoux et Haribou, 1980: 70-73): a) création d'une armée "populaire" entrainée et encadrée par des Africains de l'Ouest puis par des Tanzaniens (Relazioni Internazionali, 1977: 1102); b) création d'un secteur d'économie mixte pour importer les produits alimentaires de première nécessité; c) ébauche de décentralisation administrative qui sera consacrée dans la "Loi fondamentale" (Constitution) du 23 avril 1977 (cf. infra).

La deuxième phase dite de "démocratie populaire" (ou phase anti-féodale) a eu essentiellement pour objectif de supprimer les obstacles da nature socio-culturelle qui, jusque là, avaient empêché la modernisation de la société comorienne. Elle visait à changer les mentalités: avant d'être économique, la révolution d'Ali Soilih a été aussi–et peut-être surtout–sociale et culturelle. Ali Soilih a en effet engager une lutte contre le système féodal, la bureaucratie, la hiérarchie islamique et certaines coutumes et traditions rendues obligatoires par la religion (limitation des dépenses funéraires; les dépenses ostentatoires, formant la base du "grand mariage," sont interdites; interdiction du port du voile pour les Comoriennes . . .).

Parallèlement, Soilih va encourager l'émancipation des femmes et surtout des jeunes. La jeunesse va en effet devenir l'alliée privilégiée d'Ali Soilih au point que l'on a pu parler des Comores, en 1977, comme d'un "Etat lycéen."[14] Encadrant la jeunesse, Ali Soilih est 'a même de lui proposer une représentation politique du monde qui lui convienne. Pour abattre idéologiquement la classe politique traditionnelle qui s'appuyait sur des notables villageois et un système gérontocratique, Ali Soilih a conçu une politique de ligne kémaliste fondée sur le renversement des valeurs établies (Charpantier 1976: 109). Ce sont des "comités populaires," principalement composes de jeunes, qui vont mener campagne contre les traditions les plus rétrogrades et les pratiques obscurantistes de la société comorienne.

En Avril 1977, commence une étape importante de la révolution appelée "période transitoire." Par une ordonnance du 14 avril, le président dissout le gouvernement, toute l'administration publique ainsi que tous les partis politiques (Maestre, 1979: 26). Tous les fonctionnaires et agents de l'Etat—à l'exception des militaires—sont licenciés et renvoyés dans leurs villages d'origine. La direction du pays est assurée par un Conseil National Populaire. Caractérisée par son hypertrophie, sa concentration dans la capitale et donc, coupée du peuple, considérée comme alliée aux propriétaires terriens, l'administration comorienne constituait, aux yeux d'Ali Soilih, un obstacle à la mise en oeuvre de réformes tant au plan social qu'économique. Pour lui, cette "stratégie de la table rase" devait permettre de supprimer, au plan administratif, les séquelles de la colonisation.

Le Comité National Populaire adoptait, le 23 avril 1977, la "Loi fondamentale" (Constitution) qui instaurait une "République démocratique, laïque et sociale "et qui devait désormais régir le pays. Cette loi ne se limite pas à décrire les organes du nouveau pouvoir; elle manifeste aussi une certaine philosophie politique se caractérisant par le "pouvoir populaire" et l'autogestion.

La caractéristique essentielle de cette loi constitutionnelle est qu'elle veut instaurer un "pouvoir populaire" reposant de facon pyramidale sur les collectivités locales.[15] Le pouvoir central ne doit, en principe, s'occuper que des questions d'intérêt commun. Il comporte quatre grandes instances: la Defense nationale, les Relations exterieures, les Affaires intérieures (principalement santé et enseignement) et le Centre de planification chargé des questions de développement économique. La gestion et l'éxecution des programmes aux plan local et régional sont confiées à trois types d'instances décentralisees: les "mudirias," unités décentralisées d'autodéveloppement, regroupant de 3000 à 6000 personnes (l'archipel en comprend 55); les "bavus," au nombre de 7, regroupant les mudirias et les "wilayas," rassemblant les bavus de chaque île. Le pouvoir populaire s'exerce au niveau de chacune de ces collectivités. Dans les villages, des comités populaires de base sont élus au suffrage universel direct; les comités de mudirias et de wilayas procedent des comités populaires inférieurs. Au sommet, le Congrès national, "instance supérieure du pouvoir populaire" est constitue de tous les membres des comités de mudirias. Il est notamment chargé de proposer "les candidats à la présidence et à la vice-présidence du Conseil d'Etat," lequel constitue le gouvernement du pays (Maestre, 1978: 28).

Les bases d'une nouvelle structure de gestion et d'administration ayant ete ainsi jetées, démarre la "phase économique" de la révolution. La stratégie de développement économique mise en oeuvre, au début de l'année 1978, s'articule autour d'une double priorité: autosuffisance alimentaire et maintien du niveau des exportations. L'autosuffisance alimentaire est un objectif qui n'a de sens que si le revenu provenant de l'exportation des cultures industrielles demeure au moins constant. Dans ces conditions, la production locale de produits vivriers (auparavant importés) peut conduire à la création d'un surplus. Celui-ci peut permettre au pays d'amorcer un processus d'accumulation du capital et rendre possible l'investissement principalement dans le domaine agro-industriel. Pour atteindre ce double objectif, outre les mesures dans le domaine de la decentralisation auxquelles on a -fait référence plus haut, le Plan quinquennal[16] propose un ensemble de réformes qui touchent à l'éducation, au régime de propriété et d'allocation des terres, à la création d'un secteur d'économie mixte etc. (Gaspart, 1981: 132-133).

Mais, la plupart des mesures et réformes tant politiques, administratives qu'économiques ne verront qu'un début de réalisation car l'experience arrive prequ'à son terme. Ali Soilih a en effet dû affronter sur son chemin de nombreuses difficultés et de nombreux obstacles.

Toutes les reformes ont été menées tambour battant. En deux ans, la société comorienne, traditionnelle dans ses fondements, connaissait un souffle de changement beaucoup plus puissant qu'elle n'en avait connu en deux siècles. Des réticences et des oppositions ont donc vu le jour. Appliquées avec un peu trop de zèle révolutionnaire par des comités de jeunes, certaines réformes ont fait l'objet de maladresse dans leur application (i.e. des circulaires enjoignant aux commerçants et aux services publics de ne plus accueillir les femmes voilées . . .) Les autorités ont manifestement été débordées par ce pouvoir popularire. Les excès de celui-ci ont en fait contribué à discréditer l'expèrience et a donner de celle-ci, à l'étranger, l'image d'un "goulag sous les cocotiers" car, c'est vrai, la rèpression s'intensifiait au fil du temps.

Le président Soilih demandant par référendum, le 28 octobre 1977, la prolongation de son mandat jusqu'à l'achèvement des mudirias, n'obtient que 55% des suffrages. Les difficultés économiques et financières mais également une nouvelle campagne du "pouvoir populaire" pour bannir certaines pratiques religieuses ont accru le nombre des mécontents (Chagnoux et Haribou, 1980: 80).[17]

Au début de l'année 1978, les Comores sont menacées d'asphyxie financière et économique (longue pénurie de riz), les tensions sociales entre citadins arabisés et militaires d'origine paysanne s'aiguisent. A la suite de la découverte d'un complot, le 14 janvier, visant à renverser le président (Le Monde, 15-16 janvier 1978: 32), la répression s'aggrave: l'armèe tire le 17 mars sur la population faisant 15 morts et une centaine de blessés (Le Monde, 23 mars 1978: 4). Simultanement, on assiste à un exode de Comoriens vers la France, via Mayotte et la Réunion.[18] C'est dans une telle situation politique que s'achève la révolution comorienne: des mercenaires étrangers renversent Ali Soilih, le 13 mai 1978, lors d'un coup d'Etat qui favorise le retour d'Ahmed Abdallah au pouvoir.

La révolution comorienné a comporte un ensemble d'aspects positifs: développement des productions locales et des cultures vivrières, réallocation des terres selon leur vocation agricole, émancipation des jeunes et des femmes, priorité donnée aux campagnes et au développement rural etc. Près de quatre ans après, l'entreprise moderniste d'Ali Soilih n'est pas completement oubliée. Elle a laissé des traces dans les esprits (Le Monde, 25 avril 1981).

L'islam comorien, religion d'Etat, retrograde mais non fanatique, imprègne profondément la vie sociale. L'erreur d'Ali Soilih fut de l'attaquer de front et d'avoir encouragé une politique souvent marquée par une intolérance anti-religieuse. Pour les observateurs qui suivaient l'expérience d'Ali Soilih avec intérêt et parfois sympathie, la revolution a été victime d'un "vaste complot impérialiste" destiné à abattre un régime progressiste dans une région dont l'intérêt stratégique et géopolitique est évident (Maestre, 1979: 33). Plus réalistement, Ali Soilih n'avait pas eu une appréciation assez juste des limites des réformes qui pouvaient être imposées à la société comorienne dans des domaines-clés qui touchent à ses racines sociologiques telles que la pratique de la religion, la place assignée aux jeunes etc.

Sous la présidence d'Ali Soilih, la diplomatie comorienne poursuivait un double objectif: d'une part, obtenir la reconnaissance du nouvel Etat et de sa souveraineté sur Mayotte; d'autre part, attirer vers les trois îles des capitaux pour remplacer l'aide française.[19] En ce qui concerne le premier objectif, il a pleinement été atteint; à plusieurs reprises, tant l'OUA que l'ONU ont condamne, a une large majorite, la France pour sa politique mahoraise (cf. infra). Pour ce qui a trait au second objectif, les prets ont principalement ete fournis par les pays arabes (Lybie, Kuweit, Arabie Saoudite, Abu Dhabi). Quant à l'assistance technique, elle provenait de pays francophones tels que la Belgique, le Canada, le Sénégal, la Tunisie.

Les mois qui ont suivi le coup d'Etat ont été placés, à Moroni, sous le signe de la normalisation. Le 1° octobre 1978, un référendum constitutionnel instaurant une "République Fédérale Islamique" est approuvé par plus de 99% des suffrages exprimés. L'opinion en faveur d'une République fédérale répondait aux préoccupations du directoire politico-militaire mis en place dès le 13 mai.[20] Cet organisme à tenu a préserver la possibilité d'une réintégration ulteriéure de Mayotte au sein de la République, d'où le caractère fédéral de la Constitution. Ahmed Abdallah, candidat unique, a été élu président, le 23 octobre 1978, avec 99% des voix.

Le coup d'Etat de mai 1978 n'a pas inaugure une periode de calme politique. Le régime d'Ahmed Abdallah est loin de faire l'unanimité (malgré l'importance du score électoral realisé) et n'est pas ce que l'on peut appeler un régime stable comme en témoignent de nombreux événements récents.[21] Le président doit faire face, d'une part, à de sérieuses difficultés économiques et, d'autre part, à une opposition de plus en plus active tant à l'intérieur de l'archipel qu'à l'extérieur. De plus, il fait l'objet de vives critiques de la part d'organisations de défense des Droits de l'homme (Amnesty International, Fédération Internationale des Droits de l'Homme) (Le Monde, 4 octobre 1979; 23 janvier 1981). En exil à Paris, Ahmed Abdallah avait, a diverses reprile régime d'Ali Soilih. La situation ne semble guère meilleure sous son mandat.

Depuis la chute d'Ali Soilih, la France a ramené les Comores dans son orbite. De nombreux facteurs expliquent ce retour: les responsabilités passées et actuelles de Paris à Mayotte; la présence en France de 15000 Comoriens; le souci de contrecarrer une éventuelle mainmise étrangère sur les Comores. L'aide francaise paraît en outre cruciale pour la plus ou moins grande stabilité du régime. A l'heure actuelle, l'aide budgétaire francaise représénte plus de la moitié des dépenses de fonctionnement de l'Etat.[22] Aux termes d'un accord conclu en novembre 1978, enfin, Paris assure la défense des Comores contre agression en échange de facilitiés navales.

Par ailleurs, Ahmed Abdallah a effacé tout ce qui rappelait le régime précédent: les sociétés d'Etat ou mixtes ont été dénationalisées, le réseau des mudirias a été démantelé, les plans de réforme agraire ont été abandonnés (Leymarie, 1981b: 13). Au total, le pays paraît être retourné à un stade de non-développement.

Au plan diplomatique africain, le régime d'Ahmed Abdallah est isolé. Le coup d'Etat de mai 1978 s'appuyait sur des mercenaires étrangers qui, ultérieurement, ont occupé des postes non seulement dans l'armée mais également dans l'import-export, le tourisme. Le caractère ostensible de la présence de ces mercenaires entraîna, le 8 juillet 1978, l'expulsion de la délégation comorienne du sommet de l'OUA de Khartoum. Madagascar et les Seychelles ont décidé de ne plus reconnaître l'Etat comorien tant que celui-ci continuerait à s'appoyer sur des mercenaires étrangers. En outre, ces deux pays tout comme le Mozambique et la Tanzanie voient en l'archipel une base de tentative éventuelles de déstabilisation de la région, menées conjointement avec l'Afrique du Sud, notamment (Leymarie, 1981b: 13). Lors de la tentative avortée de renversement du président René aux Seychelles, le 25 novembre 1981, par un groupe de mercenaires venus d'Afrique du Sud, le rôle logistique des Comores a été relevé par la presse sud-africaine (Rand Daily Mail, 27 Novembre 1981: 5).

L'AFFAIRE MAHORAISE

L'affaire de Mayotte constitue un élément central de toute analyse socio-politique relative aux Comores. Cette crise domine, aujourd'hui encore, la vie politique de l'archipel et forme l'essentiel du contentieux existant entre Paris et Moroni. La crise de Mayotte permet de comprendre le mode de fonctionnement d'un système politique qui prend ses ordres à l'exteriéur—consequénce de la petite dimension.

Analyser l'affaire de Mayotte, c'est d'abord evoquer l'existence d'un soi-disant "particularisme mahorais." L'île de Mayotte est-elle différente des autres îles? Divers arguments ont été produits pour expliquer ce particularisme. D'abord un argument historique (Fichet, 1976: 424; Marinas Otero, 1978: 140): Mayotte ayant été colonisée plus tôt (1841) que les autres îles (Mohéli: 1886; Anjouan et Grande Comore: 1892), elle serait de ce fait plus francisée et plus attachée à la France. L'argument est peu convaincant. En effet, de 1841 à 1912, la France a peu fait pour assimiler la population de l'île. En outre, aucun effort de peuplement n'a été entrepris et le nombre d'Européens est toujours resté très réduit (Flobert, 1976b: 86).[23] On ajoutera que les matrones mahoraises qui forment la base même du Mouvement Populaire Mahorais (MPM) ne parlent pas le français.

Un autre argument est d'ordre ethno-linguistique. Ainsi Fichet écrit-il: "Contrairement aux trois autres îles, Mayotte est surtout habitée par des populations malgaches d'origine sakalave tandis qu'une partie des éléments blancs sont originaires de l'île Sainte-Marie, située sur la côte orientale de Madagascar, au large de Tamatave" (Fichet, 1976: 424). Selon cette argumentation, il n'y aurait jamais eu une population comorienne mais deux peuples: l'un arabisé, l'autre sakalave (Decraene, 1974: 26). De ce fait, la population de l'île serait catholique creole ou catholique malgache. Cet argument est lui aussi contestable. En réalite, la population est musulmane à 99%. Les Créoles ne représentent qu'une cinquantaine de familles et si environ 40% de la population parle le sakalave, dialecte malgache, ce groupe parle aussi le comorien et paraît moins attaché à la France que la population de villages typiquement comoriens. Meme les auteurs relativement favorables à la présence française à Mayotte indiquent qu'on chercherait en vain une justification historique, ethnique, linguistique ou religieuse au particularisme mahorais (Latrémolière, 1977: 3504).

Il est cependant vrai qu'au plan géographique, Grande Comore et Anjouan étaient plutôt tournés, dans le passé, vers Zanzibar et le continent africain tandis que Mayotte l'etait vers Nossi-Bé. Il est vrai aussi qu'à Mayotte la structure sociale n'est pas la même; les problèmes démographiques sont moins aigus qu'a la Grande Comore ou à Anjouan tandis que les hierarchies coutumieres sont atténuées (Binet, 1976: 19). Ceci ne permet pas d'affirmer pour autant qu'il y ait une race mahoraise, même s'il y a bien une spécificité mahoraise dans l'archipel.

L'existence du particularisme mahorais relève d'autres causes.[24] Pour un ensemble d'observateurs de la scène politique comorienne, c'est la décision de transférer[25] la capitale administrative des Comore de Dzaoudzi (Mayotte) à Moroni (Grande Comore) qui serait à l'origine du séparatisme mahorais (Martin, 1969: 36; Chagnoux et Haribou, 1980: 53). Saïd Mohamed Cheikh exige en effet que la capitale soit transférée dans son île d'origine. Pour lutter contre ce transfer considéré par l'ensemble de la population mahoraise comme une brimade, le Congrès des Notables de

Mayotte est créé, le 2 novembre 1958. Celui-ci se transforme en 1959, en une "Union pour la défense des intérêts de Mayotte" dont l'objectif affirmé est d'obtenir la départementalisation de l'archipel. Le déménagement des services administratifs de Dzaoudzi à Moroni commence à s'effectuer au mois de juin 1962. Ce transfert, prélude à une guerre d'usure entre Mayotte et le pouvoir central, est vivement ressenti, au plan économique, par la population mahoraise: de nombreux fonctionnaires quittent Mayotte, ce qui entraîne la perte de centaines de petits emplois subalternes (commis, plantons, domestiques, chauffeurs...) (Flobert, 1976b: 73). Beaucoup de Mahorais vont ainsi quitter Dzaoudzi pour Moroni, laissant derrière eux leurs femmes. La population féminine de l'île est ainsi particulièrement concernée par ce transfert. Ceci explique dans une large mesure le rôle important joué par les femmes dans la vie politique à Mayotte (Charpantier, 1976: 103-105).

Le transfert de la capitale n'est pas la seule explication du séparatisme mahorais. Celui-ci a également une base économique et trouve en partie son origine dans les rivalités interinsulaires dont il a été question au début de cette section. Les îles les plus *"riches"*—Mayotte et Mohéli—ont toujours craint la pression des deux autres îles, plus peuplées mais moins bien dotées du point de vue économique (Ostheimer, 1975: 79). La forte différence des densités de population entre les iles a provoqué, au fil des années, une importante immigration d'Anjouannais à Mayotte, la seule île à jouir d'une disponibilité en terres cultivables du fait d'une population relativement peu élevée et d'un régime foncier plus équitable. Cette immigration a développé chez les Mahorais un certain sentiment de xénophobie (notamment à l'égard des Anjouannais), sentiment d'autant plus vif que ces immigrants accaparaient les meilleures terres et réussissaient bien en affaires. La xénophobie n'est pas un sentiment typiquement comorien (Vallier, 1977: 14). Ce sont les Saint-Mariens installés à Mayotte et promus leaders du MPM[26] (le MPM prend, en 1966, la succession de "l'Union pour la défense des intérêts de Mayotte") qui en ont fait un instrument de propagande pour maintenir en éveil l'ardeur des militants du mouvement.

Les éléments qui précèdent—transfert de la capitale; immigration d'Anjouannais—s'ajoutent à diverses mesures vexatoires prises par les autorités de Moroni (principalement Saïd Mohamed Cheikh) à l'égard de Mayotte: brimades envers des fonctionnaires partisans du MPM; déplacement dans une autre île de l'unique médecin de Mayotte; blocage de crédits d'investissement etc. (Flobert, 1976b: 75). Toutes ces mesures ne font que renforcer le courant hostile au président et à toute politique unitaire. A la mort de Mohamed Cheikh, le prince Saīd Ibrahim amorce bien une politique d'apaisement, mais elle est de courte durée. L'arrivée au pouvoir d'Ahmed Abdallah aggrave encore les tensions.

Le problème mahorais s'est complexifié au fil des années. D'abord, parce que les dirigeants comoriens "ont préféré croire, comme le notent justement Chagoux et Haribou, que la solution de leur problème se trouvait à Paris et non pas dans l'archipel" (Chagnoux et Haribou, 1980: 57). Ceci est précisément une des conséquences de la petite dimension: le centre de décision est ailleurs.

Ensuite, la France n'a jamais eu, au cours des années 1970, une politique réellement cohérente à l'égard des Comores en général et de Mayotte en particulier. Elle n'a pas eu une politique qui aurait permis d'arbitrer clairement et de favoriser une réconciliation nationale. Son action envers les Comores s'est caractérisée par une succession de politiques hétérogènes privilégiant tantôt l'unité, tantôt la division, se ralliant à la position de l'un, puis de l'autre. Il s'agit bien en tout cas d'une politique au jour le jour, d'où l'unité d'action est absente, qui procède en réalité de l'embarras de Paris òu l'on ne savait trop comment résoudre en termes institutionnels l'imbroglio mahorais (Charpantier, 1976: 98). Il est vrai que la France se trouvait placée, dans l'affaire mahoraise, en 1973-1974, dans une position assez inconfortable. D'une part, les éléments nationalistes les plus durs, regroupés au sein du Molinaco, multipliaient les attaques contre le gouvernement francais auquel ils reprochaient de freiner le processus de décolonisation. D'autre part, une partie de la population—celle de Mayotte—rejetait toute idée de retrait hors de l'ensemble francaise (Decraene, 1974: 26-27).

Le 22 décembre 1974, un référendum est organisé aux Comores, on l'a déjà noté plus haut. A la question: "Souhaitez-vous que le territoire des Comores devienne indépéndant?", 94,56% des electeurs répondent "oui." A Mayotte, 63,82% se prononcent contre l'indépendance (Guillebaud, 1974: 5).[27] Rappelons que l'organisation de ce référendum était prévue dans la "déclaration commune sur l'accès des Comores à l'indépendance." Le problème essentiel soulevé par ce texte est qu'il est ambigu: il ne se prononce pas sur le caractère global ou non de la consultation et, par là même, la possibilité pour Mayotte de demeurer, si elle le souhaite, partie intégrante de al République française. Il n'est donc pas précisé si le decompte des voix se fera île par île ou de manière globale. Le texte prévoit une "consultation *des* populations" et non de *la* population.[28] Cela pourrait donc laisser supposer que les voix de chaque île seraient comptabilisées séparément. Cette ambigüité va peser lourd dans l'évolution politique de l'archipel et va favoriser la sécession mahoraise.

Sur ce point—scrutin global ou ile par île—, l'unanimité n'est guère de mise au sein de la classe politique française. On assiste en effet à une succession de prises de position divergentes les unes des autres, au cours des deux années qui précèdent la consultation, illustrant l'absence de politique cohérente à laquelle on vient de faire allusion. Que l'on en juge. En janvier 1972, M. Pierre Messmer, ministre d'Etat chargé des DOM-TOM, reconnaît que les habitants des quatre îles pourront exprimer séparément leur point de vue au sujet de l'indépendance. Il se prononce donc en faveur d'un scrutin île par île (Flobert, 1976b: 77-78). M. Bernard Stasi, ministre des DOM-TOM en 1973, prend position, quant à lui, en faveur d'une solution fédérale. Olivier Stirn, son successeur, se montre décidé à préserver l'unité de l'archipel (soutenu en cela par les socialistes et communistes français, ses opposants). Son projet de loi présenté, en octobre 1974, à l'Assemblée nationale française, organise une consultation globale de l'archipel.[29] Il déclare à cette occasion: "Seul le résultat global (du référendum) sera pris en considération—et le projet de loi du gouvernement le précisera expressement. La France se refuse à diviser les Comores qui ont le même peuplement, la même religion islamique, les mêmes intérêts économiques. (. . .) Et ce serait agir contre le droit des peuples à disposer d'eux-mêmes que de procéder autrement" (L'Express, 9 septembre 1974: 34).

Le Conseil des ministres français adopte, le 2 octobre 1974, un projet de loi—dont le rapporteur est M. Olivier Stirn—organisant une consultation de la population des Comores. Ce texte prévoit qu'un scrutin doit avoir lieu dans les six mois pour "savoir si la population souhaite choisir l'indépendance." Ce projet de loi manifeste la volonté du gouvernement français de l'époque de voir le scrutin se dérouler de manière globale puisqu'il y est fait référence à "la population" et non "aux populations." Les declarations du président Valéry Giscard d'Estaing, lors de sa conférence de presse du 24 octobre 1974, vont dans le même sens. Or, ce texte, devenu la loi du 23 novembre 1974, est amendé par le Sénat français qui prévoit une consultation "des populations," un classement île par île des résultats même si la proclamation se fait globalement (La Vie Publique en France, 1975: 19).

On assiste donc dans cette affaire, du côté français, d'une part à des divergences de vues entre les titulaires successifs du ministère des DOM-TOM, d'autre part, à des divergences entre le législatif et l'éxecutif, ce derniers s'inclinant devant le premier. L'ambigüité qui entachait la "declaration commune" de juin 1973 n'a pas été levée: elle aboutit à l'indépendance unilaterale et à la sécession de Mayotte. Elle pèse, aujourd'hui encore, sur l'évolution politique de l'archipel et sur les relations francocomoriennes.

Qu'advient-il, à partir de ce moment, de l'île dissidente? Le MPM ayant ainsi obtenu la partition de l'archipel suite au référendum, l'objectif suivant, c'est la départementalisation.

Le sécretaire d'Etat aux DOM-TOM annonce devant la Commission des lois de l'Assemblée nationale, le 16 octobre 1975, que Mayotte sera démocratiquement consultée sur son évolution. Un référendum est organisé le 8 fevrier 1976, à Mayotte. La population se prononce à la quasiunanimité (17886 voix sur 18093, soit 99,4%) en faveur du maintien de l'île dans l'endemble français. Mais ce référendum ne satisfait pas le MPM. Il considère que la question était "mal formulée." Un nouveau référendum est donc organisé à Mayotte, le 11 avril 1976.

Le MPM obtient que 80% des électeurs mettent dans l'urne un bulletin confectionné par lui—et donc nul—et demandant explicitement la départementalisation ("Nous voulons être département français" lit-on sur ce bulletin). On a parlé, à ce propos, de "boycott larvé." D'autre part, 97% des suffrages valablement exprimes demandent l'abandon du statut de territoire d'outre-mer et donc implicitement la départementalisation. Le référendum du 11 avril démontre la résolution des Mahorais. Finalement, le Parlement français accorde, le 24 décembre 1976, le statut très particulier—ni TOM, ni DOM—de "collectivité territoriale à caractère départemental." La situation n'a pas évolué depuis lors.

L'affaire de Mayotte a eu des implications au plan international. La controverse a mis en cause la France tant à l'ONU qu'à l'OUA. Pour les Nations-Unies, les référendums des 8 février et 11 avril 1976 se présentent comme une violation de la résolution 1514(XV) de l'Assemblée générale de l'ONU du 14 décembre 1960 qui stipule en son point 6: "Toute tentative visant à détruire partiellement ou totalement l'unité territoriale d'un pays est incompatible avec les buts et les principes de la Charte des Nations—Unies."

Selon cette résolution, les Nations-Unies estiment que les territoires non-autonomes doivent conserver, lors de leur accession à la souveraineté, les frontières qui étaient les leurs sous l'administration coloniale. Par la résolution 3385(XXX) du 12 novembre 1975 qui admettait les Comores comme 143° membre des Nations-Unies, l'Assemblée générale soulignait la nécessité de respecter l'unité et l'intégrité territoriale de l'archipel des Comores composé "d'Anjouan, de la Grande Comore, de Mayotte et de Mohéli."[30]

Entre le 4 et le 6 février 1976, le Conseil de sécurité des Nations-Unies se réunit trois fois au sujet de la situation aux Comores. Un projet de résolution considérait que l'organisation d'un référendum par la France à Mayotte constituait une ingérence dans les affaires intérieures des Comores et demandait à la France d'y surseoir.

Le Conseil de sécurité n'a pu adopter ce projet par suite du veto de la France (UN, Security Council, 1976: 5; Landskron, 1977: 111).

L'argumentation développée par la France est la suivante: le respect de l'intégrité territoriale héritée des limites des territoires coloniaux—résolution 1514(XV)—est un usage ou un idéal qui le cède en importance à l'obligation de l'autodétermination. En d'autres termes, pour la France, dans cette affaire l'autodétermination est le principe suprême même si la sagesse politique conseille d'éviter, là où cela est possible, la balkanisation de régions qui ont un intérêt à rester homogènes. C'est seulement, poursuivent les Français, pour des raisons de commodité que les quatre îles de l'archipel ont été réunies en 1912 dans une même entité administrative. Cette mesure n'a jamais prétendu préjuger le caractère propre de chacune de ces îles ni assimiler Mayotte aux trois autres îles qui ne sont tombées sous le contrôle de la France qu'à la fin du 19° siècle.[31]

Au débat du Conseil de sécurité de février 1976, la délégué de la Guinée-Bissau, représentant le groupe africain, a clairement posé le problème: "L'OUA a toujours défendu le principe de l'autodétermination. Le cas de Mayotte n'est pas la même chose car il constitue une manipulation politique de partis locaux par le gouvernement français en vue de préserver une certaine influence dans cette région, dans un avenir immédiat" (UN, Security Council, 1976: 7). Les référendums des 8 février et 11 avril 1976 ont été condamnes par l'Assemblee generale des Nations-Unies à une large majorité (UN, General Assembly, 1976: 1-2).

L'intérêt de la France pour Mayotte s'explique, en grande partie, pour des raisons d'ordre stratégique (cf. infra). Elles ne sont pas les seules. Des raisons de politique intérieure française ont également joué. Il a pu aussi s'agir, comme l'écrivent Chagnoux et Haribou, "d'une manifestation de grogne de la vieille garde UDR—solidement implantée à la Réunion—à la fois contre les forums internationaux et contre une série de réformes sociales imposées peu avant par le président Giscard d'Estaing: l'affaire de Mayotte a été aussi sans doute l'occasion d'une petite revanche en politique intérieure française."

Quelle peut etre, à moyen et long terme, l'évolution de l'affaire mahoraise? Malgré l'absence de cohérence de la politique du gouvernement français envers l'île dissidente et ses tergiversations, on peut en tout cas distinguer clairement une chose: les autorités françaises ne veulent pas doter l'île du statut départemental. Le fait que l'île ait recu le statut de "collectivité territoriale" est très significatif de ce point de vue.

On espérait à Moroni, au début du second semestre 1981, qu'après l'élection à la présidence de la République du socialiste François Mitterrand, la France accélérerait le "lâchage" de Mayotte. Qu'en est-il? Dans le "project africain" du Parti socialiste français rédigé avant la victoire électorale, on note: "L'île de Mayotte doit redevenir partie intégrante de l'archipel des Comores" (Le Monde, 22 mai 1981). A l'heure actuelle, les déclarations officielles au sujet de Mayotte sont inexistantes. L'incertitude de toute perspective de règlement a contribué à reveiller l'opposition a Ahmed Abdallah et pourrait mettre en difficulté son régime. La position de la France socialiste est caractérisée par un certain attentisme qui contraste avec la netteté des résolutions adoptées sur les Comores par le Parti socialiste lorsque celui-ci était dans l'opposition. Ce retard apporté au règlement du problème mahorais irrite Moroni (Le Monde, 20-21 décembre 1981). Au plan diplomatique, enfin, l'affaire de Mayotte a été gelée: la réunion du comité ad hoc de l'OUA sur Mayotte qui devait avoir lieu en mai 1981 à Moroni, n'a pu se tenir, faute de participants et le sommet africain de Nairobi n'a pris aucune initiative.

L'IMPORTANCE STRATÉGIQUE DES COMORES

De nombreux observateurs de la scène politique comorienne soulignent l'importance stratégique de l'archipel. (Latrémolière, 1977: 3504; Flobert, 1976a: 302-308).

L'océan Indien est loin d'être, aujourd'hui, le "lac de paix" que certains pays riverains voudraient en faire. On a en effet assisté, au cours des dernières années, à une militarisation progressive de cet océan, principalement dans le secteur occidental, là où précisément se trouvent les Comores. De nombreux facteurs ont accru le caractère névralgique de l'océan Indien: l'émergence de régimes radicaux dans des pays riverains: Sud-Yémen, Mozambique, Seychelles, Ethiopie; l'extension des activités des mouvements de libération en Afrique australe; l'instabilité permanente dans la

Corne orientale de l'Afrique (conflits de l'Ogaden et de l'Erythrée); l'importance du trafic pétrolier (Bowman, 1979: 1-10). En outre, après la révolution islamique en Iran, la guerre du Golfe et l'intervention soviétique en Afghanistan, l'océan Indien est devenu l'un des principaux points chauds maritimes du globe.

La situation géographique des Comores permet à celles-ci de contrôler le trafic pétrolier en provenance du Golfe arabo-persique et d'Indonésie en direction des Etats-Unis et de l'Europe via le Cap. L'obligation de contourner le Cap, à partir de 1967, a donné naissance à une génération de super-pétroliers de plus de 100.000 tonnes de jauge qui ne peuvent plus emprunter désormais le canal de Suez. Le trafic pétrolier annuel transitant au large des Comores est évalué à près d'un demi milliard de tonnes de pétrole brut (Latrémolière, 1978: 11). Vingt-sept navires en moyenne, dont seize pétroliers, empruntent cette voie quotidiennement (Monde Diplomatique, 1976: 19). Mayotte n'est pas la mieux située de ce point de vue dans la mesure ou les pétroliers naviguent habituellement entre la Grande Comore et Mohéli. L'avantage de Mayotte c'est de disposer d'un lagon coralien abrité qui constitue l'un des meilleurs points de mouillage de ce secteur de l'océan Indien avec Antseranana (ex-Diego Suarez) et Port-Louis. Mais cette rade n'est pas aménagée.[32]

Dans l'affaire de Mayotte, la France a été sensible à l'aspect stratégique. On rappellera, à cet égard, le mot du général de Gaulle s'adressant aux Comoriens, à Moroni, le 10 juillet 1959: "Vous êtes ici à un point essentiel du monde."[33] Mayotte constitue avec Djibouti et le département de la Réunion, un des points d'appui indispensables du dispositif stratégique français dans l'océan Indien (Le Monde, 24 mai 1979: 18). Les forces francaises de l'océan Indien se répartissent comme suit: Djibouti: 4500-5000 hommes; la Réunion: 3200 et Mayotte: 350.[34] Outre ces trois bases, la France maintient sur cinq îles minuscules de petits détachements armés: Juan de Nova, Europa, Bassas da India, l'archipel des Glorieuses et l'îlot de Tromelin. Ces îles, servant de "bases-ricohet," sont régulièrement revendiquées par Madagascar (Leymarie, 1981a: 217-221; Gavshon, 1981: 297).[35] L'importance de ces points d'appui n'est pas reconnue par tous les stratèges français. En 1975, l'amiral Schweitzer estimait que "les bases construites à grands frais hors des territoires nationaux soulèvent des problèmes politiques tels que les inconvénients sont plus grands que les avantages. L'époque actuelle est aux flottes de haute mer, disposant d'une logistique de ravitaillement et de navires-ateliers pour leurs réparations qui les rendent autonomes" (Monde Diplomatique, 1976: 21). De ce point de vue, Mayotte, en raison d'un environnement hostile (Comores, Madagascar, Mozambique) ne serait pas un appui très sûr pour la France.

S'il convient de reconnaître l'importance des bases flottantes, les points d'appui terrestres ne doivent pas être sousestimés. Dans la pratique, on observe un intérêt constant des Américains pour les facilités qui leur sont accordées à Diego Garcia, Masirah, Mombasa ou des Soviétiques pour des bases telles que Aden, Socotra, Maputo ou Antseranana (Le Monde, 15 février 1981: XIX).

Le renversement du président Soilih, en mai 1978, est lié, partiellement, à l'importance stratégique de l'archipel et la France avait tout à gagner à voir ce régime renverse. L'arrivee au pouvoir, a Moroni, de Ali Soilih, jugé trop "radical" par Paris, inquiétait les stratègès français. A leurs yeux, l'evolution politique de l'archipel vers un régime "a la chinoise" représentait deux dangers, outre celui de la contagion: d'une part, elle risquait d'interdire a la France l'utilisation de la rade de Mayotte, avec les conséquences qui en découlaient pour le ravitaillement pétrolier. D'autre part, cette évolution pouvait rendre plus difficile la défense du département de la Réunion déjà affaibli, au plan interne, sous la pression du courant autonomiste. De ce point de vue, si l'on a pu contester l'unité politique de l'archipel, il est plus difficile de cóntester son unité stratégique. (Latrémolière, 1977: 3505). Certains organes de presse francais ont avancé que le coup d'Etat contre Ali Soilih avait été "téléguide" depuis Paris et la Reunion, par les services francais de renseignements (SDECE).[36] Il est évidemment malaisé de confirmer l'hypothèse. Il faut cependant convenir que le changement de regimé arrangeait bien la stratégie française dans l'océan Indien.

On remarquera enfin le président Abadallah, conscient de la situation stratégique de son pays, est prêt à monnayer, contre le retour de Mayotte dans l'ensemble comorien, l'accord d'une base française aux Comores à l'image de ce qui s'est fait entre les Etats-Unis et Cuba (cf. la base de Guantanamo) (Le Monde 16 octobre 1981).

CONCLUSION

Dans l'histoire recénte des Comores, on peut distinguer trois périodes: la période qui va de 1946 (année où l'archipel devient un territoire d'outre-mer) à l'independance; la présidence d'Ali Soilih (début 1976- mai 1978); le retour au pouvoir d'Ahmed Abdallah.

La première période est marquée, on l'a vu, par une agitation politicienne qui a bien peu à voir avec les problèmes socio-économiques auxquels est confronté le pays. Les rivalitiés insulaires, personnelles et claniques ont déterminé, au cours de la plus grande partie de la période, une effervescence un peu vaine.

La dépendance politique est apparue clairement: en dépit d'un élargissement continuel de l'autonomie locale, le sort de l'archipel se jouait à Paris, au ministere des Départements et Territoires d'Outre-Mer. La classe politique traditionnelle n'était porteuse d'aucun projet politique et économique: vouloir l'indépendance, mais qu'en faire? La marche vers l'indépendance permettait à la bourgeoisie marchande d'accroître son hégémonie sur la société comorienne.

Par une politique erratique et incohérente, la France, de son côté, a peu fait pour préparer, politiquement et économiquement, le pays à acceder à la souveraineté.

Avec la présidence d'Ali Soilih, le contraste est net. En dépit des excès et des outrances que l'on a relevés, cette période se caractérise par une volonté de s'attaquer aux vrais problèmes de la pauvreté et du sous-développement. La dépendance politique n'est plus alors qu'un souvenir: le cordon ombilical a été coupé. Mais, la parenthèse est de courte durée.

Avec Ahmed Abdallah, ce sont les politiciens "vieille manière" qui reviennent sur le devant de la scène. On est ramené en 1975. L'histoire des Comores? Pleine de bruit sans aucun doute, et d'un peu de fureur aussi.

NOTES

1. La superficie du pays généralement admise est de 2236 km^2 (Mantoux, 1974: 41). Cette superficie est cependant calculée sur la base de cartes déjà anciennes au 1/40,000. On a retenu ici les surfaces correspondant aux cartes plus récentes au 1/50000 (Chagnoux et Haribou, 1980: 11). Pour une présentation géographique succincte des Comores, voir par exemple, DONQUE, 1970: 39-42.

2. Cette moyenne recouvre un déséquilibre démographique interinsulaire: la densité est la plus élevée à Anjouan (361 hab/km^2) et la plus basse à Mohéli (62 hab/km^2).

3. La surface agricole utile (terres cultivables + pâturages) est de 1232 km^2 (Chagnoux et Haribou, 1980: 85).

4. Pour une analyse des problèmes agricoles de l'économie comorienne, voir par exemple Boisson (1977: 485-500) ou Gaspart (1981: 123-143).

5. Pour l'histoire des Comores antérieure à la colonisation, voir Martin (1969: 8-19).

6. Il s'agit essentiellement de la Société Coloniale Bambao (SCB), de la Société de Nioumakele (NMKL) et de la Société des Plantes à Parfum de Madagascar (SPPM) à Mayotte.

7. Le fait que l'actuel président des Comores, M. Ahmed Abdallah est appelé ironiquement dans l'archipel, le président "import-export" n'est pas uniquement anecdotique . . .

8. Il s'agit initialement d'un Conseil général qui, en 1952, devient Assemblée territoriale, et doté de compétences plus étendues que ses homologues métropolitains.

9. Pour une vue des revendications politiques du Molinaco voir Boina (1969: 29-32 et 1972: 13-14).

10. Les prises de position du Molinaco n'avaient en effet pratiquement aucun impact dans l'archipel.

11. cf. partie consacrée à l'affaire mahoraise pour une analyse de ce scrutin.

12. Ce qui était prévu par la "Déclaration commune" en son point n° 1 ("L'accès à l'indépendance").

13. Les militants du FNU s'étaient prononcés en décembre 1974 en faveur de l'indépéndance de l'archipel. Leur opposition à Ahmed Abdallah résultait essentiellement d'une conception differente des modalités d'accession à cette indépendance.

14. Le droit de vote est abaissé à 15 ans.

15. Voir titre II: "Les circonscriptions territoriales" (art.8-12), Loi fondamentale, 25 avril 1977, Moroni.

16. Voir Plan intérimaire, 1978.

17. Ali Soilih avait connu de réelles difficultés économiques dés le début de sa présidence du fait de la suppression totale de l'aide française, difficultés accrues à la suite du massacre de Majunga. A la fin de l'année 1976, un conflit qui oppose l'ethnie malgache Antaïsaka et des Comoriens installés à Madagascar se solde par la mort de 1400 Comoriens. A la suite de ces événements, les autorités de Moroni rapatrièrent 17000 personnes: en deux mois, la population des trois îles indépéndantes augmenta de 5 à 6%. L'éruption du volcan Karthala, au début de 1977, accrut encore ces difficultés.

18. Des témoignages rendent compte de la réalité de cet exode et des motivations politiques de ces "boat-people" (Le Monde, 4 mars 1978; 18 avril 1978). Sans nier la réalité matérielle des faits, les autorités de Moroni en donnent une interprétation différente: elles accusent les forces françaises stationnées à Mayotte de se livrer à des "actes de piraterie" dans les eaux territoriales comoriennes en "enlevant" des piroguiers aux abords de l'île d'Anjouan (Le Monde, 10 mars 1978).

19. On notera qu'au moment de la suspension de l'aide française, celle-ci s'élevait à 7 milliards de F.CFA (1 US $ = 250 F.CFA en 1975; 328 CFA, en avril 1982) sur un budget d'un peu plus de 8 milliards pour l'ensemble du territoire (Vallier, 1977: 16).

20. Le "directoire politico-militaire" est dirigé, dès le 13 mai, par Said Atthoumani, un ancien ministre de Ahmed Abdallah. Il est remplacé, quelques jours plus tard, par Abdellahi Mohamed qui devient chef de gouvernement (Le Monde 17 mai 1978).

21. Contestation étudiante à l'automne 1979 (Le Monde, 9-10 septembre 1979); grèves en février 1980 (Le Monde, 29 février 1980); peu de temps après, la population et les élus d'Anjouan—fief du président—demandent la démission du gouverneur de l'île (Le Monde, 31 aout-1 septembre 1980: 12). Saïd Ali Kemal donne sa démission d'ambassadeur des Comores à Paris (Le Monde, 24 juillet 1980), réclame la démission du président Abdallah et fonde un "Comité national de salut public" (Le

Monde, 16 octobre 1980); un coup d'Etat est déjoué le 15 février 1981, le but des conjurés étant de "mettre fin à la faillite économique et à la corruption du régime"; arrestation de Mouzaoir Abdallah, ancien ministre (Le Monde, 10 novembre 1981) dissolution du Parlement et du gouvernement le 25 janvier 1982.

22. Le déficit de trésorerie atteignait, en 1981, 1,5 milliard F.CFA.

23. Trois chiffres témoignent du fait que la colonisation plus ancienne ne la différencie pas du reste de l'archipel: deux-tiers des Mahorais souffrent de paludisme, 98% sont analphabètes et 5% à peine comprennent le français.

24. Il convient d'avoir à l'idée qu'aux Comores, si particularisme il y a, il concerne davantage Anjouan dont l'autorité du président Abdallah, Anjouannais lui-même, ne réussit pas toujours à maîtriser les effets (Latrémolière, 1978: 11).

25. Vote de l'Assemblée territoriale du 14 mai 1958.

26. Le MPM a longtemps monopolisé l'activité politique à Mayotte. D'autres partis politiques ont cependant vu le jour, au fil du temps: le PRDM (Parti pour le Rassemblement Démocratique des Mahorais), favorable au retour de Mayotte dans l'ensemble comorien; le RMPR (Rassemblement Mahorais pour la République), émanation locale du parti français RPR; l'UDM (Union Democratique des Mahorais), constitué par les Mahorais qui ont quitté Madagascar.

27. Selon les leaders du Mouvement Mahorais, l'organisation du référendum était entachée de violations de règles de droit (Revue Française d'Etudes Politiques Africaines, 1975: 81-94).

28. Le point 1 de ce texte stipule: "L'accès à l'indépendance procédera d'une consultation *des* populations de l'archipel à une date qui sera déterminée d'un commun accord, dans les cinq années au plus, à compter de la date de la signature de la présente déclaration."

29. Ce projet de loi se conforme ainsi aux recommandations de l'OUA et de l'ONU en la matière. Olivier Stirn attire cependant l'attention sur la nécessité de mettre en oeuvre une politique de régionalisation devant permettre la sauvegarde des intérêts de la minorité mahoraise.

30. Dès avant le premier référendum de 1974, l'Assemblée Générale des Nations-Unies affirmait l'unité et l'intégrité territoriale de l'archipel dans sa résolution 3291 (XXIX) du 13 décembre 1974.

31. Un auteur note à ce sujet: "Les fondements du nationalisme comorien sont les mêmes que ceux de tous les Etats du tiers monde issus de la décolonisation. Ils résident dans une communauté d'histoire et non dans le souvenir d'un Etat unitaire pré-colonial qui, la plupart du temps, n'a pas existé. Le contexte revient à mettre en cause la légitimité deppresque tous les pays d'Afrique noire, comme la notion d'intangibilité des frontières coloniales, simple traduction juridique de ce nationalisme." (Latrémolière, 1978: 11).

32. L'aménagement de la rade de Mayotte (1000 km^2) pourrait faire de cette île le "verrou" du Canal de Mozambique (Vallier, 1977: 14).

33. On notera, en passant, que, lors de son voyage de 1959, c'est Moroni et non Dzaoudzi qu'a tenu à visiter le général de Gaulle témoignant ainsi qu'il reconnaissait, à défaut d'une tradition mono-étatique, un fait comorien indépendant de toute allégeance à Dzaoudzi, symbole de la souveraineté française (Latrémoliere, 1977: 3503). Ceci contraste largement avec l'attitude des gaullistes du Parlement français, les plus ardents à favoriser la partition du territoire.

34. Les forces françaises à Mayotte comprennent le détachement de légion étrangére de Mayotte (DLEM) fort de 240 hommes provenant du 2° régiment étranger (Bonifacio) et du 1° régiment étranger de Cavalerie (Orange), un détachement de gendarmerie (50 hommes), le patrouilleur l'Epée, un remorqueur et trois chalands de transport amphibies (Le Monde, 24 mai 1979).

35. L'archipel des Glorieuses est également réclamé par les Comores (Le Monde, 20-21 janvier 1980).

36. Afrique-Asie, 12 juin 1978; Le Nouvel Observateur, 22-28 mai 1978; Marchés Tropicaux et Méditerranéens, 9 juin 1978.

REFERENCES

Africa Research Bulletin (1975) "95% vote for independence." (January 15): 3466.

Afrique-Asie (1978) (Juin 12): 33.

Afrique Contemporaine (1975) "Indépendance et coup d'Etat." 81 (Septembre-octobre): 16.

––– (1978) "Texte de la Constitution comorienne." 100 (Novembre-décembre): 13-19.

BINET, J. (1976) "Les Comores au seuil de l'indépendance." Afrique Contemporaine 84: 16-20.

BOINA, A. B. (1969) "Colonialisme et anticolonialisme aux Comores." Revue de Politique Internationale (Belgrade) 472: 29-32.

––– (1972) "Les Comores et leur lutte de libération." Revue de Politique Internationale (Belgrade) 524-525: 13-14.

BOISSON, J. M. (1977) "Les Comores." Annuaire des Pays de l'Océan Indien (Aix-Marseille) 4: 485-500.

BOURDE, A. (1965) "The Comoro Islands: problems of a microcosm." Journal of Modern African Studies 3, 1: 91-102.

BOWMAN, L. W. (1979) "Security issues in the western Indian Ocean." Presented at the International Conference on Indian Ocean Studies, Perth, W. A., August 15-22.

CHAGNOUX, H. et A. HARIBOU (1980) Les Comores. Paris: Presses Universitaires de France.

CHARPANTIER, J. (1976) "Référendums mahorais, lois françaises et hégémonie politique comorienne." Revue Francaise d'Etudes Politiques Africaines 126: 96-118.

CRUSOL, J. and L. CRUSOL (1980) "A programme for agriculture in island plantation economies." World Development 8,12: 1027-1033.

DECRAENE, P. (1974) "Comores: Mayotte à l'encan." Revue Française d'Etudes Politiques Africaines 106: 25-27.

Documents de l'actualite internationalé [Ministère des Affaires Etrangères, Paris] (1973) "Déclaration commune sur l'accès des Comores à l'indépendance." (Aôut 12): 523-527.

DONQUE, G. (1970) "L'archipel des Comores." Revue Française d'Etudes Politiques Africaines 50: 39-51.

Express [Paris] (1974) (Septembre 9): 34.

FICHET, M. (1976) "Les Comores, Mayotte et la France." Est et Ouest 584: 423-425.

FLOBERT, T. (1976a) Les Comores. Evolution juridique et socio-politique. Aix-Marseille: Travaux et mémoires de la Faculté de droit et de science politique.

——— (1976b) "Histoire et actualité du Mouvement Mahorais." Revue Française d'Etudes Politiques Africaines 121: 70-90.

GASPART, C. (1981) "The Comoro Islands since independence: an economic appraisal," pp. 123-143 in A. Kerr (ed.) The Indian Ocean: Resources and Development. Nedlands and Boulder: University of Western Australia Press and Westview Press.

GAVSHON, A. (1981) Crisis in Africa. Battleground of East and West. Harmondsworth: Penguin.

GUILLEBAUD, J. C. (1974) "Le référendum sur l'indépendance des Comores." Le Monde (sélection hebdomadaire) 1365: 5.

JUNQUA, D. (1975) "Comores: un inquiétant exemple de décolonisation à la française.' " Le Monde Diplomatique 253: 15.

LANDSKRON, W. A. (1977) "Comoros-Mayotte," pp. 111-112 in Annual Review of United Nations Affairs 1976. New York: Oceana.

LATREMOLIERE, J. (1977) "Les Comores et leur avenir." Marchés Tropicaux et Méditerranéens (Décembre 23): 3503-3505.

——— (1978) "La France et le nouvel Etat comorien." Afrique Contemporaine 100: 10-12.

La Vie Publique en France (1975) "Comores: les voies de l'independance." (Juillet 25): 17-21.

Le Monde (quotidien) 1978: 15-16 janvier, 4 mars, 10 mars, 23 mars, 18 avril, 17 mai; 1979: 24 mai, 9-10 septembre, 4 octobre; 1980: 20-21 janvier, 29 février, 24 juillet, 16 octobre; 1981: 23 janvier, 25 avril, 16 octobre, 10 novembre, 20-21 decembre.

Le Monde (1979) "La strategie francaise en océan Indien." Mai 24.

——— (1981) "Océan Indien, nouveau coeur du monde." Fevrier 15.

——— (1981) "Le projet africain du Parti Socialiste est de nature a seduire les partenaires de la France sur le continent noir." Mai 22.

Le Monde Diplomatique (1976) "Grandes manoeuvres dans l'ocean Indien." Decembre.

Le Nouvel Observateur (1978) Mai 22-28.

LEYMARIE, P. (1981a) Ocean Indien. Le nouveau coeur du monde. Paris: Editions Karthala.

——— (1981b) "Le nouvel imbroglio comorien." Le Monde Diplomatique 331: 13.

Loi fondamentale (1977) Avril 25.

MAESTRE, J. C. (1979) "L'éxperience révolutionnaire d'Ali Soilih aux Comores 1976-1978." Annuaire des Pays de l'Ocean Indien 4: 25-41.

MANTOUX, T. (1974) "Notes socio-économiques sur l'archipel des Comores." Revue Française d'Etudes Politiques Africaines 100: 41-60.

Marchés Tropicaux et Méditerranéens (1978) (Juin 9): 51.

MARINAS OTERO, L. (1978) "Comoros: macroproblemas en la genesis de un microestado." Revista de Politica Internacional (Madrid) 155: 123-148.

MARTIN, J. (1968) "Les notions de clans, nobles et notables. Leur impact dans la vie politique comorienne d'aujourd'hui." L'Afrique et l'Asie 81-82: 39-63.

––– (1969) "L'archipel des Comores." Revue Francaise d'Etudes Politiques Africaines 44: 6-39.

OSTHEIMER, J. M. (1975) "The politics of Comorian independence," pp. 73-101 in J. M. Ostheimer (ed.) The Politics of the Western Indian Ocean Islands. New York: Praeger.

Plan Intérimaire de cinq ans pour le développement économique et social 1978-1982 (1978) Fevrier.

Rand Daily Mail (1981) (Novembre 27): 5.

Relazioni Internazionali [Milano] (1977) "La prospective delle Comore in un'intervista del presidente Soilih." (Novembre 12): 1102.

Revue Française d'Etudes Politiques Africaines (1975) "Mémoire des députés du Mouvement Mahorais sur le référendum du 22 décembre 1974 aux Comores." 110: 81-94.

SAINT-ALBAN, C. (1973) "Les partis politiques comoriens entre la modernité et la tradition." Revue Française d'Etudes Politiques Africaines 94: 76-91.

SELWYN, P. (1975) "Introduction: room for manoeuvre?" pp. 8-24 in P. Selwyn (ed.) Development Policies in Small Countries. London: Croom Helm.

TAYLOR, C. L. (1971) "Statistical typology of micro-states and territories. Towards a definition of a micro-state," pp. 183-202 in J. Rapaport, E. Muteba, and J. J. Therattil (eds.). Small States and Territories. Status and Problems. New York: Arno.

United Nations, Security Council (1976) Critiques sur un projet de référendum aux Comores. Chronique mensuelle 13,3: 5-14.

United Nations, General Assembly (1976) Résolution adoptée par l'Assemblée Générale. Question de l'île comorienne de Mayotte. (A/RES/31/4). Octobre.

VALLIER, A. (1977) "Les Comores indépendantes: bilan en 1977." Afrique Contemporaine 92: 14-22.

WOOD, D.P.J. (1967) "The smaller territories. Some political considerations," pp. 23-34 in B. Benedict (ed.) Problems of Smaller Territories. London: Athlone.

World Bank (1979) Les Comores. Problèmes et perspectives d'une économie insulaire de petite dimension. Washington, DC: Author.

10

MAURITIUS: THE MEADE REPORT
TWENTY YEARS AFTER

PERCY SELWYN
Institute of Development Studies,
University of Sussex

In 1960, a commission consisting mainly of specialist advisers in British Colonial Office but chaired by Professor J.E. Meade was appointed by the Government of Mauritius "to survey the present economic and social structure of Mauritius and to make recommendations concerning the action to be taken in order to render the country capable of maintaining and improving the standards of living of its people, having regard to current and foreseeable demographic trends." This study was conducted in tandem with one by Titmuss and Abel-Smith (known as the "Titmuss Report"), which was more centrally concerned with social and demographic issues (Titmuss and Abel-Smith, 1961).

The Commission's report (Meade et al., 1961), generally known as the "Meade Report," had a substantial impact in Mauritius. Its general approach has been reflected in a variety of government policies as well as in the climate of opinion. In this chapter, I shall first summarize the main arguments of the report and then consider how adequate they were to the circumstances of 1960. I shall then discuss how well the report stands up in the light of subsequent events.

THE REPORT

The report started with a description (mainly based on the Titmuss Report) of the population explosion in Mauritius after World War II. The rate of natural increase had risen from about 0.5 percent per annum in the years before the war to nearly 3 percent per annum in the late 1950s. This reflected a moderate increase in the birthrate (from 33 per 1000 in 1936-1940 to 41 per 1000 in 1958) combined with a substantial fall in the death rate (from 28 per 1000 in 1936-1940 to 12 per 1000 in 1958). The principal cause of this change was the virtual elimination of malaria during the 1940s. Calculations made for the Titmuss Report had shown that, if fertility rates remained at their existing levels and the progress of medicine and public health brought mortality rates down to levels obtaining in medically advanced communities, the population would increase from its existing level of some 600,000 to 3 million by the end of the century. Even if the birthrate were substantially reduced, the population of working age would increase by 50 percent over the coming fifteen years.

This population growth would imply a substantially increased demand for resources for three reasons:

(1) capital would be required to create additional jobs;
(2) a high level of investment would be needed merely to maintain existing levels of average income: Assuming an average capital/output ratio of 4:1, and population growth of 3 percent, a net investment rate of 12 percent would be needed merely to prevent a fall in average incomes; and
(3) more resources would be needed to meet the additional demand for social and economic services.

Thus the report was concerned centrally with two closely related questions: How could more jobs be created, and how could average incomes be, at the least, prevented from falling? This concern with employment recurs frequently. Thus: "The major objective of future economic planning must be to keep unemployment as low as possible." But the emphasis is also on "productive" employment. The aim was to encourage both jobs and growth, but with a strong emphasis on jobs.

The principal constraint on the provision of jobs was seen as the lack of resources—of capital. Hence priority should be given to the encouragement of industries or other activities with a low capital/labor ratio. But for such labor-intensive activities to be economic, it was necessary that wage rates should be stable. Restraint in wage rates did not mean that living standards could not rise. But improvements in living standards had to be brought about in ways that did not affect going wage rates—for example, through social welfare measures and food subsidies. There were limits on what could be redistributed in this way through the tax system, but "In the conditions of Mauritius, low wages (to stimulate expanded employment) plus a moderate dose of social-security benefits or of cost-of-living subsidies (to support the standards of living) together make up a very sensible policy. But high wages plus social-security plus cost-of-living subsidies would spell inevitable ruin."

The provision of jobs was not merely a function of the supply of capital. "It does not follow . . . that, if funds are provided, then all the available labour will in fact be automatically employed. The provision of capital on the sort of scale required is a necessary but not a sufficient condition for the solution of the problem of employment." It was necessary to examine the employment prospects of individual sectors in order to identify both the problems facing them and possible policy measures.

The traditional industry in Mauritius, employing over half the labor force and responsible directly or indirectly for over half of the country's output and over 98 percent of visible exports, was sugar production. It seemed unlikely that the sugar industry would employ substantially more people. Total exports of sugar would probably be constrained by market limitations. In any event, as output increased, labor productivity would also rise. Moreover, because of institutional arrangements, the production of sugar was greater than could be justified on grounds of comparative advantage. Credit, marketing arrangements, research, and technical advice were readily available for sugar production, but were virtually nonexistent for other crops. Sugar was sold in different overseas markets under a variety of arrangements, marginal sugar being sold on the so-called free market. The free market price was then well below the average export price. But the proceeds of sugar exports were averaged out among producers. Thus the marginal price paid to the individual producer was higher than the marginal price received by the country. The price signals provided by the marketing system thus reinforced specialization in sugar production. For all these reasons, it would be desirable to restrain the growth in output of sugar and encourage that of other crops. Various measures were proposed—an export tax on sugar, the switching of loans by the government agricultural bank away from sugar toward other crops, and far greater relative emphasis on research on crops other than sugar.

The report's concern about wage costs is reflected in its discussion of agricultural prospects: "The production of tea—which is one of the most promising of alternative crops—requires considerable amounts of labour. This makes it a particularly appropriate crop. . . . But at the same time it means that its profitability and success will depend largely on wage restraint."

One approach to the problem of wage costs would be through greater emphasis on small planters using family labor:

> Where the production of sugar cane, of tea, or groundnuts ... is undertaken by such small planters, the income earned by the planter and his family is automatically adjusted to the price at which the product can be sold and to the productivity of the planter himself. . . . The standard of living of the planter could be raised as his productivity increased; but there would not be the same danger that an inflexible money wage cost would make Mauritian tea uncompetitive on the world market.

But although the diversification of agriculture, and in particular the growing of food crops, would be beneficial both for nutritional and balance of payments reasons, it would not provide many jobs:

> One cannot rely upon the sugar industry to provide any substantial volume of increased employment, and other agriculture is likely to provide employment for only a strictly limited, if appreciable, labour force. It is, therefore, to the institution and expansion of manufactures that one must turn to seek productive employment for substantial numbers.

The expansion of manufacturing industry was thus seen as a central element in employment policy. It was, however, likely to be difficult. Whereas sugar manufacturing was highly efficient and progressive, other industries were "for the most part at a rather primitive stage of development, carried on on a small scale and often struggling to keep alive." There were virtually no artisan-type industries. Mauritius lacked raw materials. The domestic market was small; production must therefore be on a small scale unless costs could be low enough to allow for industrial exports. There was a lack of industrial experience or know-how. Education was mainly academic; there was very little technical or commercial education. There would probably be a shortage of capital for new industries. Existing financial institutions were unsuitable for the provision of industrial capital. Moreover, the communal structure of Mauritian society involved the fragmentation of the potential capital market; surpluses accumulated by one community would not be available for investment in activities undertaken by another. The capital market was thus even less effective than it need be.

The report proposed a mixture of policies in this sector. After emphasizing again the need for wage restraint, it proposed improvements in technical education, an increase in industrial credit through the Agricultural Bank (which should become a national development bank), the establishment of industrial estates, the use of government purchasing so as to encourage local industry, and the revision of the customs tariff so as to give greater assistance to local industry. The report was cautious on tax concessions to new industry and was opposed to the investment allowances that the government was granting since these would give most aid to capital-intensive industries. Any government assistance should be selective and should provide most help to labor-intensive industry. But if foreign firms came to Mauritius with their own capital resources, there was no particular need to insist on their being labor-intensive, since such enterprises would have useful spinoff effects in terms of technical knowledge, business experience, and managerial ability.

This general argument was supplemented by more detailed consideration of particular issues, covering labor policy, education, administration, agriculture, industry and finance. The final summary contains no less than 129 recommendations (although some of these are of the "we are against sin" kind. Thus "a greater ruthlessness should be exercised in pruning government departments of unnecessary staff" or "recurrent government expenditure should be closely scrutinised with a view to eliminating unnecessary spending"). But this brief account brings out the main emphasis of the report, even if it omits most of the detail.

The Mission did not commission any research; nor did it have access to any studies on such central issues as the factors affecting family size, the problems and attitudes of small and medium planters, or the nature and potential of the labor force. Although the Mission tried to overcome these deficiencies by taking evidence from as wide a cross-section of Mauritians as possible, and, in the case of population policy, accepting rather uncritically the proposals of the Titmuss Report, this was undoubtedly a major weakness in its work. Much of its analysis and many of its proposals were thus based on theoretical reasoning rather than on empirical data. No doubt this was inevitable in a rapidly executed study; but where, as we shall see, policies recommended by the report have turned out to be irrelevant, this may well reflect the lack of such detailed work.

CRITICISMS OF THE REPORT

Much of the Meade Report's general approach is now familiar. ILO employment mission reports started from much the same standpoint. But it was by no means a typical attitude at the time; the common starting point of a team report (as in many of the World Bank country studies of the time) would be to equate the economic development problem with the economic growth problem. The Meade Report was indeed concerned with economic growth; one of the fears it expressed very strongly was that economic growth might not keep pace with population growth, and that there would be a fall in average incomes leading to a fall in standards of living. But standards of living were placed first; economic growth was regarded as a means rather than an end.

In many ways the report was conservative, however. It took the institutional structure of Mauritius—both internally and internationally—as a datum, and made proposals for adjustments within that structure. King (1979) has drawn attention to two areas in which this was so—income distribution and the mechanism of the open economy. Although I believe that King's arguments are exaggerated and in certain respects wrong, his general point is well taken. It is therefore worth considering in some more detail the approach of the report to these two issues.

The Meade Mission was well aware of the extreme concentration of wealth, income, and economic power among a small group of people in the country. There were scarcely any statistics on any of these aspects of inequality. But the facts were well enough known. Moreover, a study carried out in 1974 in the Ministry of Finance produced substantial evidence of the concentration of ownership and control of the principal enterprises in Mauritius—a situation that had not changed to any marked degree since 1960. But although the Mission was conscious of the situation, it did not propose any measures to reduce such inequalities. Meade himself, in two subsequent papers (1961 and 1967), did in fact explore the implications of different distributions of wealth—and in particular, land. But the report itself says nothing about this. It did, however, express fears that existing inequalities could well increase, and several of its proposals were designed to prevent this. Thus part of its argument against high wage rates was that this would create a privileged group of people with jobs at the expense of mass unemployment. Again, the report wished to limit the expansion of sugar production, but was opposed to production quotas, which would create a privileged group of people (with quotas) over and against the rest of the community. Thus the report, while accepting existing inequalities, was concerned that these should at least not be increased.

This limited approach could be criticized on two grounds. First, an elimination of extremes of inequality could help to improve the standard of living of the very poor. Thus a land redistribution program could in certain circumstances help those without land or with very little. There are suggestions of such an approach in the Meade Report's support for small planters as against wage employment on large estates. But this was proposed, not as a measure of income redistribution, but as a means of encouraging labor-intensive farming.

The second argument, which is referred to by King, is that a redistribution of income in favor of the poor would increase the demand for locally produced products compared with imports, and would thus improve industrial prospects (see also Seers, 1969). This assumes that import propensities are higher among the rich than among the poor. In a very open economy, where virtually all foodstuffs are imported and nearly all manufacturers employ imported raw materials and other imported inputs, this is doubtful. Although household expenditure surveys have been carried out in Mauritius for different income groups, these neither distinguish between imports and local products nor provide any information on *marginal* expenditure. But there is no evidence that rich and poor consume a substantially different mixture of imports and local products. This particular objection, then, does not appear to have much substance.

The one area in which a redistribution of incomes in favor of the poor might help local demand would be the reduction in levels of saving, much of which, as both Meade and King show, as exported. A more equal distribution would reduce savings and the export of capital and increase local demand for goods and services. If, as King argues, the main constraint on growth in small, open economies is not capital but the size of the market, this could expand production possibilities. But this is to present such constraints in terms of alternatives: limits are laid down either by the supply of capital (as is emphasised by Meade) or by the size of the market. But such an economy may suffer from both constraints; if capital is scarce, measures likely to reduce the level of savings through increasing consumption, while raising the level of demand (much of which would in any event leak out in the form of imports), might appear a poor alternative to measures designed to prevent the export of capital (e.g., through more effective exchange controls).

The second area in which the Meade Report was conservative was in its acceptance of the mechanisms of the open economy. It showed full awareness of the institutional structures—monetary system, trading arrangement, institutionally maintained export specialisation, and so on—and described their implications.

The economy of Mauritius is a very open one—that is, a high proportion of its income is derived from exports and a large part of its expenditure is on imports. . . . Production of goods and services for the home market is of smaller importance in the total economy than in most countries. This has certain important consequences. First, the secondary effects on local incomes of any investment are fairly limited. . . . Secondly, it is not possible for Mauritius to generate its own internal inflation. An increase in internal demand is immediately reflected in an increase in imports. . . . Mauritius cannot, in present circumstances, use monetary and credit expansion to stimulate the local economy.

This is followed by a significant footnote:

We are ignoring at this point the fact that, under the present currency arrangements (i.e., the colonial "sterling exchange" standard) such policies are not in any case possible. *We consider that, by and large, these institutional arrangements reflect the economic facts on life in Mauritius* [emphasis added].

The report does indeed make several proposals that would have the effect of moderating the extreme openness and external dependence of the economy. These include tariff protection and measures to counteract institutional arrangements favoring sugar over local food crops. But these were marginal changes; it was assumed that Mauritius had no alternative to its existing basic structure.

One final impression. The report emphasized that the free market had not worked in Mauritius. Institutional factors had caused a divergence between private and social costs and benefits. But solutions could be found through making the price system more effective, and in particular through the use of taxes and subsidies. Thus the tendency to overproduce sugar could be counteracted by the imposition of an export tax on sugar; wage rates could be kept down by the use of food subsidies and other social benefits; labor-intensive industries could be encouraged through wage subsidies; population growth could be limited through tax arrangements favoring the "three-child family."

The report was thus strongly in the classical tradition. Possibly its comparative conservativeness was one factor in its success. In looking through both its general argument and its specific proposals, I am impressed by how much its approach became both the foundation of successive development plans and the conventional wisdom in Mauritius, as well as by how many of its proposals were implemented. If the purpose of a visiting mission is to have some impact on policy, a conservative bias and an avoidance of criticism of fundamental structures will undoubtedly improve its prospects. In certain circumstances the analysis and suggestions that can be made within such a framework will be seriously inadequate. There are countries in which a visiting mission has the choice between advising revolutionary change (which will be ignored) or marginal change (which will be irrelevant). But the situation may not be so clear cut. The political and social situation may leave room for maneuver without revolutionary change. Measures that will lead to rising standards of living among the majority of the people, and that will reduce the absolute incidence of poverty, will be possible broadly within existing structures. This was probably the case in Mauritius in 1960.

THE MEADE REPORT TODAY

So far I have considered the Meade Report on its own terms—that is, a document for the early 1960s. In the rest of this chapter I shall look at certain themes and proposals in the report in the light of subsequent experience. I shall be concerned with five areas: population growth, employment, the welfare state, diversification away from sugar, and economic dependence.

Population

As we have seen, population growth was at the center of the Meade Report's approach. The population explosion directed attention to the employment problem. Possibly the most remarkable change in Mauritius since the Meade Report has been the fall in rates of population growth. (see Table 10.1).

Table 10.1 shows that, in spite of a continuing fall in the death rate, the rate of natural increase fell by some 1.2 percent between 1955-1959 and 1971-1975, although it rose slightly in the later 1970s.[1] This reflected a substantial fall in the crude birthrate, which in turn reflected a major fall in fertility rates. The net reproduction rate, which was 2.5 in 1962, fell to 1.4 in 1975 and 1.36 in 1978. How did this happen?

There are several possible interpretations. One is that the Meade and Titmuss Reports had drawn attention to the population problem, and that the gradual development of official policy (family planning assistance and propaganda, the limitation of family allowances to three children) and the activities of the Mauritius Family Planning Association successfully convinced large numbers of parents of the possibility and desirability of limiting the size of their families. Indeed, the annual reports of the Mauritius Family Planning Association strongly suggest that the fall in fertility rates was the result of their efforts by way of assistance and propaganda.

TABLE 10.1   Island of Mauritius: Birthrates and Death Rates

Period	Crude Birthrate	Crude Death Rate	Rate of Natural Increase
1936-1940	33.1	27.7	5.4
1955-1959	41.6	12.0	29.5
1971-1975	25.0	7.8	17.3
1976-1978	26.1	7.6	18.5

SOURCE: Bi-Annual Digest of Statistics.

There may be some truth in this view. Undoubtedly the activities of both government and the Family Planning Association facilitated access to means of family limitation. Moreover, there was a major shift in public (or at least publicly known) attitudes. In 1960, the then minister of finance was subjected to the most violent abuse in the press for intending to implement the proposals in the Meade and Titmuss Reports on the tax treatment of large families, and the government was compelled to withdraw its proposals. Today, not only are tax arrangements along these lines accepted, but there is regular family planning propaganda on the television, with virtually no vocal opposition. The change in the public's attitude is striking.

But none of this explains why so many people decided to have smaller families. The most plausible hypothesis that I can suggest is that this is part of a major social change that has taken place in Mauritius over the past generation. In earlier times, the possibilities of movement from one social group or employment category to another were very small, and the children of, say, sugar laborers would expect to remain sugar laborers. Such a view has, however, become less and less acceptable. One possible explanation of this change was the transfer of political power from a noninterventionist colonial power, which ran the country in tacit association with a white plantocracy, to an elected government that presented possibilities of personal advancement to far wider sections of the community. Education was seen as the key to this advancement. Table 10.2 briefly summarizes what has happened.

By 1978, 70 percent of all boys and 66 percent of all girls between the ages of 5 and 19 were enrolled in schools. Virtually all children go to primary school. The major change has been in secondary school enrollment, which increased more than fivefold between 1959 and 1979.[2]

This educational expansion has had two effects. First, the average age of marriage has risen substantially since the early 1960s. Data produced by the Central Statistical Office show that there were increases of up to five

TABLE 10.2   School Enrollment

Year	Primary	Secondary	Total
1959	126,173	15,437	141,610
1975	149,838	63,472	213,310
1978	138,352	80,939	219,291

years in the average age at which girls in certain communities married, but all communities showed some increase. Incidentally, girls accounted for 47 percent of all secondary school enrollment in 1978; it was only in Form VI that the disparity between boys and girls was at all substantial. Second, there was a positive incentive for parents to have fewer children. If the children were to have better jobs than their parents, this would be costly both in terms of earnings foregone and of actual costs of schooling. Therefore, there were advantages in having smaller families.

Neither the Meade Report nor the Titmuss Report showed any awareness of these possibilities. The Meade Report took a very cautious view of educational expansion: government should not press ahead with compulsory primary schooling, and the temptation to expand (rather than to improve) secondary education should be resisted. This view was based on the apparent demand for people with educational qualifications and the shortage of available resources. It ignored the wider social implications of educational expansion, and although it recognized the very substantial public demand for more education, it did not associate this with forces that would render its analysis obsolete.

The available statistics also suggest a substantial narrowing of the gap between the marriage and fertility patterns of the different communities—that is, the emergence of a "Mauritian" rather than an Indo-Mauritian, Franco-Mauritian, Creole-Mauritian, or Sino-Mauritian structure. The reasons for this are not clear; the available statistics do not suggest any increase in the extent of urbanization (although, in a small country, the distinction between "urban" and "rural" is questionable). Communal divisions are still powerful. But increasing mobility and, possibly, the national identity created by political independence, may well be undermining some of the old divisions. Part of this change would be the emergence of a common Mauritian attitude to ward both the appropriate age of marriage and the desirable size of family.

Thus, although we cannot identify the exact causes of the decline in fertility since the early 1960s, it seems at least probable that they are part of a process of social change that was foreseen by neither Meade nor Titmuss. Indeed, if either Meade or Titmuss had suggested that such changes were probable, they would have been considered utopian. Moreover, with hindsight we can see that the actual proposals of Meade and Titmuss—and in particular the use of the income tax system for lowering the birthrate—were largely irrelevant. Even though the number of taxpayers rose substantially over the decades following Meade—partly as a result of the erosion of the real value of the tax allowances through inflation—they still numbered only some 24,000 in 1976-1977 out of a total adult population of over 450,000. Tax allowances would thus be a feeble instrument for influencing population growth—if indeed they had any effect at all.

Employment

The Meade Report pointed out that whatever happened to the birthrate, the number of people of working age would increase by 50 percent over the coming fifteen years. In fact, the number of people between the ages of 15 and 59 rose by 51 percent between 1962 and 1977. Thus the emphasis on the need for job creation was well justified, even if we ignore the need to provide employment for those without jobs at the time of the report.

Table 10.3 compares employment in "large" enterprises (i.e., those employing ten persons or more) in 1959 and 1978. The figures are not strictly comparable; in particular, that for employment in the sugar industry for 1959 was an average, whereas the 1978 figure was for the month of September—which is a period of comparatively high employment in sugar. Average employment in sugar during 1978 was probably between 1000 and 2000 less than that shown in the table. The figures for employment in tea and other agriculture are similarly not completely comparable.

Even with these reservations about the statistics themselves, the change they show is remarkable. The Meade Report had been pessimistic in its forecast of future employment in agriculture. The figures confirm this view. There was probably an absolute decrease in agricultural employment over the period. But in spite of this, total employment appears to have more than doubled—that is, it increased more than in proportion to the number of people of working age.[3] This partly reflected the increased participation of women in the labor force. Women and girls accounted for 17 percent of the employed labor force in 1962, and 20 percent in 1972. Nearly 80 percent of the employees in the Industrial Free Zone in 1977 were women. But there was certainly a fall in unemployment.

TABLE 10.3 Employment 1959 and 1978 (enterprises employing 10 persons or more)

	1959 (average)	1978 (September)	Increase, 1959-1978 Numbers	Increase, 1959-1978 Percentage	Percentage of Total Increase, 1959-1978
Sugar	57,448	54,054[c]	−3,394	−5.9	−3.0
Tea	2,003[a]	5,096	3,093	154	2.8
Other agriculture	3,786[b]	1,652	−2,134	−56.4	−1.9
Manufacturing and processing[c]	3,203	32,797	29,594	924	26.5
Government	10,663	46,341	35,678	335	31.9
Development Works Cooperation	—	8,071	8,071	—	7.2
Local authorities	1,152	5,145	3,993	347	3.6
Docks and stevedoring	2,144	5,226	3,082	144	2.8
Construction	2,955	9,309	6,354	215	5.7
Wholesale and retail trade		6,026			
Restaurants and hotels	3,025	3,174	27,425	907	24.5
Other		21,250			
Total	86,379	198,141	111,762	129	100

a. Excluding small planters and government.
b. Including government sack factory.
c. Excluding sugar.

The way in which employment increased was not foreseen, however. Meade had seen manufacturing as the sector likely to produce more jobs. Employment in manufacturing rose by over 900 percent over the period—although from a very small base. But this increase accounted for only about a quarter of all the additional jobs created. Some 42.7 percent of the additional employment was in government, the Development Works Corporation (a parastatal body carrying out construction and other work for government departments), and local authorities. The figures under-estimate the growth in public sector employment. Over the period, other parastatal bodies were created. The employment statistics do not list them separately, but if they were included, it is probable that the public sector would be seen to have provided at least 50 percent of the additional jobs created since 1959.

As we have noted, the Meade Report emphasized the need for the creation of *productive* employment. This was not clearly defined, and possibly the Mission was not entirely clear about what it did mean. There are several possibilities. First, "productive" may have been intended to apply to activities that met social wants in a cost-effective way. Such a meaning would make no distinction between wants met through the market and those met by government—between shirts and schools, between hotels and hospitals. But it would imply that people engaged in meeting nonmarket wants should do so in a reasonably efficient way, that the public sector should not employ large numbers in "make-work" schemes, and that only those needed for specific tasks should be employed in carrying them out. Second, and more narrow, "productive" may have been intended to cover the supply of marketed or marketable goods and services—implying that the employment problem should not be met by a sizable expansion of the public sector. Lastly (and this is an argument of which there is no trace in Meade), in view of the highly open nature of the economy, its heavy dependence on imports, and the need to be able to pay for those activities that added to exports or saved imports—that is to say, to the supply of "tradables" as opposed to "nontradables."

Since Meade assumed the continuation of the existing monetary mechanisms under which the scope for budgetary and balance-of-payments deficits was very limited, it is hardly surprising that the last of these interpretations was not in the forefront of its arguments. But the notion of "productive" employment probably included elements of both cost-effectiveness (or the avoidance of feather-bedding) and marketability.

Undoubtedly much of the additional employment created over the period has not been "productive" in either of these senses. Some of the growth in public sector employment could best be described as a form of redistribution of income. The employment policy of the government in the 1970s included a *Travail Pour Tous* programme (included in the Development Works Corporation figures shown in Table 10.3) under which the gap between the permanent employment being created in the private and public sectors of the economy and the employment target would be bridged. Thus not only did government institute policies that, it was hoped, would lead to full employment; it also accepted responsibility for providing jobs directly for anybody who could not find one in other ways.

No studies have been carried out on the long-run implications of this policy. Both the sugar and tea industries claim, however, that it has had the effect of reducing the supply of labor, and may well compel them to mechanize, with a consequent loss of jobs. Moreover, the increase in public sector employment was undoubtedly one factor in the serious deterioration in the balance of payments during the late 1970s (see below).

The other main element in the Meade Report's employment strategy was wage policy. As Lamusse (1980) points out, government became closely involved in wage policy during the 1960 and 1970s. Partly there appears to have been a concern with improving the position of the poorest employees—and in particular those in the sugar industry. But apart from this, government as a major employer could not dissociate itself from broader wage and salary policy—especially in the light of the sudden rise in inflation after 1973. Wages rates remained fairly stable throughout the 1960s. One element in wage stability was price stability; the consumer price index rose by only some 19 percent between 1962 and 1971. Since 1972, Mauritius, like most other countries, has experienced a much higher rate of inflation. This was primarily the result of the very substantial increase in import prices. The rate of inflation rose to some 30 percent in 1974, but fell thereafter, ranging between 10 percent and 15 percent in the later 1970s. In 1979, however, a 23 percent devaluation following from a balance-of-payments crisis led to a sharp increase in the rate of inflation, which was running at about 25 to 30 percent in 1979-1980.

Prices would have risen much more rapidly if government had not subsidized wheat and rice. The cost of these subsidies was running at well over Rs 100 million per annum in the late seventies—or about 7 to 10 percent of total budgetary expenditure. Since price rises have been the main issue in pay negotiations since 1973, it is reasonable to suppose that wage increases have been less than they would have been if food had not been subsidized. But it is not clear what effect this has had either on the level of employment or on the relative labor intensity of the employment that has been created. During the period from 1959 to 1970, while wages and prices were fairly stable, employment appears to have risen on average by about 3.5 percent per annum; between 1970 and 1977, when both wages and prices rose rapidly, if erratically, employment rose by over 5 percent per annum. These figures, of course, prove very little, but they suggest that it would be simplistic to assume a direct relation between wage levels and the creation of jobs.

Many of the jobs that have been created in the private sector—and especially in export industries—have been for women. The low level of female wages was undoubtedly a major factor in attracting such industries. But such employment, although adding to family incomes, does little to reduce unemployment, since it brings onto the labor market people who otherwise would be outside it. In any event, the low level of women's wages reflected less food subsidies or government policies of any other kind than it did the lack of effective trade union organization among women workers. Moreover, many doubts have been expressed about the benefits to the country of the development of foreign-owned export industries employing low-wage female labor. (see, for example, Commission Justice et Paix, 1974). The profits of such industries are exported, they pay no taxes in Mauritius, and they have very weak local linkages. Their local benefit consists solely of the wage costs; the lower these costs, the less is this benefit.

Wage policy, however, remains a central issue in Mauritius. Wage and salary increases in the 1970s helped to worsen both budgetary and balance-of-payments deficits. During 1976 and 1977, wage awards generally were in excess of increases in the price level. At the same time both government's finances and the balance of payments were adversely affected by a substantial deterioration in terms of trade. The effect of wage increases on the rate of job creation is debatable, but they certainly involved heavier claims on resources. Where, in an open economy such as Mauritius, the resources available at any time depend largely on the volume of exports and the terms of trade, a deterioration in the terms of trade combined with an increased demand on resources will rapidly lead to balance-of-payments difficulties. I will return to this point later.[4]

The Welfare State

As we have seen, the Meade Report put some emphasis on the expansion of social provision by the state as a means of moderating wage increases while at the same time improving the level of living of the poor. The past twenty years have indeed seen a major expansion in public

TABLE 10.4   Social Expenditure in the Recurrent Budget

	Rs million	
	1958-1958	*1979-1980 (est.)*
Food subsidies	—	130
Education	18.6	303
Health	14.9	172
Budgetary contribution to social security	15.8	149
Total	49.3	754

spending on the social services. Table 10.4 shows the increase in budgetary expenditure on major items of social provision.

The actual proportion of the recurrent budget devoted to these items remained unchanged at 42 percent, but the level of spending rose fifteen times in current prices, and possibly five times in constant prices. Even so, the information in Table 10.4 is incomplete. It excludes certain items, such as water subsidies, which are only partly social in their impact, as well as others, such as housing, where the extent of government subsidy is very difficult to determine.

This expansion of social welfare activities was not carried out in the context of the Meade intellectual model. It reflected a long-standing commitment of the Mauritius Labour party to welfare-type spending. As far back as 1949, future Prime Minister Ramgoolam was arguing in favor of food subsidies, old age pensions, health insurance, and improved educational services (Hazareesingh, 1979: 77-79). At the same time, he proposed the levying of a sugar export tax in order to pay for social expenditures. There was no suggestion that such welfare provision should be in place of higher wages; no connection was made between wages and social welfare. The Mauritius Labour party's commitment to social welfare derived more from British fabian thinking than from any general development strategy.

The extension of welfare activities can be seen qualitatively as well as quantitatively. There is now free (although not universal) secondary and university education; following a report by Brian Abel-Smith and Tony Lynes in 1975, a contributory National Pensions Scheme was established, operating side by side with existing non-contributory benefits; government has been heavily involved in promoting cooperatives; there has been a substantial (if intermittent) government housing program. These involvements have had varying degrees of success; the cooperative movement in particular has a spotty history. As a "bundle" of policies, they raise issues that were hardly considered in Meade and that have indeed received insufficient analysis in the ensuing years.

Mauritius, like Sri Lanka, has adopted a style of development emphasizing public sector investment and institutions in the context of a so-called mixed economy, together with the growth of a welfare state. The reasons for such policies are complex and go back to the colonial era in each country. But little has been done to analyze the effects of the Mauritian welfare system on the lines of studies carried out in Sri Lanka (see, for example, Richards and Gooneratne, 1980). The issues raised by Meade twenty years ago are clearly too narrow. Following the Meade Report, we might ask what effect the welfare system has had on levels of wages and employment. What has been its budgetary impact? In their work on Sri Lanka, Richards and Gooneratne are indeed concerned with the impact—especially of food subsidies—on employment. But they raise other major questions. Who have been the beneficiaries of welfare spending? What has its impact been on the poorest members of the community? What has its effect been on economic growth? They do not arrive at simply answers, but they recognize that the questions need to be asked.

Thus if we look at the welfare elements in Mauritian policy, it is at least arguable that some parts of this policy have been regressive in their impact. Almost certainly, rich families benefit more than poor families do from educational spending, merely because the children of rich families are likely to stay longer at school and to be more than proportionately represented in higher education (which is far more costly per head than primary education is). Again, subsidies on water and housing are erratic in their incidence, but since the poorest people are those most likely to be without a piped water supply and better-off people obtain income tax concessions on mortgage interest payments, it is possible that these programs too have their regressive elements. Benefits from the National Pensions Scheme must be judged in the context of the overall structure of contributions and outgoing payments.

This is not to argue that Mauritian welfare programs have not helped the poor. But it is to question Meade's implicit assumption that programs ostensibly designed to help those in need would in fact do so. As the series of working papers prepared for the ILO's World Employment Programme Research has shown, the impact of public spending on poverty and employment is frequently difficult to identify, but the distribution of benefit is frequently substantially at variance with the stated aims of welfare programs. Bonnen (1970) suggests the questions that should ideally be asked about such programs: What is their purpose and who are their intended beneficiaries? Who actually benefits? What are the total benefits of the program? What is the distribution of benefit and, in particular, what is the distribution of benefit between actual beneficiaries and intended or potential beneficiaries? Schaffer (1978) has drawn attention to the issue of who obtains access to such potential benefits.

Thus Meade's approach to welfare-type spending has proved simplistic. The notion of the "social wage," implicit in Meade, raises issues that have not been examined in Mauritius (and, indeed, are rarely examined anywhere). It is too easy to confuse stated intentions, or budgetary classifications, with social impact. With the growing pressure on resources in the 1980s, there will doubtless be increasing interest in trying to identify the effects of these programs—both on the economy as a whole in terms of growth, employment and the balance of payments, and on the welfare of those most in need.

Diversification of the Economy

A main emphasis of the Meade Report was on the need to diversify the economy away from sugar. The two principal sectors in which such diversification was hoped for were agriculture (and in particular in tea and food crops) and manufacturing industry. The report did not consider that there was much scope for the growth of tourism in view of the island's remoteness and poor communications.

In any event, restrictions on sugar markets have been less severe than the Meade Report supposed—in part because of the collapse of the International Sugar Agreement. Whereas Meade talked in terms of a market limit of less than 600,000 tons, the five-year plan for 1975-1980 included a target of 800,000 tons production by 1980—the constraint being the ability of the industry to produce rather than to sell sugar. Any revived international sugar agreement, while doing something to stabilize the free market price, may however involve limits on Mauritius's total sugar exports.

But although there has in the event been no difficulty in disposing of Mauritius's sugar production, government's stated policy has for some years been to encourage the production of crops other than sugar. Some of the measures proposed in the Meade Report—such as the export tax on sugar, the creation of an Agricultural Marketing Board, and the shifting of the emphasis of the state's development bank away from sugar, have been adopted. Comparative statistics on the production of crops other than tea and tobacco are very poor, but, apart from an expansion in tea production, the results have not been encouraging. Between 1959 and 1972 the area under agriculture appears to have increased from 221,100 acres to 262,500 acres[5] —or by 41,400 acres. Of this increase, 38,400 acres, or 93 percent, was accounted for by an increase in the land under sugar. The area under tea rose by over 11,000 acres, but there appears to have been a fall in the area under other crops. The tea expansion program, which appears from these figures to have been comparatively successful, has in fact faced severe problems, and the 1975-1980 plan not only did not provide for any expansion in the area under tea, but also implied that there was a possibility that this area might fall. What went wrong?

First, the export tax on sugar. Various reasons were given in the report for imposing such a tax. As we have seen, it was intended to counteract the "almost irresistible upward trend in the output of sugar," by bringing the marginal return to the individual producer more into line with the national marginal return. It would restrain the production of the least efficient and highest-cost producers. Moreover, it was difficult to assess small planters to income tax, and the export duty would fall on people who were able to pay income tax but did not do so. Thus the proposed tax on sugar production would be "both economically sound and socially just."

The government accepted the principle of the sugar tax (which had as we have seen proposed by the Mauritius Labour Party as far back as 1949), and it has been levied at various rates ever since. But its effect on sugar output appears to have been negligible. Balogh and Bennett (1963) argued that the tax was mistaken because there was a backward sloping supply curve for sugar. There is no evidence for this. But the other factors making for sugar specialization are so powerful that the elasticity of supply for sugar is certainly extremely low. As far as the discouragement such a tax would give to the least efficient and highest-cost producers, the flat rate *ad valorem* duty proposed by Meade was replaced by a sliding scale under which the smallest (and probably least efficient) producers were entirely exempted. It was indeed unrealistic to expect that a government whose support lay very substantially among small and medium planters would apply such a tax to them in its full rigor. In any event, the main achievement of the tax has been to raise revenue; in 1979-1980, the export duty was estimated to yield some 9 percent of all government revenue. As a tax, it has clearly come to stay. But nothing is left of its original rationale.[6]

Another proposal for the encouragement of food crop production was the establishment of an Agricultural Marketing Board. The main purpose of the Board was to offer guaranteed minimum prices for crops other than sugar. The report suggested, however, that it would be wise in the first instance to restrict the Board's activities to a limited number of nonperishable crops. Potatoes and onions were specifically referred to. Today, the Agricultural Marketing Board exists, but it has still not expanded its operations beyond these products, plus maize and garlic. Production of potatoes averaged 3800 tons per annum in the years from 1955 to 1959, but this reflected a fall from previous higher levels; 7000 tons had been produced in 1952-1953.

Production averaged over 9,000 tons per annum between 1972 and 1975 and was over 12,000 tons in 1978. This increase may be partly the result of a potato subsidy operated through the Marketing Board (which could have had the effect of diverting land from other food crops to potatoes). But in general food production in the 1970s has been stagnant. The main growth appears to have been with the sugar companies, which instituted a program for food crop production under the leadership of the Mauritius Chamber of Agriculture (a body representing mainly the sugar estates). But there is little evidence that the Agricultural Marketing Board has had any impact on the total output of food crops.

The Meade Mission was indeed aware of the management problems that would face such a board. In the event, the Board, which has a (possibly undeserved) reputation for incompetence and bad judgment, is widely believed to have done little part from providing jobs for its officials. But although its uselessness is widely suspected, there is virtually no possibility that it will be abolished. The decision to establish an institution is frequently irreversible; like other countries, Mauritius lacks any machinery for institutional sanitation—that is, for flushing unwanted and useless institutions out of the system. Visiting missions frequently propose the creation of institutions to carry out specific jobs. If government accept their proposals, the country may be burdened with maintaining such institutions indefinitely, however useless they may turn out to be.[7]

As we have seen, the Meade Report hoped to encourage labor-intensive crop production through the support of small planters whose incomes would depend on their productivity rather than on a rigid wage rate. An attempt was made to expand tea production on this basis, using what were called "project planters." But the attempt has failed. It has not proved possible to insulate the tea planter economy from the wage economy. Most of the project planters abandoned their tea plots, and the public sector was compelled to take them over. No study has been made of the experience and motivations of these planters, but it appears likely that the returns to the labor they would have been required to expend compared unfavorably with their possible earnings elsewhere. Moreover, the tea-growing areas are remote and unattractive—the establishment of "tea villages" has done little to attract planters. The creation of a tea planter class might have been possible if there had been mass unemployment; in any event, tea planters had an alternative. The wage costs of growing tea were replaced by the opportunity costs facing the planters, and the planters decided that these were too high.

The sector in which diversification has been most successful is manufacturing. Industrial output expanded very substantially, accounting in 1978 for 17 percent of the GNP. This was accompanied by a large increase in industrial employment and exports. Whereas the Meade Report had seen the growth in manufacturing as principally for the domestic market, today the scope for most such industries is very limited, although there will undoubtedly be further backward linkages from existing industries now relying on imported inputs. But because of the narrowness of the domestic market, the main emphasis in the 1970s has been on export industries. This has given rise to a whole range of problems that were not foreseen by Meade. Who was to start such industries? What would be the role of Mauritian capital and enterprise? Would the pattern of such development be such as to reinforce the existing concentration of wealth, income, and economic power? Or were there possibilities that industry could be developed in other ways? If foreign investors were necessary, on what terms should they be brought in? What should be the markets for Mauritian industry, and how could access to them be obtained? It is not reasonable to criticize the Meade Report for not considering these questions; manufacturing in 1960 was at such a primitive level that *any* industrial growth appeared desirable. But today such an attitude is no longer possible.

A sector that was virtually ignored by Meade was tourism. The report was highly sceptical about the prospects for the industry as well as about the wisdom of devoting resources to its expansion. But this has been one of the most rapidly growing sectors during the past twenty years. Tourist nights increased more than tenfold between 1963 and 1978. Unfortunately, official data on the contribution of the industry to employment and incomes are inadequate. Dinan estimates the direct employment created by tourism in 1977 at some 5,500, and indirect employment at possibly as much as 10,000, while its direct contribution to GNP was some Rs 50-55 million—or rather more than 1 percent. Here too a range of questions has arisen that were not foreseen by Meade. Can Mauritius gain more of the economic benefit accruing from tourism? If the ratio of net to gross foreign exchange earnings from tourism in Mauritius is only some 10 percent (de Kaudt 1979: 82), how can this be increased? How can the competition for scarce resources (beaches, infrastructure services, and so on) best be contained?[8] What is the scope for effective physical planning? Can the social costs of tourism be limited? Like the sugar tax, tourism has come to stay, but many countries have found it an uneasy and unpredictable element in their society. Any fresh study of the "economic and social structure of Mauritius" could not ignore the problems of living with tourism.

The Open Economy

One of the most significant changes in Mauritius since the Meade Report has been the modification of the institutional arrangements that reinforced the open economy. Instead of the quasi-automatic colonial currency system, Mauritius now has a central bank that issues currency, has powers over the commercial banks, and is government's banker. The links between branch commercial banks and their head offices abroad have been weakened; exchange controls have been tightened, and the export of capital has become more expensive. The link between the rupee and sterling has been abandoned. None of this was proposed by Meade.

Some of these changes have undoubtedly been beneficial. The imposition of exchange controls has been effective in reducing the export of capital. The Meade Report pointed out that the surplus from the sugar industry was either reinvested in sugar or exported, mainly to South Africa and Rhodesia. Since the strengthening of exchange controls, much of the surplus from sugar has been reinvested in Mauritius and has helped to build up the manufacturing and tourist sectors. This has had the indirect effect, however, of extending the economic power of the plantocracy. The link between the rupee and sterling was broken in the beginning of 1976 because of the inflation that it was feared would result from the further depreciation of sterling. Thus the subsequent fluctuations in the value of sterling—variations that were irrelevant to the situation or needs of Mauritius—have not been allowed to influence the working of the Mauritian economy.

But the creation of an independent monetary system has had more complex effects. Under the previous system, as Meade pointed out, it was impossible for Mauritius to suffer from balance-of-payments difficulties; a fall in export earnings would be translated into a fall in local incomes and government revenue. The commercial banks might draw on their head offices for funds, but there were no means of creating purchasing power internally. This is no longer so. We can illustrate this by looking at the events of the late 1970s.

In 1976, the terms of trade deteriorated by 27 percent, and there were further deteriorations of 10 percent in 1977 and 8 percent in 1978. At the same time, wages and salaries continued to increase. If there had been no central bank, government and the private sector would have been compelled to discharge employees or impose wage reductions. The banks would have adopted a tight money policy. In the event, both the central bank and the commercial banks substantially increased their credit to the public and private sectors in spite of credit controls. Commercial banks' claims on the private sector rose by 112 percent between the end of 1975 and 1978, while the "local assets" of the central bank increased by Rs956 million over the same period, or by over 5000 percent. In a larger country with a substantial domestic economy this would probably have been inflationary, except insofar as it encouraged local production. In Mauritius, the effect was felt mainly on the balance of payments. Overseas reserves fell disastrously. By August 1979, they had fallen to Rs54.5 million—some 2 percent of the annual value of imports. The overall balance of payments deficit in 1979 was estimated at Rs620 million—or 20 percent of the value of imports.

Government was compelled to go to the IMF for assistance. An "adjustment program" was agreed with the fund, including a 23 percent devaluation of the rupee, a substantial reduction in the budgetary deficit (including a freezing of existing levels of food subsidies), and tight credit controls.[9] Fears were expressed that recourse to the IMF would very substantially reduce Mauritius's freedom of action. But such fears miss the point. The constraints existed, whether the IMF was involved or not. The actual policy measures may have been different if the fund had not been asked for help, but radical steps would have been needed in any event.

Thus an independent monetary system in Mauritian conditions had the short-term effect of softening the impact on employment and real incomes of a deterioration in the terms of trade. But it did so at the expense of the foreign reserves, and in effect only postponed the day when hard decisions were needed. At some stage a choice had to be made between full employment at rather lower levels of real income, and employment for a privileged group at higher levels of real income. The existence of a central bank enabled government to postpone the choice; it did not cause the need for such a choice to go away.

CONCLUDING REMARKS

The Meade Report undoubtedly performed a useful function. It drew attention to genuine problems; some of its solutions were sound on a technical level; it encouraged local discussion of important issues. Its weaknesses were probably those of any visiting mission—an excessive use of theoretical concepts without a sufficient consideration of how far these applied to the particular circumstances. In the case of the Meade Mission, there was overreliance on market-type solutions—in other words, on the use of taxes and subsidies to remedy what were seen as distortions in the system. On the other hand, the system itself was by and large accepted. This conservatism probably enabled the useful parts of the report to be accepted and implemented. Without it, the report would merely have gathered dust in some government department.

The report failed to identify two major long-term issues. First, its discussion of population problems did not foresee the social changes that would, within a decade, render its analysis obsolete. Second, it did not see that industrial growth in the long run meant production for export, and that this could mean an increase in the country's external dependence. But I suspect that mission reports in general have a poor record in identifying long-term trends.

A mission that went to Mauritius today would certainly identify a very different group of problems. It would still be necessarily employment oriented. But its discussion of employment would be profoundly affected by educational changes over the past decades. It would give far more attention to the world economic system and its impact on Mauritius. It would be more concerned with the growing pressure on real resources—urbanization, the impact of tourism, and the effects of industrial growth. It would try, to a greater extent than did the Meade Report, to identify the causes of poverty and the impact of existing poverty-oriented programs. And it would be especially concerned with the problem of productivity in both the public and private sectors. But all this is merely to say that each age throws up its own questions. It is no real criticism of a report of 1960 that it does not answer the very different questions of the 1980s.

NOTES

1. The increase in the birthrate in the late 1970s may have reflected an increasing number of marriages, resulting from the baby boom of the late 1950s and early 1960s.

2. By far the greater part of this increase was in nongovernmental schools, which accounted for 93 percent of all secondary enrollment in 1978. Most of these schools were indeed supported by government, but they all depended more or less on fees. In 1977 government agreed to pay fees of pupils in all secondary schools.

3. It should, however, be emphasized that these figures are incomplete since they exclude small-scale and self-employment—e.g., small plantations, most fishermen, retail trade, domestic servants, taxi drivers. If there had been a census in 1981, it might have thrown light on what had been happening to employment in these sectors.

4. More recently, government has attempted to restrain wage increases and has used the occasion of devaluation to reduce real wage levels—with what long-term success is is not possible to say.

5. The "effective area" under cultivation is, however, less than this. In 1978, the effective area under sugar cane, tea, and tobacco was only 231,000 acres—93 percent of which was under sugar. There are no corresponding data for land under food crops, nor indeed would such figures be meaningful, since much of the expansion in food crops during the later 1970s was in cane interlines.

6. Kaldor (1980: xxiv), drawing on many years' experience as a would-be tax reformer, has pointed out that the intellectual work of such reformers can rarely take into account the precise form in which the basic ideas will be carried into practice. Results may diverge greatly from original intentions, so that the objectives of the tax have not been met and yet the illusion may have been created that they have.

7. A similar point is made by Shaw (1973): "The art of closing down obsolete institutions is underdeveloped."

8. This competition is not merely between Mauritians and tourists; it is equally between rich Mauritians (who try to monopolize access to the beaches) and poor Mauritians.

9. For details of the program, see Ringadoo (1980).

REFERENCES

BALOGH, T. and C.J.M. BENNETT (1963) Report of the Commission of Enquiry (Sugar Industry) 1962. Mauritius Legislative Council Sessional Paper 4.

BONNEN, J. T. (1970) "The absence of knowledge of distributional impacts: an obstacle to effective policy analysis and decisions," in R. H. Haveman and J. Margolis (eds.) Public Expenditures and Policy Analysis. New York: Rank McNally.

Commission Justice et Paix (1974) L'Industrialisation á Maurice (December).

de KADT, E. (1979) Tourism: Passport to Development? New York/Paris: World Bank/UNESCO.

DINAN, P. (1980) Dix Ans d'Economie Mauricienne. Port Louis: Editions IPC.

HAZAREESINGH, K. [ed.] (1979) Selected Speeches of Sir Seewoosagur Ramgoolam. London: Macmillan.

KALDOR, N. (1980) Reports on Taxation. London: Duckworth.

KING, J. (1979) Mauritius, Malthus, and Professor Meade. Sussex: IDS Communication 49, 1970.

LAMUSSE, R. (1980) "Labour policy in the Plantation Islands." World Development 8 (December).

Mauritius Government (1975) Five-Year Plan for Social and Economic Development, 1975-80. Port Louis: Government Printer.

MEADE, J. E. (1961) Mauritius: a case study in Malthusian economics." Economic Journal 71 (September).

――― (1967) "Population expansion. The standard of living and social conflict." Economic Journal 77.

――― et al. (1968) The Economic and Social Structure of Mauritius. Mauritius Government Sessional Paper 7 (1961). Reprinted by Frank Cass, London.

RICHARDS, P. and W. GOONERATNE (1980) Basic Needs, Poverty and Government Policies in Sri Lanka. Geneva: ILO.

RINGADOO, V. (1980) Budget Speech (June 3). Port Louis: Government Printer.

SCHAFFER, B. (1978) Official Providers. Paris: UNESCO.

SEERS, D. (1969) "A step towards a political economy of development: illustrated by the case of Trinidad and Tobago. Social and Economic Studies (September).

SHAW, E. S. (1973) Financial Deepening in Economic Development. London: OUP.

ABOUT THE CONTRIBUTORS

ROBIN COHEN is Professor of Sociology at the University of Warwick and formerly Professor of Sociology at the University of the West Indies, Trinidad. He has published widely in the field of international labor studies. He has been associated with the Sage series on African Modernization and Development since its inception, having served as a member of the International Advisory Board, contributed to the series, and co-edited Volume 2, *African Labor History* (1978), with Peter Gutkind and Jean Copans.

DANIEL DOS SANTOS is an Angolan national who knows Cabinda, the subject of his chapter, from first-hand experience. He has studied in Canada and is presently a member of the Department of Sociology, Université de Montréal.

CLAUDE GASPART is the Director of the Interdisciplinary Centre for Research and Applied Technology in Development at the University of Louvain, Belgium. He specializes in African affairs. He has lectured in growth and development economics at the University of Constantine (Algeria) and acted as an adviser to the Algerian government in the field of small-scale industries. He is also President of the International Association for Micro-states Studies.

ARNOLD HUGHES studied at the University of Wales (Aberystwyth) and Ibadan University, Nigeria. He is Lecturer in Political Science at the Centre of West African Studies, University of Birmingham. He has written extensively on various aspects of African politics and has published in the *Canadian Journal of African Studies, Political Studies,* and *African Affairs.* In recent years he has been a frequent visitor to The Gambia and has published over twenty papers and articles on the politics of that country.

RAPHAEL KAPLINSKY has worked at the Institute of Development Studies at the University of Sussex since 1970, with the exception of a few years (1974-1978) at the Institute for Development Studies in Kenya. His two major areas of research are technology and transnational corporations.

JOONEED KHAN was born in Mauritius in 1944 and educated at the Curepipe Royal College, the University of Windsor, and the Université de Montréal. Co-founder of the Mauritian Militant Movement (MMM), he returned to Canada in 1970, where he has since worked as an editor with the Canadian Press news agency and as foreign news editor and analyst with the Montreal daily, *La Presse.*

DEIRDRE MEINTEL studies at the Catholic University of America (Washington, D.C.) and received a Ph.D. from Brown University (Providence, Rhode Island) in 1978. She taught at McGill University (Montreal) for five years and is currently co-director of a research project on immigrant women workers in Montreal. Her academic interests focus on ideologies of class, race, ethnicity, and sex.

MIGUEL SANCHEZ-PADRON was born in 1945 and studied at Bilbao, Oxford, and London (Birkbeck College). He has taught at the University of Bilbao and is now teaching Development Economics at the University of La Laguna, Tenerife (Canary Islands). He worked at the Institute of Development Studies (University of Sussex) and has done field work in Mexico. He has published articles on industrial relations in Mexico and on the Canary Islands and has co-authored a book on the Canaries, *Desarrollo del subdesarrollo: especulación y necesidades* (1977).

PERCY SELWYN is a Fellow at the Institute of Development Studies at the University of Sussex. He was Senior Economic Adviser in the British Colonial Office and Commonwealth Office, and has worked in Lesotho and in Mauritius (where he had earlier been a member of the Meade Mission). He has written extensively on small countries, islands, and related topics. He is author of *Industries in the Southern African Periphery,* and of a study of island problems for UNCTAD, among others. He has recently been involved in studies of Anguilla and the Seychelles. His present interests are in the field of public expenditure planning.

IBRAHIM K. SUNDIATA is an Associate Professor of History at the University of Illinois at Chicago. He has also taught at Rutgers University and Northwestern University, where he received his Ph.D. in 1972. Professor Sundiata has undertaken research in both Equatorial Guinea and in

Liberia, and has received Woodrow Wilson and Fulbright-Hays awards. He is a past member of the Board of Directors of the African Studies Association.

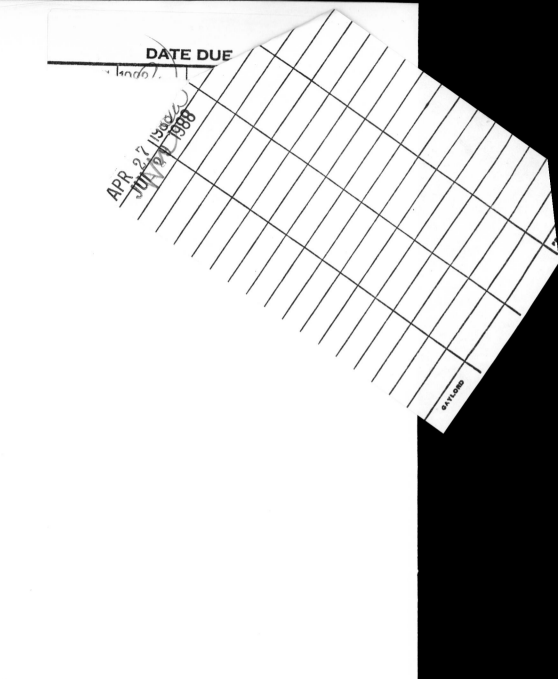